IMAGES
of America

PORT HUENEME

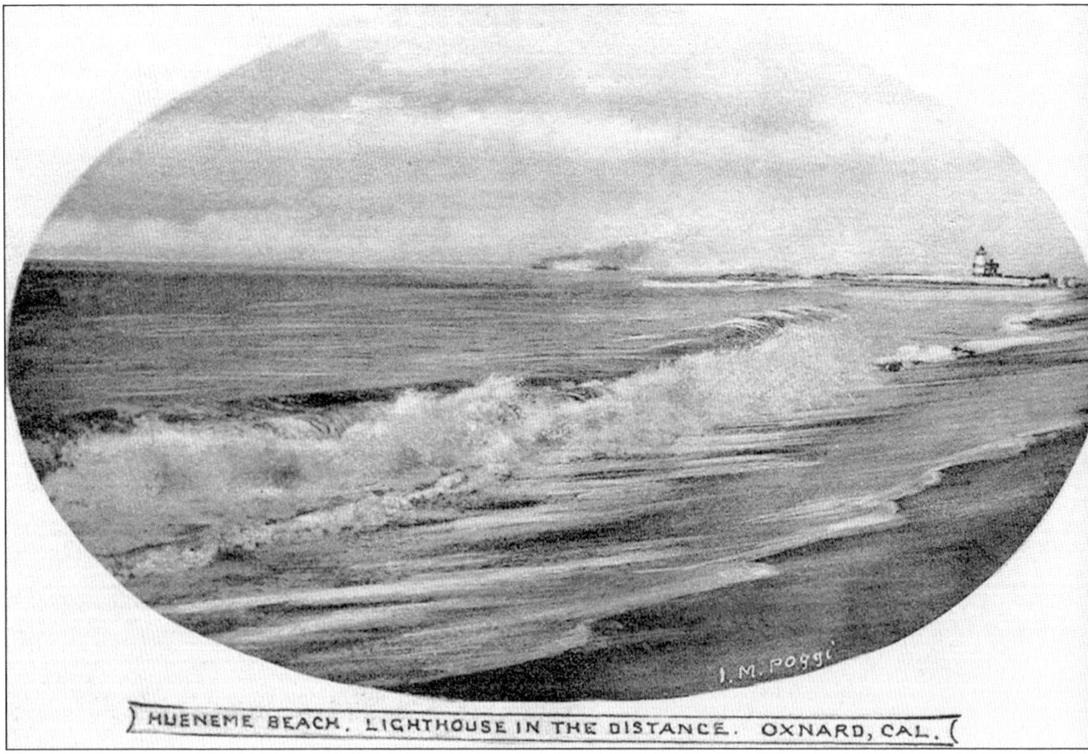

ON THE COVER: Sacks of barley, a leading export crop between 1870 and 1890, are ready for transport to one of the many ships that anchored at the end of the Hueneme Wharf. (Courtesy of the Port Hueneme Historical Society.)

IMAGES
of America

PORT HUENEME

Jeffrey Wayne Maulhardt

ARCADIA
PUBLISHING

ISBN 978-0-7385-3064-2

Published by Arcadia Publishing
Charleston, South Carolina

Printed in the United States of America
Library of Congress Catalog Card Number: 2005930093

For all general information contact Arcadia Publishing at:
Telephone 843-853-2070
Fax 843-853-0044
E-mail sales@arcadiapublishing.com
For customer service and orders:
Toll-Free 1-888-313-2665

Visit us on the Internet at www.arcadiapublishing.com

This book is dedicated to my mom, Jean Marie Maulhardt, and to my extended family from the Port Hueneme Little League. There are too many families, friends, and coaches to thank individually, for fear of not mentioning someone who at one time or another contributed to my wonderful childhood days.

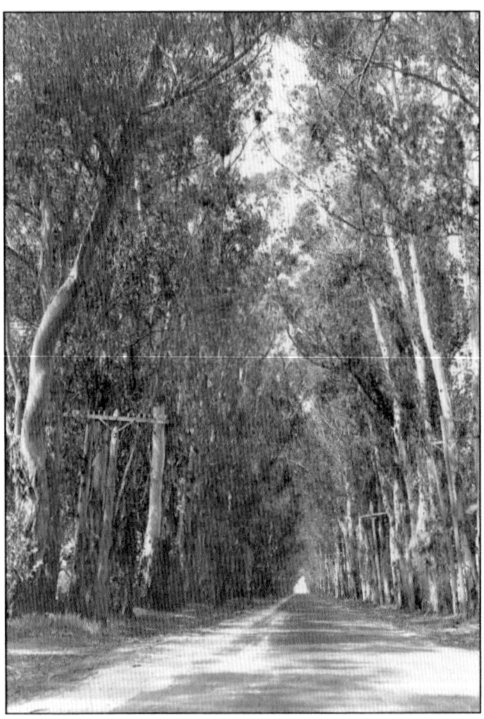

Thomas Bard planted seedlings shortly after he relocated to Hueneme from Ojai in 1871. With a keen interest in horticulture, Bard imported thousands of varieties of plants over the years and planted over 2,000 seedlings himself. He eventually planted 40 acres of trees, a total of more than 60,000 trees. Pictured here are eucalyptus trees along Fourth Street (Ventura Road).

Contents

ACKNOWLEDGMENTS

First on my list of acknowledgements is Dorothy Ramirez, who not only allowed me unlimited access to the collection of the Hueneme Historical Society but also gave me hours of her time while I scanned images used in this publication. Also, thank you to Helen Brant and Laura and Ray Prueter. Special thanks goes to Jeannette Moranda for allowing me to come over to her historic home and browse through the pictures and articles belonging to her late husband, Walter Bill Moranda. Also, I appreciate the follow-up phone calls and all the legwork it took to find that extra name, date, or place. Thanks to Ted Moranda for the entertaining memoirs in his book *Paul 'n Me and Old Hueneme* and for sending me some personal photographs at a moment's notice. I am also indebted to the efforts of Powell Greenland for authoring the definitive history, *Port Hueneme: A History*. Thanks to my good friend and fellow history enthusiast Eric Daily, who deserves credit for making this book a little more special by giving me the opportunity to plow through his collection once again and by graciously allowing me to scan whatever I needed. Thanks to Hueneme legend Larry Miller, Ed Maulhardt, and Craig Maulhardt for providing sports pictures. David Davis's help was indispensable, and he provided access to several invaluable photographs from his personal collection. Charles Johnson of the Ventura County Museum of History and Art provided me with treasured images from the library's archives. Thanks to Rita Borchard Edsall, whose pictures I scanned years ago and still seem to find a place for them in my books. Thank you to our original family historian, Richard Maulhardt, and his wife, Ruth. Their early and long-lasting support has encouraged me to keep scanning and to keep typing. My eternal gratitude goes out to Grandpa Robert Louis Maulhardt for all the "quarters" he gave us at the Hueneme Little Field (A quarter could by five Reese's cups!) and for providing a role model for all my brothers and me. Thanks to Pat Weigel for talking Mom into getting us into baseball. Thanks to all the friends I grew up with at the Hueneme Little League—though we don't see each other as much, we are still a family.

Thanks to Mom for taking us to the Hueneme beach almost every day in the summer after baseball was over. Thanks to my brothers, Ed, Tim and Craig, for supporting me in all of my many ventures and to my sister, Julie, for teaching us all humility.

INTRODUCTION

The name of the city of Port Hueneme has changed as much as the direction of the city itself. Originally *Wene'me* meant and was a "resting place" for the many Chumash Indians who paddled up and down the coast from Santa Monica to San Luis Obispo. Soon after the establishment of the mission at San Buenaventura, the "point" was abandoned by the Chumash in favor of mission life. For the next 80 years, Hueneme and the majority of the 44,000-acre Rancho El Rio de Santa Clara o la Colonia was void of activity, save for cattle grazing for a short period in the late 1850s by the original grantee, Raphael Gonzalez, and his family.

In 1856, Lt. James Alden, who was in charge of the Coast and Geodetic Survey, penned a new spelling for the area on his map of the West Coast—Point Hueneme. It wasn't until Christian Borchard and his son John Edward Borchard planted the first commercial crop—barley—in 1867 that a new direction for the plain was established. Also at this time, Pennsylvania-born Thomas Bard, who originally oversaw the development of Thomas Scott's oil industry in the Ventura/Ojai area, envisioned a wharf to export farming goods as part of a thriving agricultural industry. But first, Bard had to clear up a boundary dispute caused by vague border descriptions of the Rancho Colonia. Scott, Bard's boss, owned approximately five-sevenths of the rancho, or over 32,000 acres. The remaining acreage was owned by the Gonzalez family and sold shortly after to the "New Californians." It was the Scott-owned property that fell into dispute.

Unlike many Midwestern states that offered homestead property of 160 acres, most California land was divided up during the Mexican ownership of California between 1834 and 1846. Beginning in 1834, California governors handed out over 100 land grants, 17 in Ventura County. The grants were large enough for livestock grazing, usually 11 leagues, or approximately 40,000 acres. The scarcity of land for new settlers to buy and settle led to land disputes. In the case of Rancho Colonia, 17,000 acres came under fire when squatters claimed a triangular piece of land between Mugu lagoon and the slough near Point Hueneme. The name *Wynema* was reestablished by one of approximately 100 men who formed the Squatters League and were led by W. E. Barnard, H. P. Flint, G. S. Gilbert, Daniel Dempsey, and Robert G. Livingston. In 1870, Barnard and three partners established the Wynema Lighter Company to transport goods to and from the point area and out to awaiting ships. Barnard, along with partners Flint and Gilbert, also established the Pioneer Store. Further cementing his position of power in the area, Barnard became the first postmaster general and the area's correspondent to the *Ventura Signal*.

Thomas Bard, on the other hand, had his work cut out for him. In addition to fighting the boundary dispute in court, he had to fight to get a foothold in the area where he planned to develop a wharf. By February 1871, Bard established the Hueneme Wharf and Lighter Company to challenge Barnard's company. Tensions between the established "squatters" and Bard's interests soon reached boiling point. In a move that echoed the strategy of the squatters, Bard and his men fenced off an area in which he intended to "squat" in order to start his wharf. In May 1871, a near "war" between Bard and Barnard, whose men were equipped with rifles, was avoided when the two men came to an agreement to settle the matter in court. Bard proved victorious and offered the "squatted land" for sale or lease to his former foes. Bard's diplomatic patience was a prelude to his later political ambitions, which culminated in a seat in the U.S. Senate in 1900. Bard and Barnard ended up becoming longtime friends.

In 1872, Secretary of the Interior Columbus Delano confirmed Bard's claim to reestablish the original boundaries of Rancho Colonia, thus giving Bard the power to sell or lease the 17,000 acres of land in dispute. By June, Bard platted the town of Hueneme. The next year, on January 1, 1873, Bard was among the leaders, along with Angel Escandon and William Dewy Hobson, who helped break off the southern portion of Santa Barbara County into a new district, Ventura County. With this new configuration came a new voting district, the Hueneme Township, which included the plains area south of the Santa Clara River. The name was officially changed from Wynema to Hueneme when a post office was established on August 10, 1874. For the next 24 years, Hueneme was the bustling agriculture hub in the county.

Things changed drastically for the wharf town when the Oxnard brothers decided to build a $2-million factory in the middle of the plain in 1898. With the building of this factory, area farmers switched to planting sugar beets, which were shipped by rail out of Oxnard, bypassing the town of Hueneme altogether. Soon, businesses, homes, and families were transported across the fields to the new hub of agricultural activity, Oxnard. Among the longtime Hueneme businesses that left were Lehman and Waterman, general merchandise; Harry Witman, hardware and plumbing; the McCoy brothers' restaurant and saloon; I. M. Poggi, druggist; and B. F. Korts, the town's butcher.

For the next two decades, Hueneme was a glorified ghost town. Weekends and holidays were the exception after 1905, when the Bakersfield & Ventura Railway laid down tracks from Oxnard to the beach community of Hueneme. For 22¢, one could get a round-trip ticket to the beach. Richard Peacock, who owned a confectionary store in Oxnard, rented a piece of land next to the beach from the Bard family and opened up a resort. By the late 1920s, Henry Horsewood purchased the business, and the resort became known as Horsewood's up until the tropical storm of 1939, when the resort, boardwalk, and wharf were destroyed.

In 1922, two packinghouses were built for Sunkist, one next to the wharf and the other next to present-day Ventura Road and the beach road. This brought a little vitality to the area but nothing like the pre–sugar factory days. The year 1937 brought the formation of the Harbor District plans to develop a shipping port, but World War II derailed the longtime efforts of Richard Bard and others when the Navy took over the harbor and much of the beach area.

With the addition of the new harbor, the citizens of Hueneme went to the polls to vote on a name change that would reflect their new status as a port town. On May 1, 1940, the name officially became Port Hueneme. Eight years later, on March 16, 1948, residents went to the polls again to vote on incorporation. The 2,875 citizens voted overwhelmingly for cityhood. Bert Dahl was selected as the first mayor, and he was joined on the council by John Priegel, George Moranda, Ansgar Larsen, and Ralph McKeehan. The charter council and its succeeding members helped shape Port Hueneme into a jewel of a beach community that has fostered pride in anyone who has every lived, worked, or been associated with the city.

One

Wynema
A Bustling Town

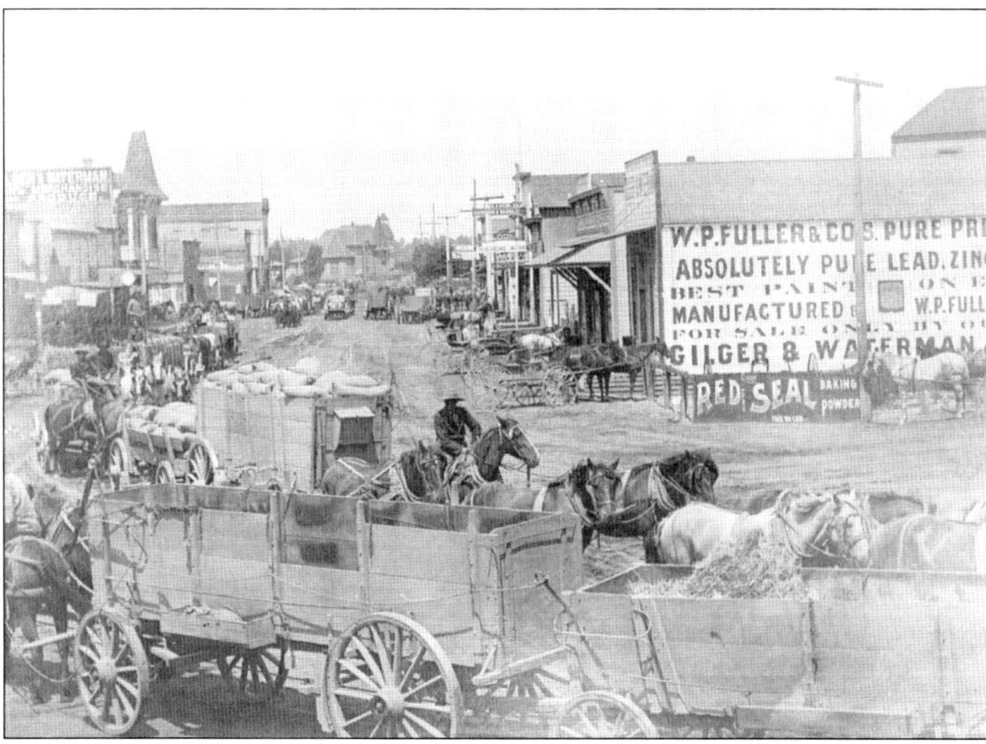

Hueneme was a busy grain port for the 30 years between 1870 and 1900. Wheat, barley, and corn were the most abundant produce during this time. Here, a line of wagons wait their turn to unload their produce at one of the several warehouses near the wharf. The steeple of the Methodist Episcopal Church is visible in the background.

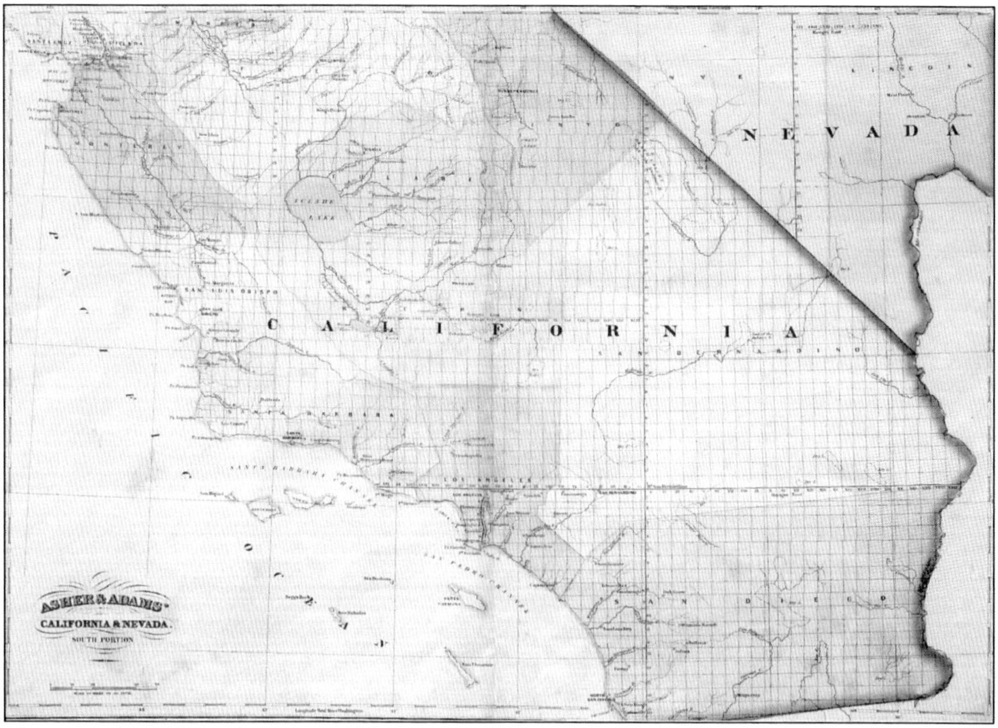

This map depicts Southern California in 1872, but by January 1873, Ventura County had been partitioned off from Santa Barbara County. Thomas Bard was instrumental in creating the new county, which had a population of 3,100, 65,000 acres of tillable land, and 310,000 acres used for grazing. There were also 64,717 grapevines, 11,580 almond trees, 8,699 walnut trees, 127 orange trees, and 50 lemon trees. Sheep, hogs, and cattle made up the top three livestock at 107,800, 4,450, and 4,030 respectively.

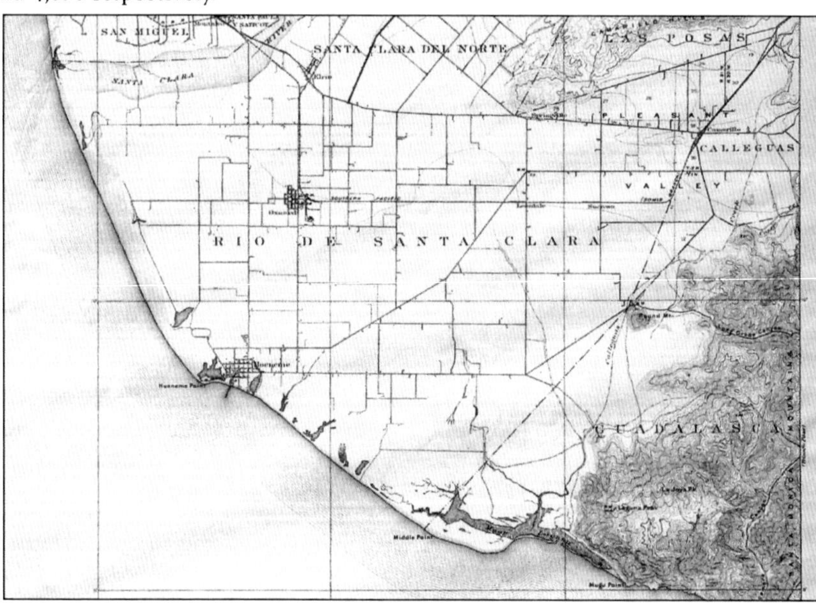

This map by the U.S. Department of Interior was completed in 1901 and shows the center of town for both Hueneme and Oxnard.

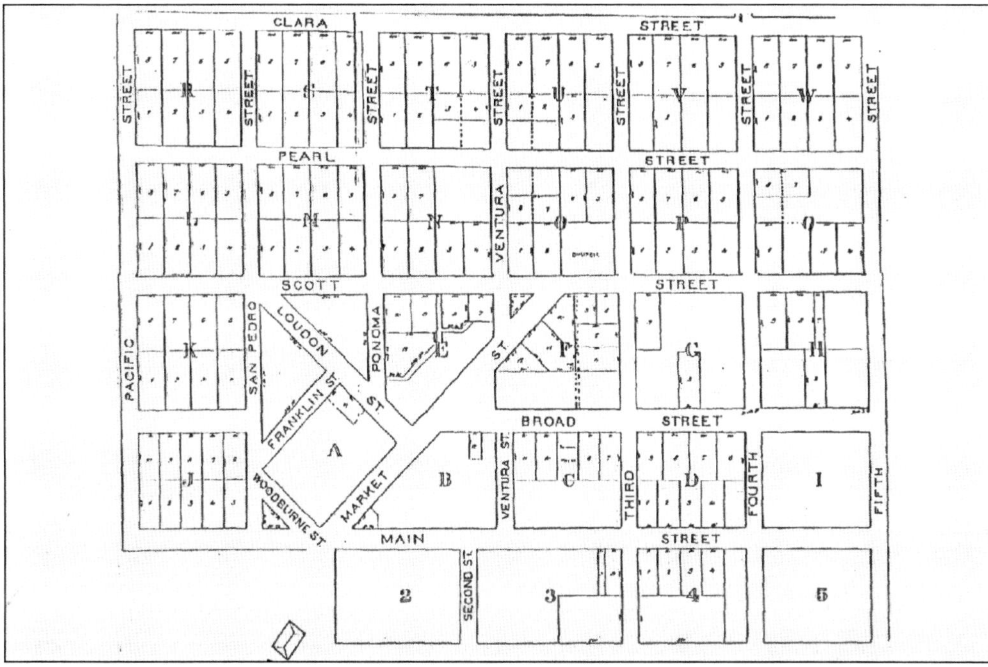

The town site of Hueneme was laid out by Thomas Bard in 1872, and Bard selected names from his past for use in his new hometown. Scott Street came from his employer, Thomas Scott. Franklin Street was derived from the county of Bard's birth, while Woodbourne was the name of his former residence. Clara was named for his sister in-law Clara Gerberding. Market Street was also a name from his Pennsylvania upbringing. Broad Street, which met up with Market Street at a diagonal, was later changed to Hueneme Road.

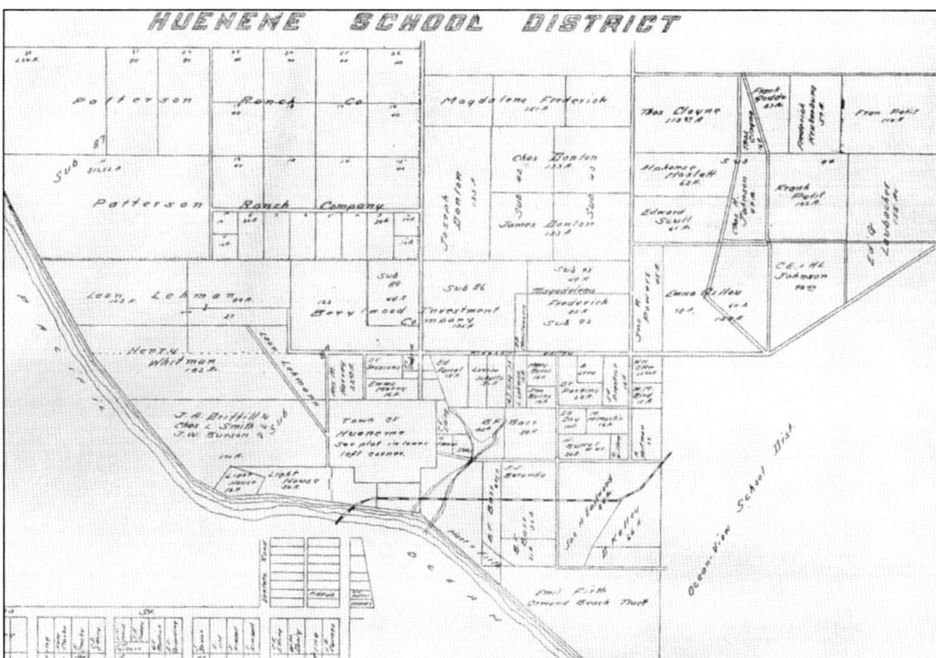

This map shows the Hueneme School District boundaries in 1913.

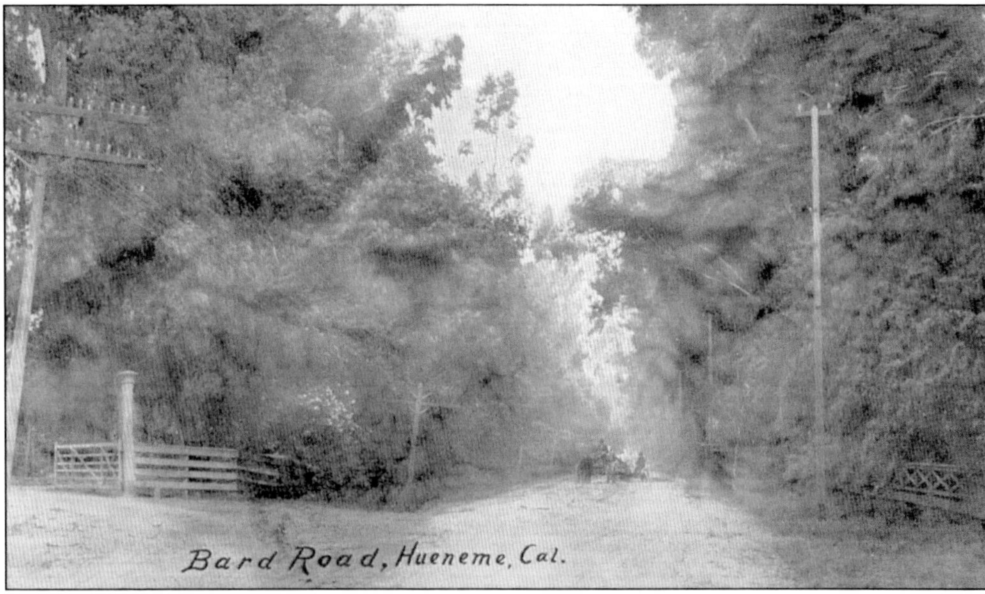

Thomas Bard planted eucalyptus as a windbreak, and because the trees grew rapidly, the wood could also be used as firewood for the formerly treeless plain. Bard purchased his seedlings from Elwood Cooper of Santa Barbara, who had introduced the native Australian eucalyptus tree to California. Cooper also imported ladybugs from the Orient to fight the clack scale—a black scale disease that was threatening the orchards in Santa Barbara.

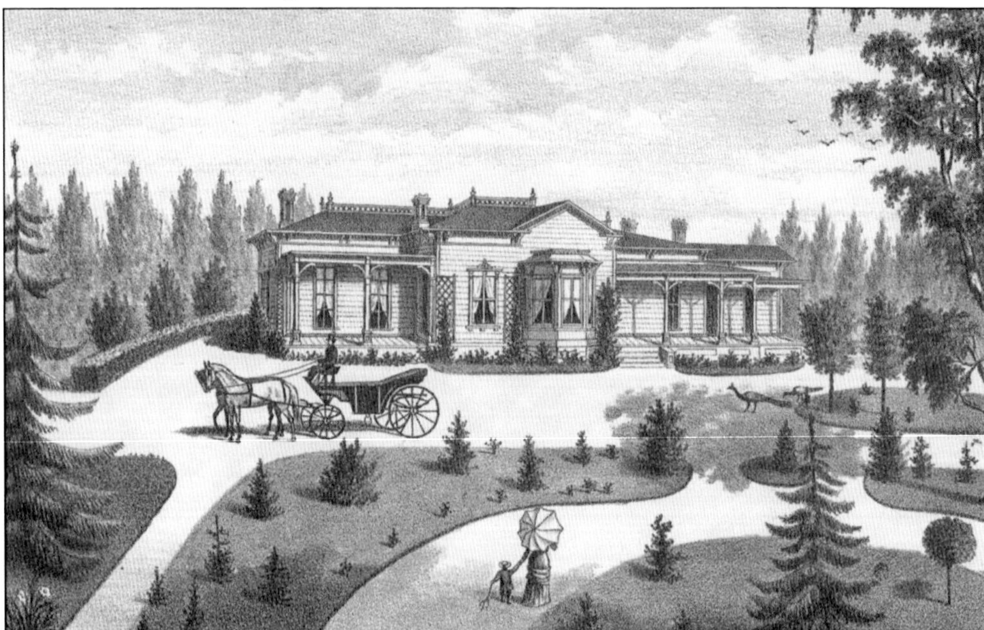

When Thomas Bard first moved to Hueneme, there was only one fruit store, one livery, one butcher shop, one hotel, one barber shop, and one lumber yard. With the building of the wharf, this would all change. Bard built three homes in Hueneme. The first, built in 1874, was a small bungalow that served as a temporary home until he could build the larger, one-story, six-room home he named Berylwood, pictured here.

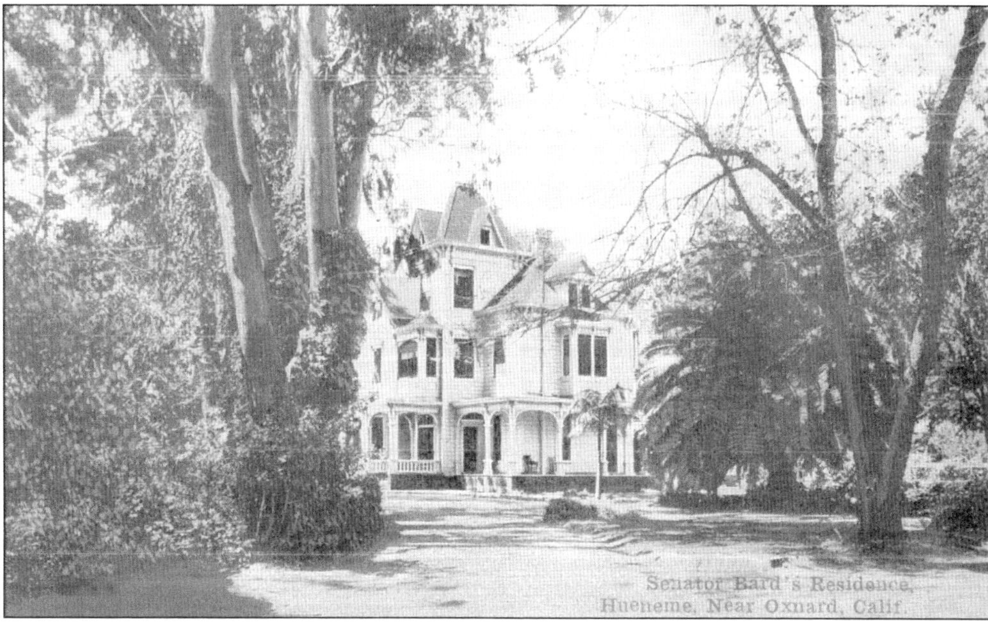

When Thomas Bard's wife, Mollie Gerberding, arrived at her new home in 1876, she was extremely disappointed to find the land to be so barren, flat, and treeless. Bard immediately set out to increase his tree plantings as well as expand the size and grandeur of his residence.

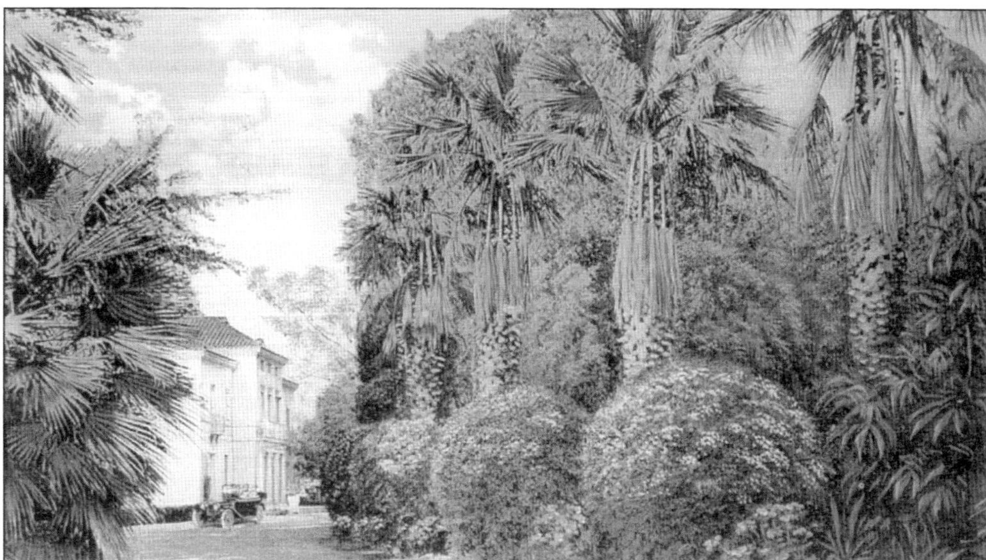

In 1912, Bard built one of grandest homes in Ventura County. Designed by Myron Hunt, the new stucco-and-tile Berylwood took 18 months to complete. One reason for the new home was Thomas Bard's dilated heart condition, which led his doctor to suggest that an elevator be installed to accommodate Bard's movement to his second-story bedroom. The structure now serves as the officers' club for the Naval Construction Battalion Base, as well as home to the organization that helps preserve the mansion and its associated history, the Friends of the Bard Mansion. The Bard family retained ownership of the 20 acres surrounding the home and leased it to the Navy from 1944 to 1951, after which they sold the land and residence for $149,500.

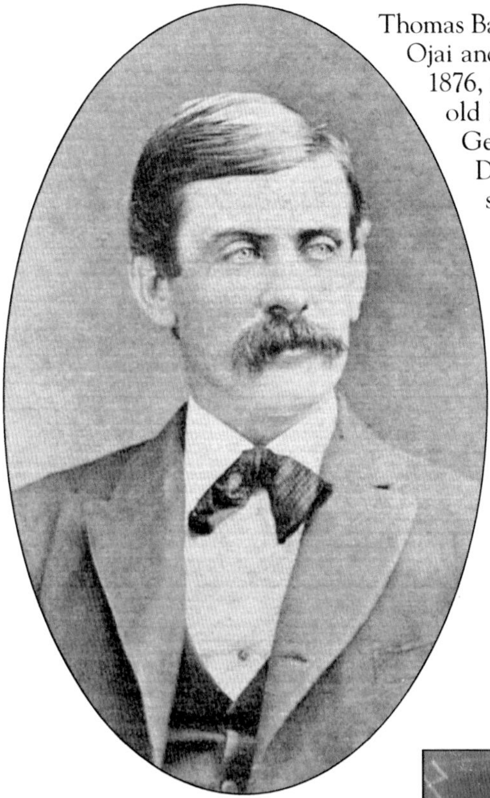

Thomas Bard moved to Hueneme in May 1874 after selling Ojai and Canda Larga properties for Thomas Scott. By 1876, the 34-year-old Thomas Bard married 18-year-old Mary "Molly" Gerberding, the sister of Clara Gerberding, who was married to Bard's brother Dr. Cephas Bard. Thomas and Molly Bard raised seven children, losing one child, Robert, at 22 months. Thomas Bard passed away in 1915, but his wife lived at the Berylwood home until 1934. She passed away in 1937 in Ojai.

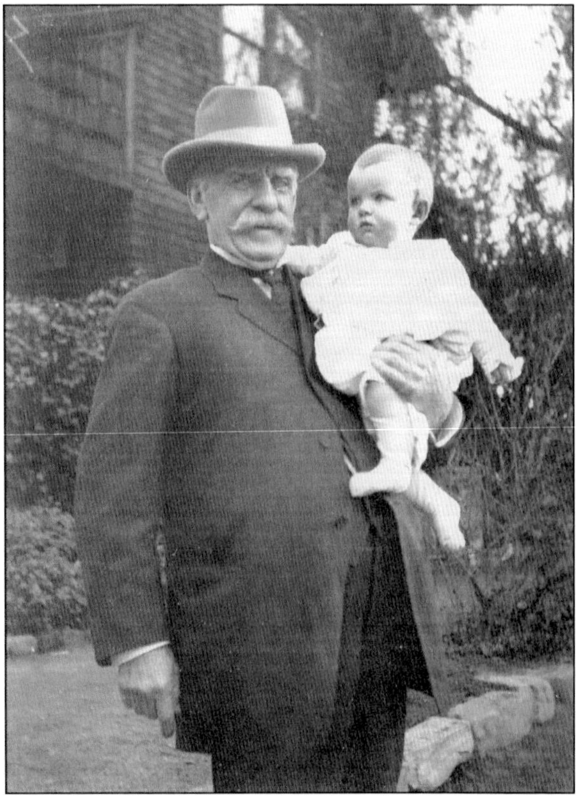

In addition to being one of the first "realtors" of Ventura County, Bard was an accomplished politician and county advocate. He served as the first supervisor for the Hueneme Township in 1873 and topped off his political career by serving as a U.S. senator from 1900 to 1905. His son Richard Bard became active in community affairs by heading the group that developed the harbor. The Bard family also donated some land for the Bubbling Springs Park as well as portions of the Hueneme beach.

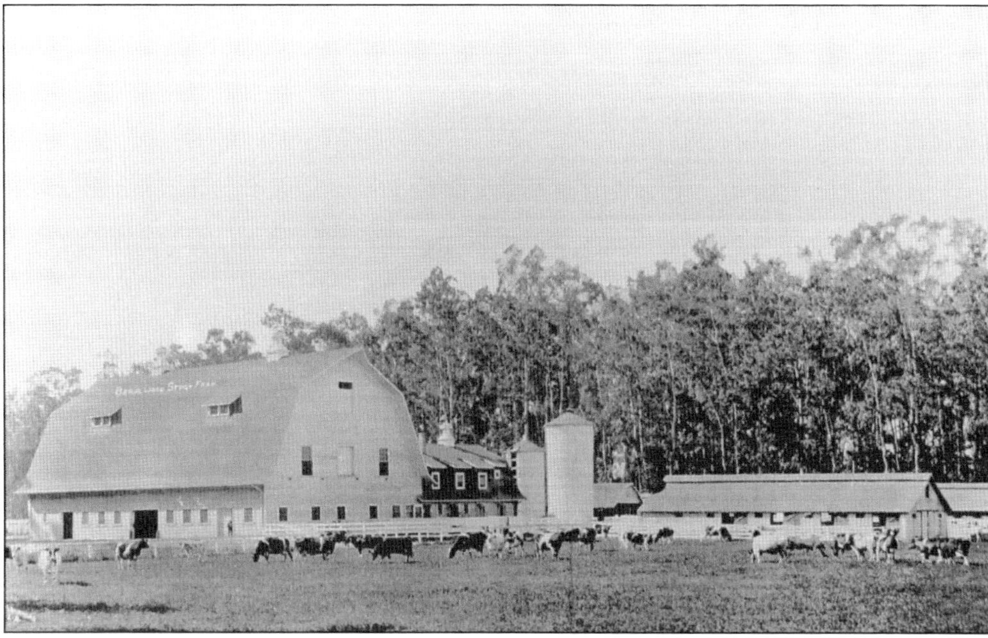

The Berylwood Stock Farm was located on the Thomas Bard property.

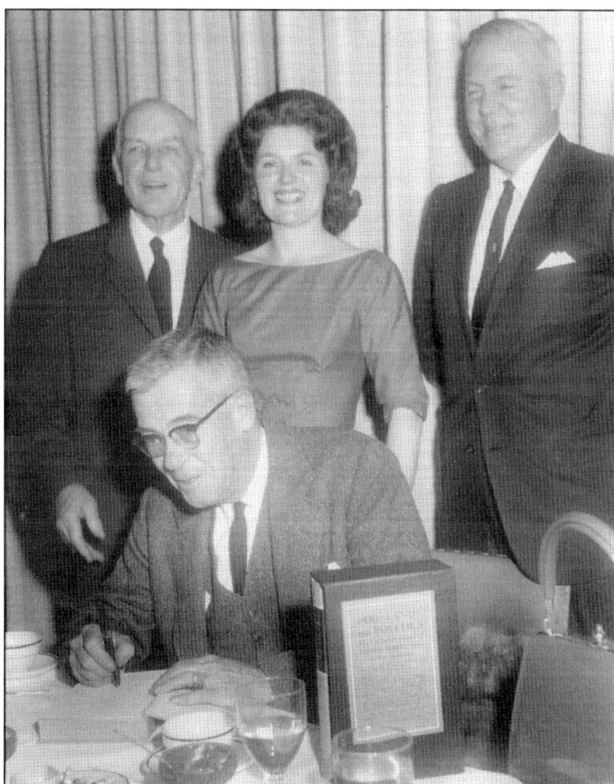

William H. Hutchinson signs copies of his two-volume biography of Thomas Robert Bard, published by Oklahoma Press in 1964. Pictured on the left is Richard Bard, the son of Thomas Bard, and to the right of Bard is Mrs. Duane O'Hara.

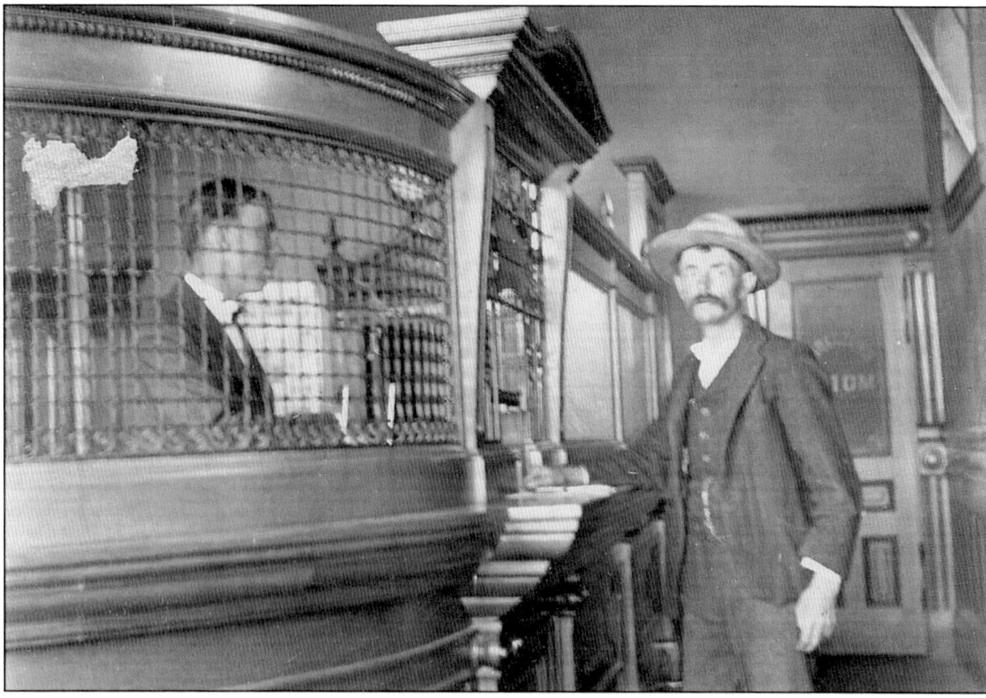

This 1890s interior view of the Bank of Hueneme features teller Fergus Linn "Ted" Fairbanks and customer Joseph Mehn. The Fairbanks family arrived in Hueneme in 1881, and Ted's father served as an assistant wharfinger—a position that put him in charge of the wharf and warehouses. The younger Fairbanks went to work for the Bank of Hueneme around 1896.

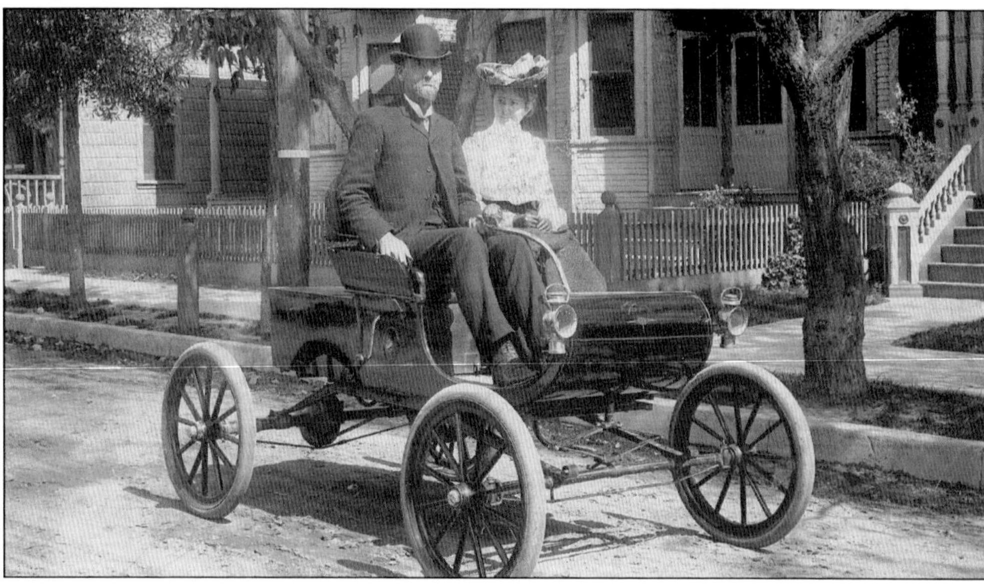

Dr. Oscar V. Sessions is said to have owned the first automobile in Ventura County, an event announced by the *Free Press* in December 1896. Born in Anna, Illinois, in 1852, Sessions attended Northwestern University Medical School and relocated to Hueneme in 1882. He turned over his practice to Dr. Livingston in 1903 and moved to Los Angeles to write, lecture, and travel. He devoted his later years to archeological excavations in Mexico.

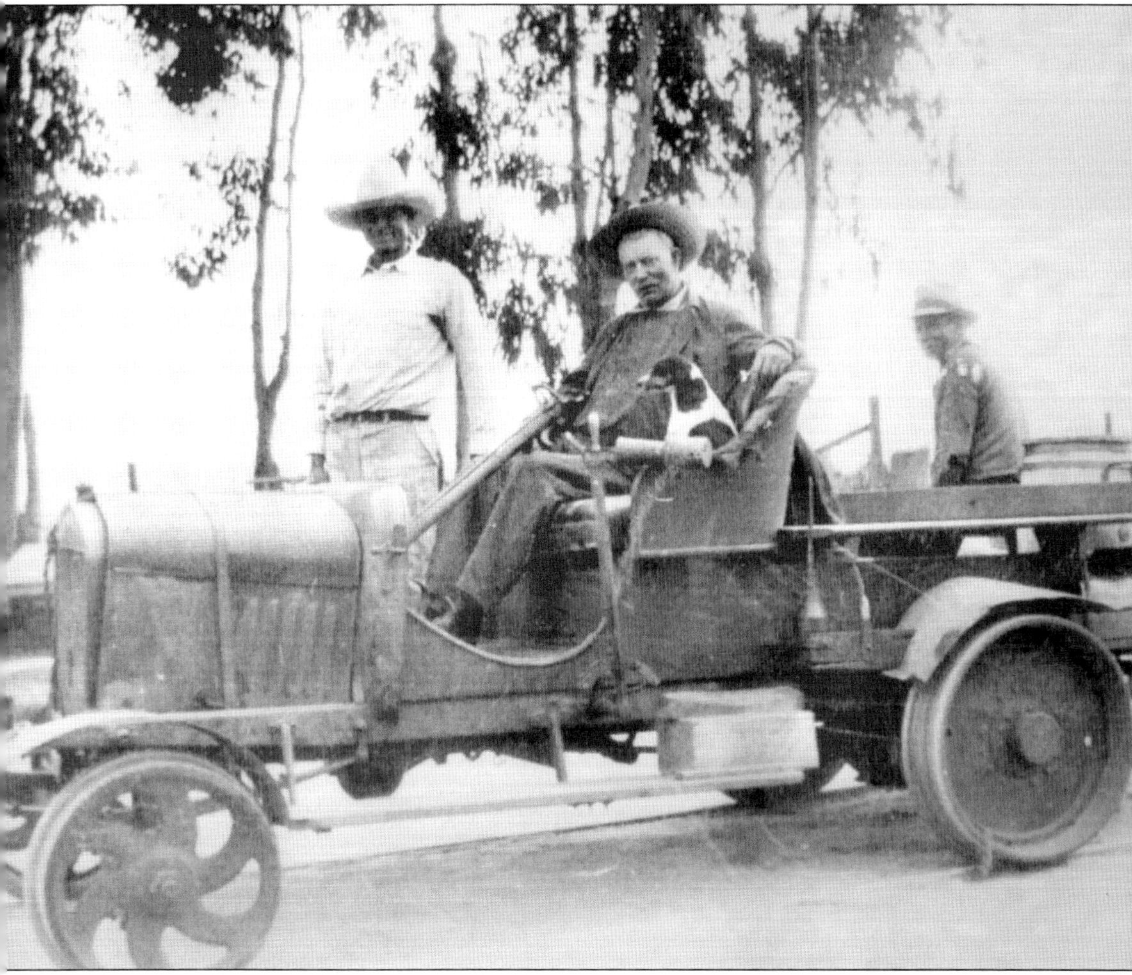

This vehicle served as a repair car for the Ventura County Railway. The converted truck had a Studebaker body, a Cadillac rear end, and a four-cylinder Ford Model T engine. The "machine" could travel up to 30 miles an hour.

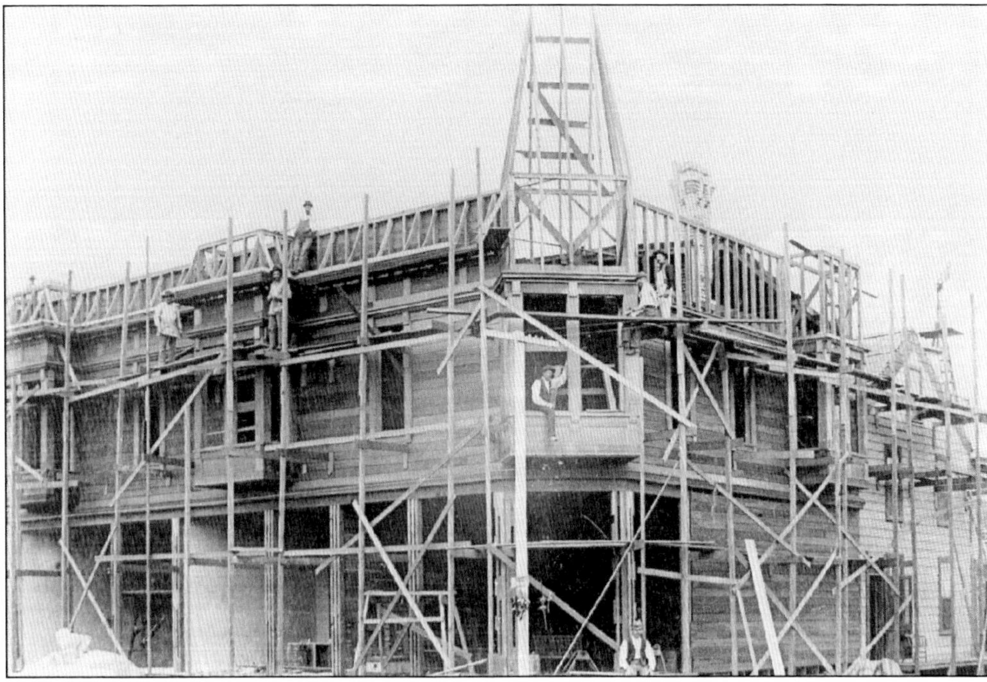

Construction of the Seaside Hotel began construction in 1894, and once completed, the first-class hotel became the resting place for vacationers, as well as businessmen traveling through the area. The men who worked for Oxnard Construction Company and who built the Oxnard Beet Sugar Factory stayed at the Seaside Hotel.

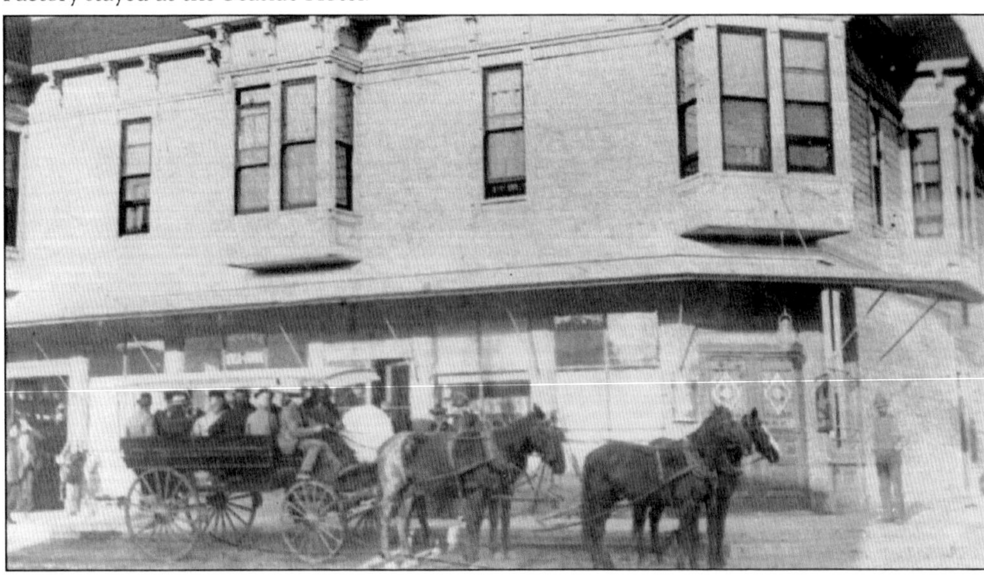

The proprietor of the Seaside Hotel, which was located on Market Street, was J. E. McCoy. In addition to renting a fine room at the hotel, patrons could get a game of billiards, eat in the restaurant, and belly up to the bar. Though the Seaside Hotel did abandon its original site for the growing town of Oxnard, the hotel suffered a worse fate when it burned to the ground in a fire in 1904. Pictured here, the Hueneme Stagecoach and Livery, run by Bart Pitts, stops at the hotel to load up with passengers.

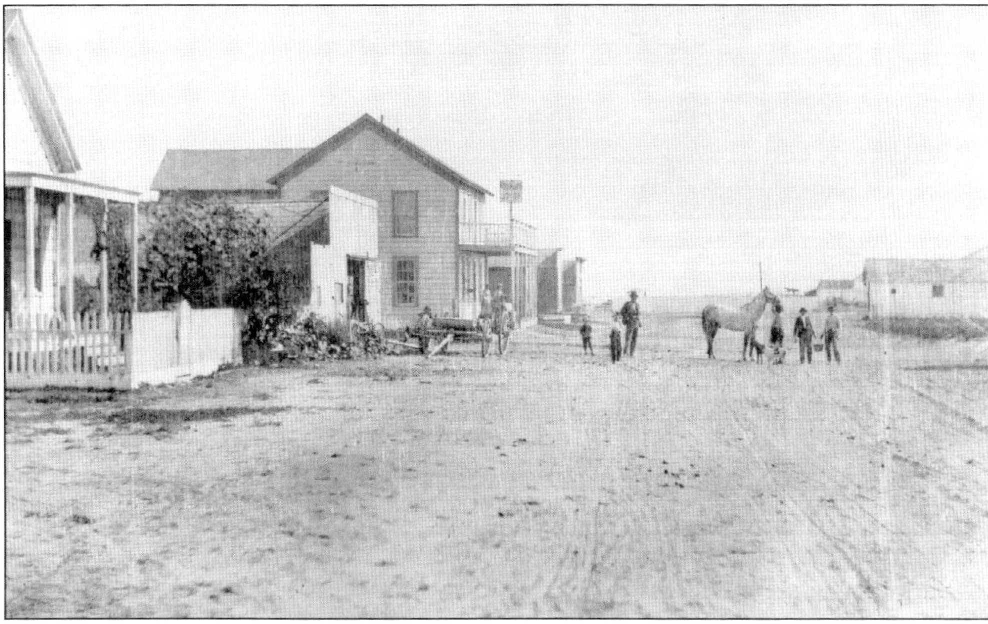

This 1870s view of Wynema shows the location of the Pioneer Hotel. D. D. McCoy, the proprietor of the hotel, also joined forces with D. W. Pierpont in 1875 to operate a butcher shop.

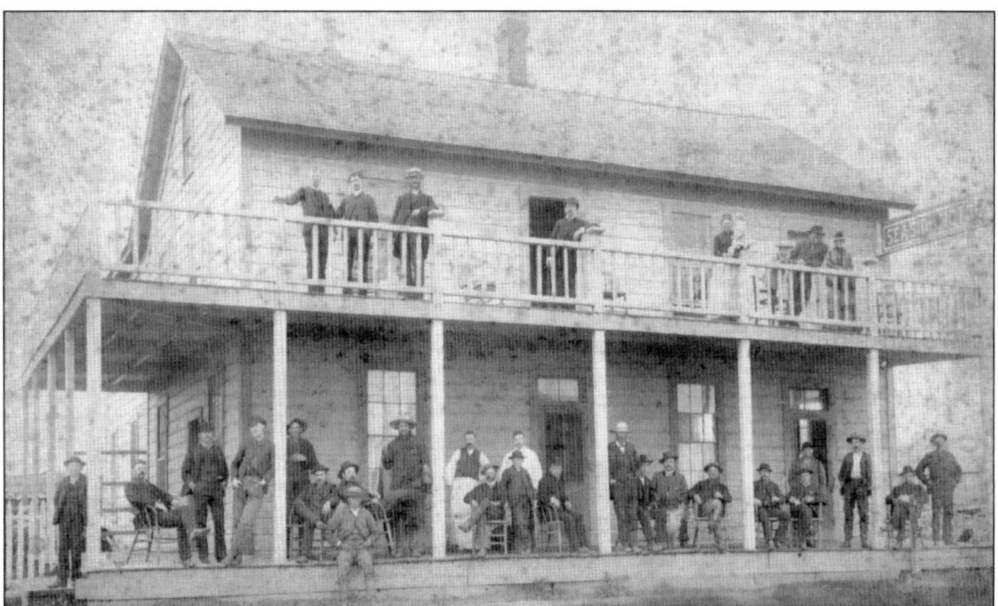

Though the two pictures on the opposite page are listed as the Seaside Hotel, the hotel in this picture displays a sign stating that it is also the Seaside Hotel. Either the photographs on the opposite page are a new version of the old hotel or they are of the Hueneme Hotel.

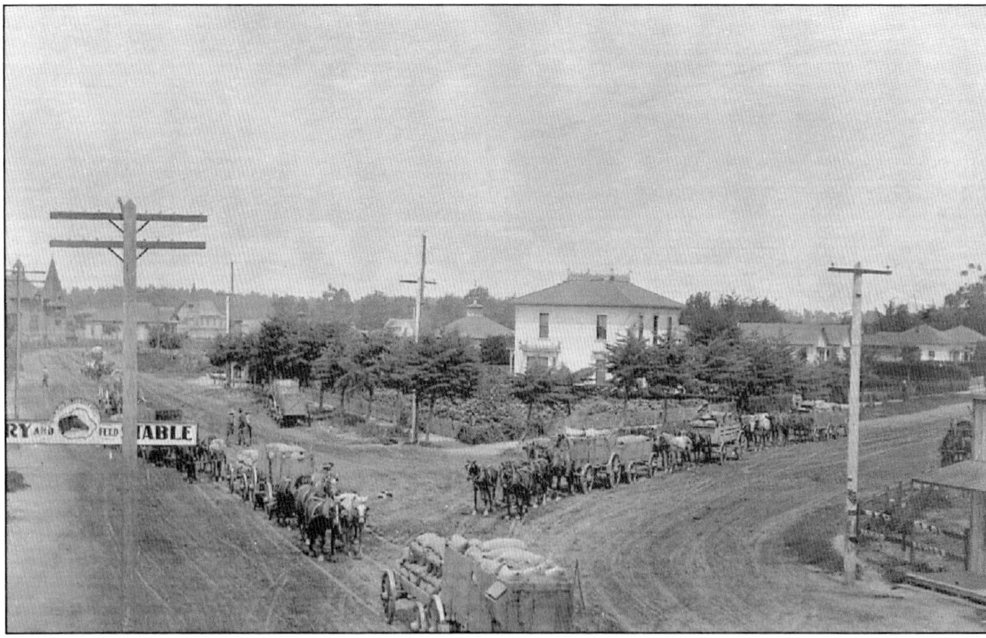

This view shows the intersection of Main and Market Streets in the 1890s. The warehouses in Hueneme had the capacity to store 325,000 sacks. Among the items exported out of the area in the 1890s included wheat, lima beans, corn, barley, oats, hogs, wool, fruit, livestock, oil, and asphaltum.

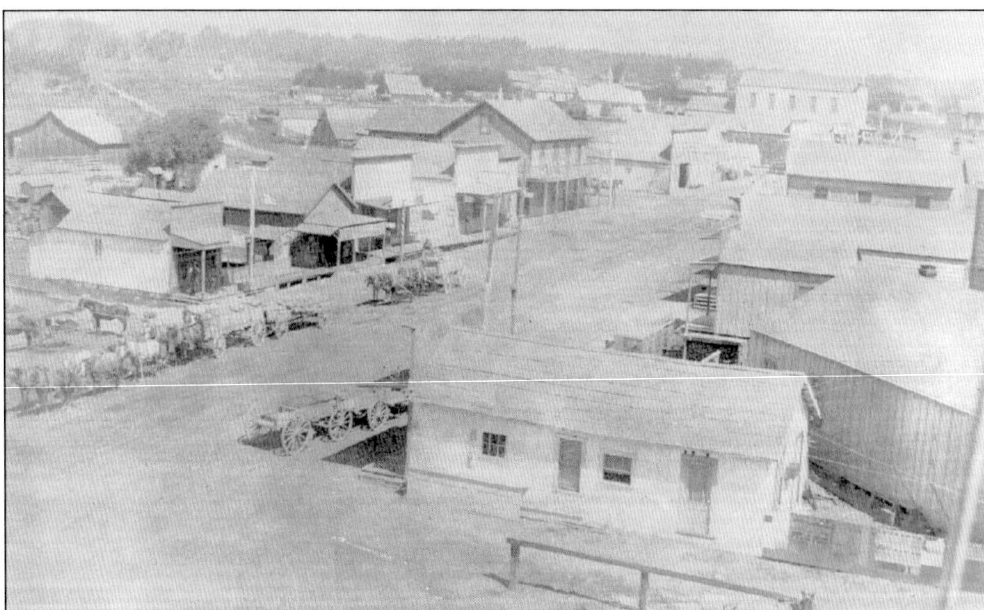

In addition to the many businesses that were springing up around Hueneme, the women of the community formed a lodge of Independent Order of Good Templars in 1879. The lodge began with 20 members, and within a short time, Mrs. Emily Pitts-Stevens had encouraged 128 members to pledge their allegiance to the group that fought against the consumption of alcohol.

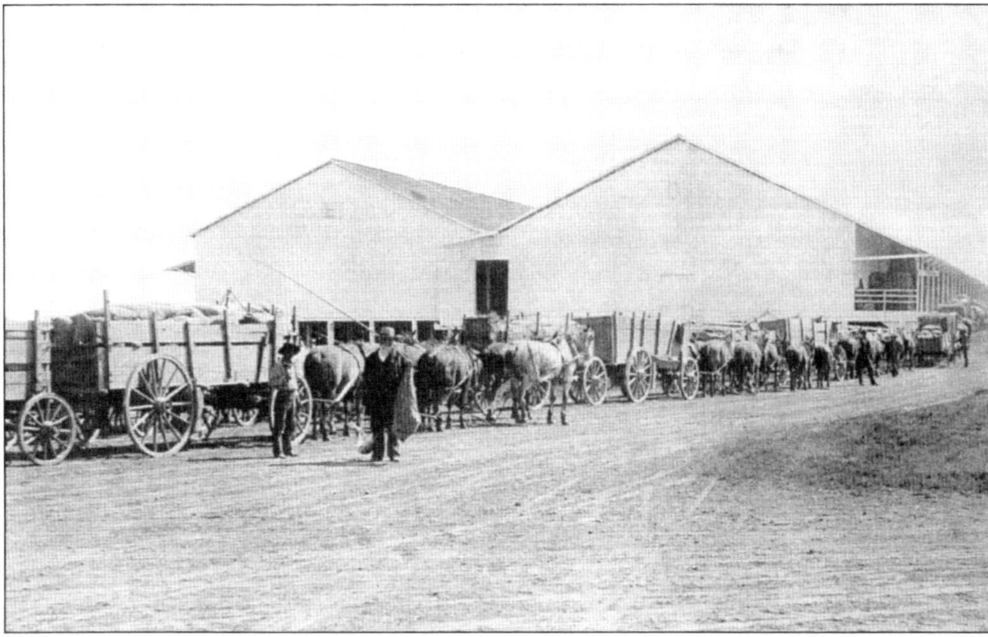

Patience was needed during harvest time. Here Elijah B. Fairbanks, the head of the wharf beginning in 1881, directs traffic to the warehouses. Fairbanks's boss was A. J. Salisbury, Thomas Bard's partner in the wharf business.

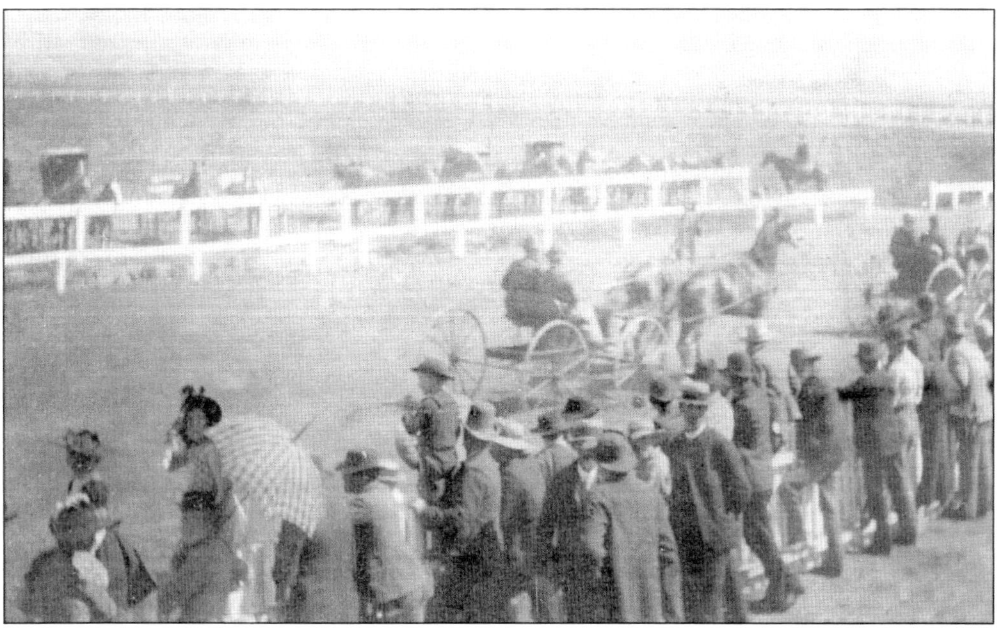

The Hueneme Racetrack and Fairgrounds, pictured *c.* 1891, were located on the former Lehman ranch and, later, the Naval Construction Battalion Center, just northwest of the town of Hueneme. Horse racing was a popular sport in the area at the time. Bets were taken on four races a day for both runners and trotters. William Zeller was in charge of the race entries, Charles Donlon took charge of the livestock entries, Leon Lehman served as superintendent of the pavilion displays, and David Perkins was in charge of the farm products exhibits.

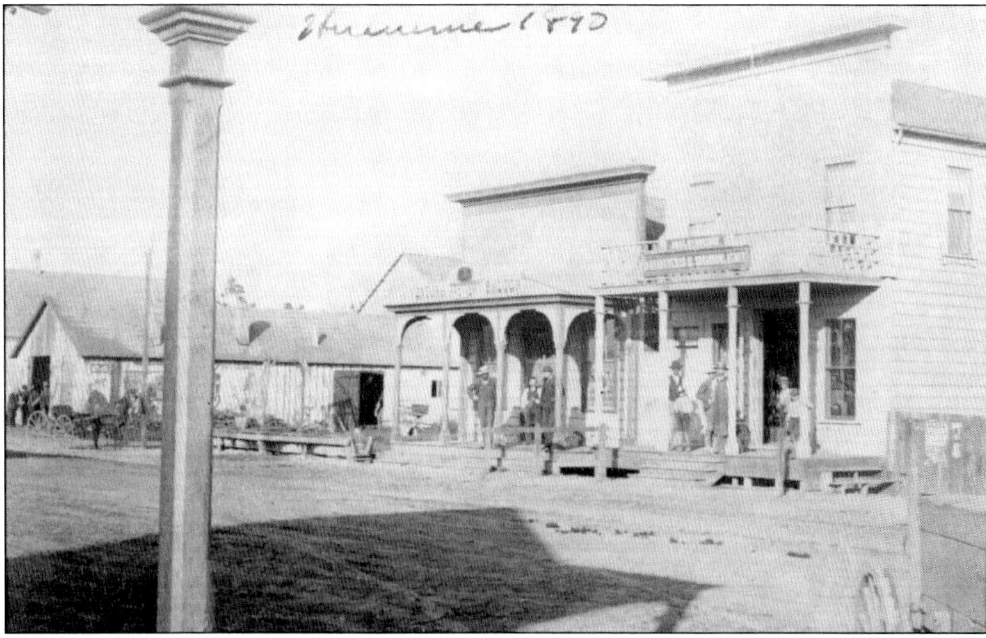

The businesses along the dirt road of Market Street in Hueneme in the 1890s included the Ventura Brewery Saloon and Joseph P. Mehn's Harness and Saddlery shop. Mehn also sold bicycles as early as 1898. Though Mehn did not move to Oxnard, his clients did. Ten years later, in 1908, Joseph Mehn was listed in the Ventura County directory as a notary public. (Courtesy of the Ventura County Museum of History and Art.)

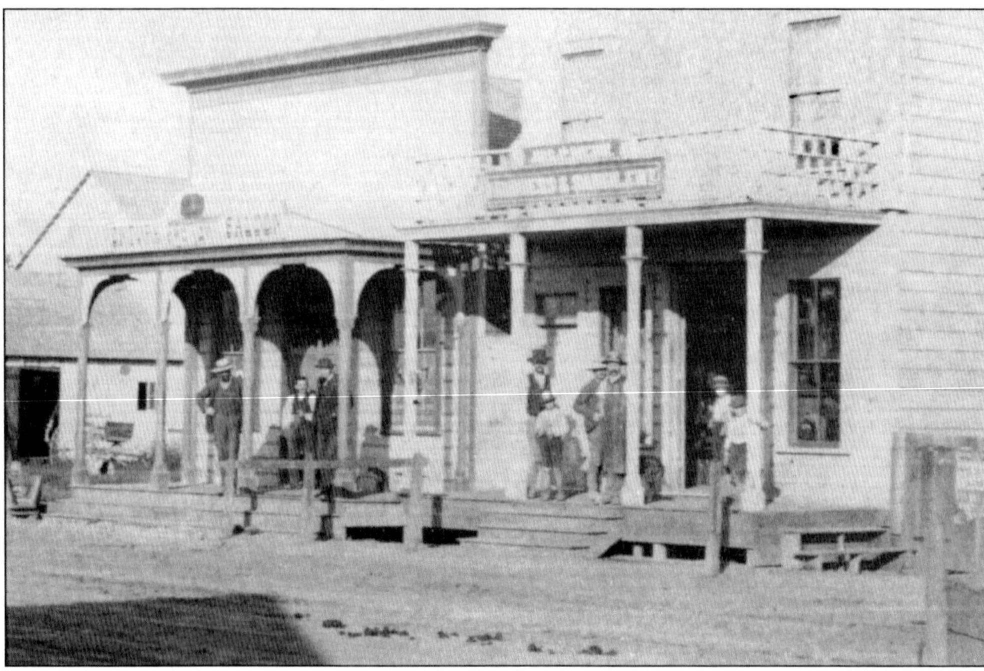

In this close up of the citizens of the day all but one are sporting a hat and most of the men have facial hair. Clothes could be purchased at Wolff and Lehman's store, the largest mercantile establishment in the county at the time.

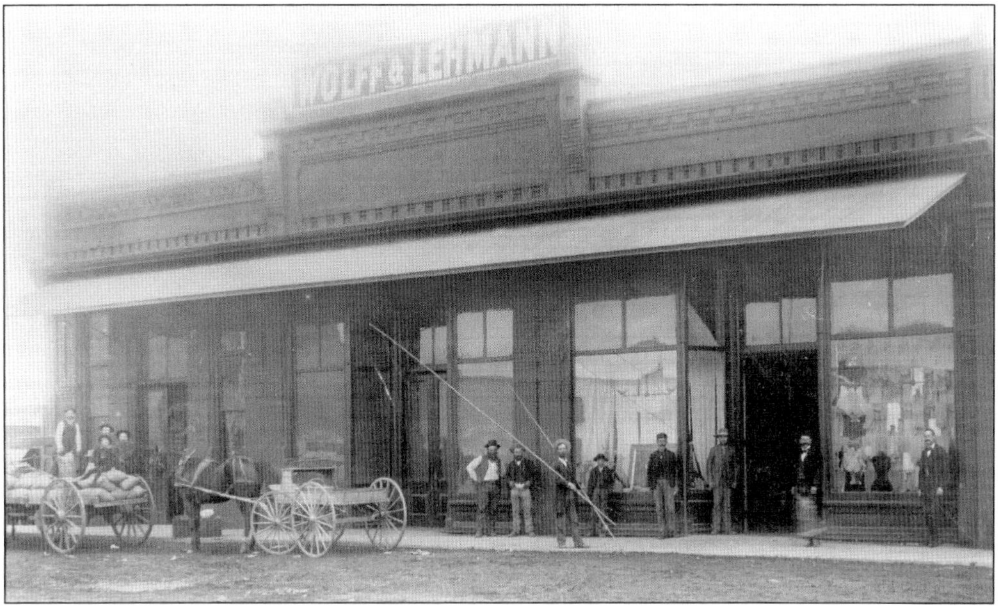

Wolff and Lehman received their shipments from the *Alcatraz*. Whenever she came into port, the townspeople knew they could restock at the store. (Courtesy of the Ventura County Museum of History and Art.)

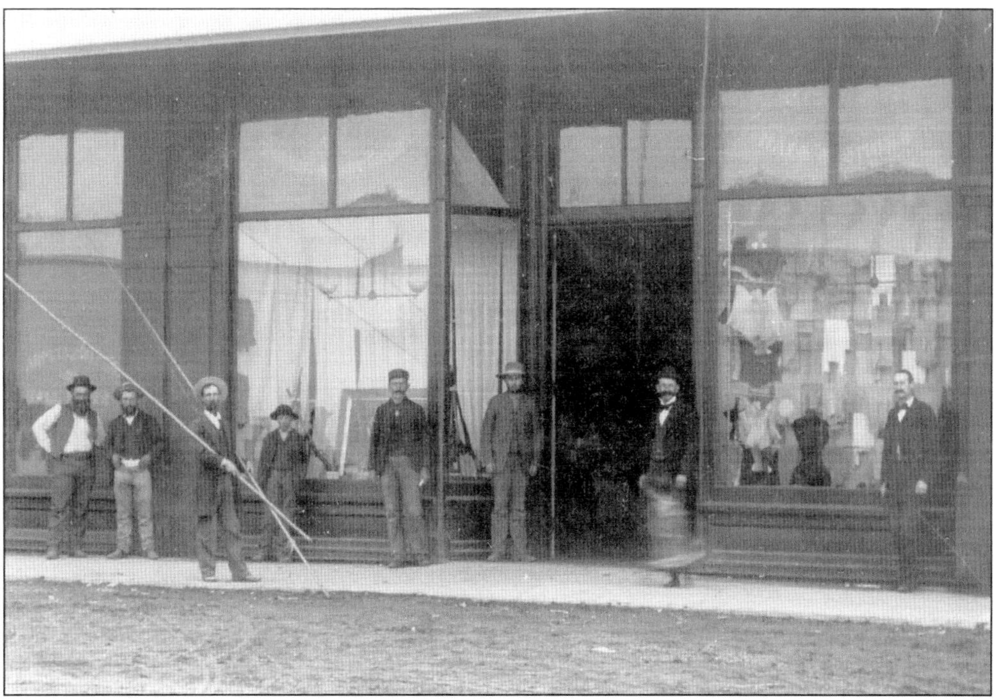

In March 1894, a fire swept through a block of buildings along Main Street, including the Wolff and Lehman building. The replacement building, seen in this picture, utilized brick and glass in its construction, but by 1898, Wolff and Lehman had joined the exodus to Oxnard.

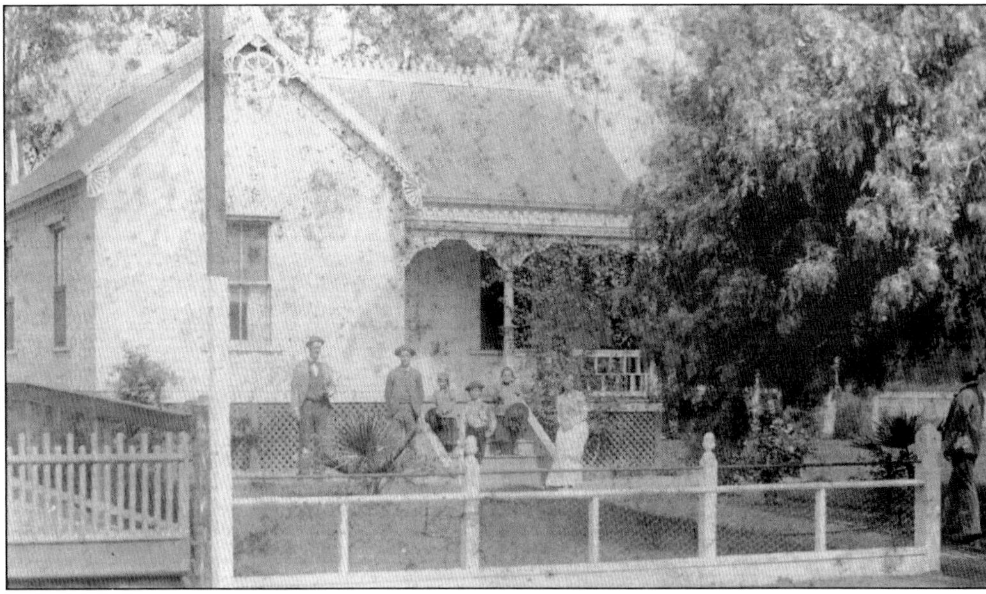

Pictured here is the C. G. Witman home in the 1880s. Son Harry W. Witman ran a hardware and plumbing business in Hueneme before relocating to Oxnard and expanding the business. (Courtesy of the Ventura County Museum of History and Art.)

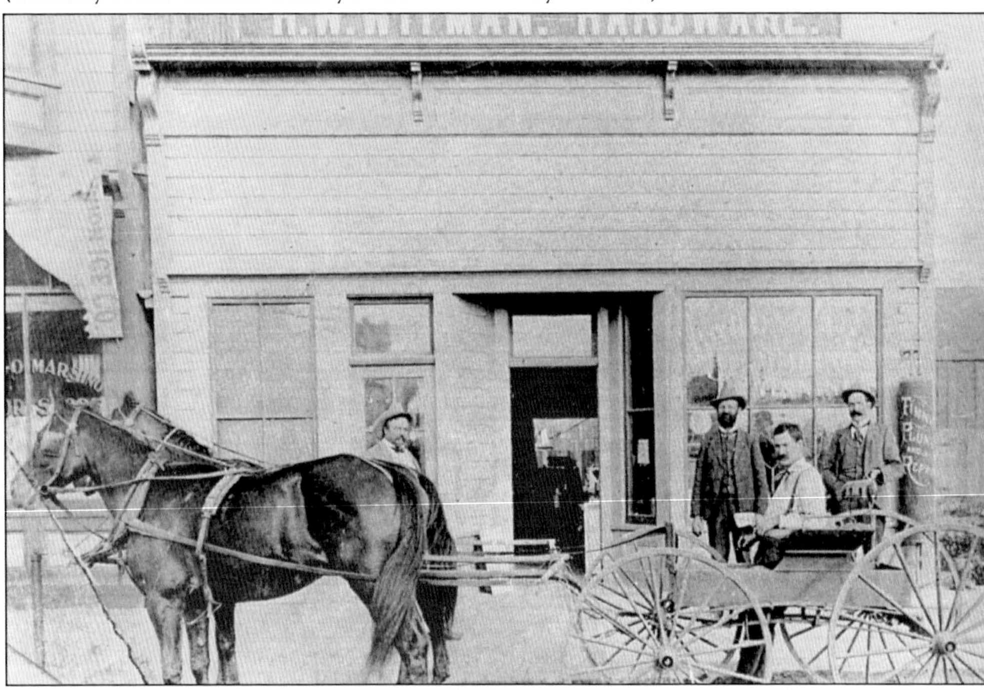

Witman's Hardware store met the needs of the town of Hueneme, but with the explosive growth of Oxnard, Harry Witman became one of that town's leading boosters. He guaranteed to sink a producing artesian well anywhere on the plain for $100 or he would return the money. Witman was part of several groups, including the Shriners, Elks, and Eagles organizations, and he was also influential in encouraging the big league New York Giants to come to Oxnard for an exhibition game in 1913.

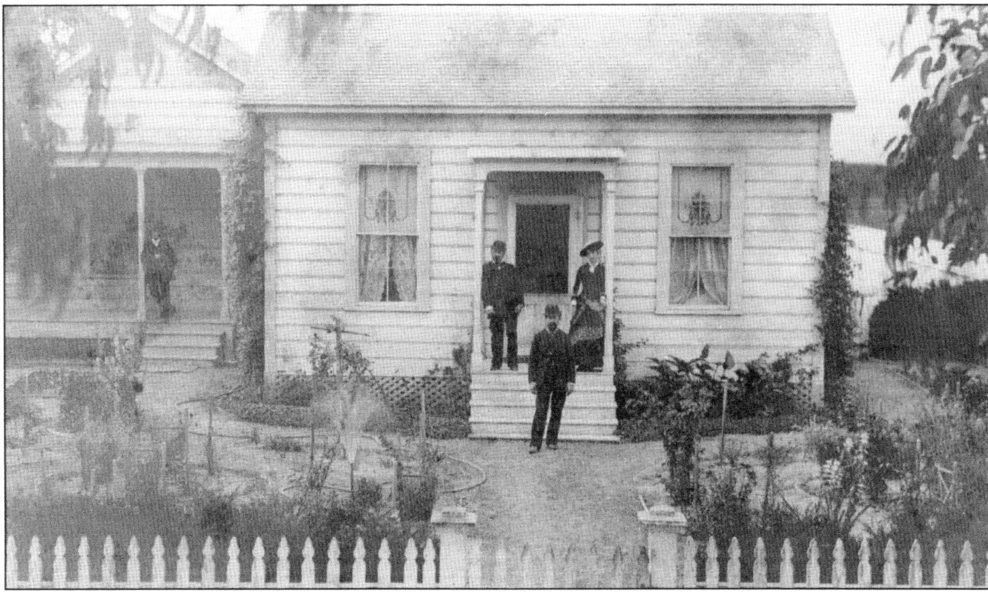

Abraham "Achille" Levy came to Hueneme in 1873 via France, and he went to work for his cousin Moise Wolff at his general merchandise store. In 1876, after Levy became a United States citizen, the two formed a partnership. Levy went back to France in 1881 to bring back a wife to his adopted country. Like Thomas Bard's wife, Lucy Levy was not impressed with the modest home of her husband and its undeveloped surroundings. The Achille and Lucy Levy home in Hueneme is pictured here in the 1880s. (Courtesy of the Ventura County Museum of History and Art.)

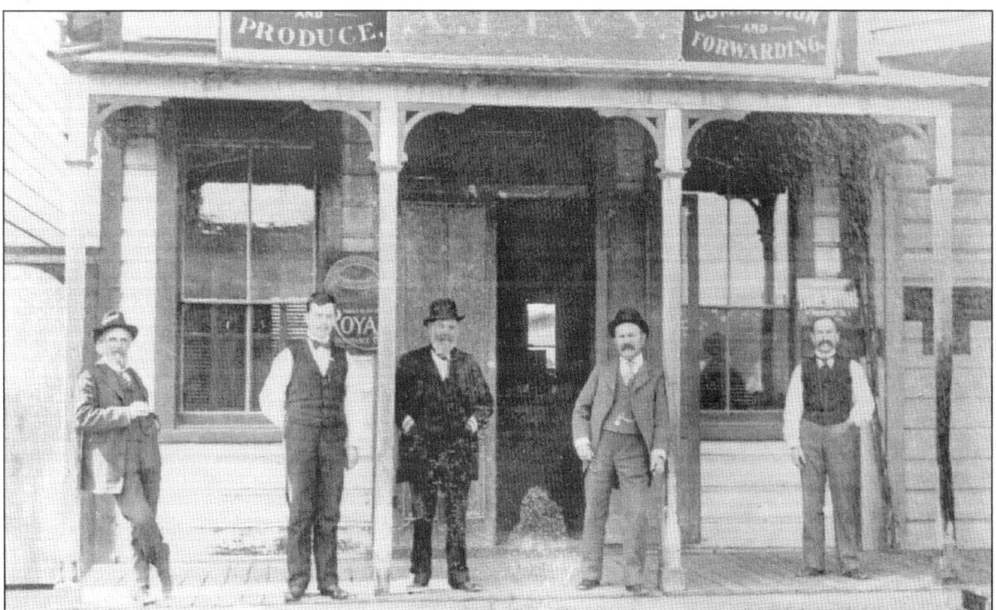

After returning from France in 1882, Levy (second from the right) began a commodity brokerage firm while still in partnership with Wolff. The partnership lasted another three years before it was dissolved. Wolff found another partner in Leon Lehman, and Levy took on brokering and banking. He eventually became one of the most prominent bankers in California when he established the Bank of A. Levy in 1905.

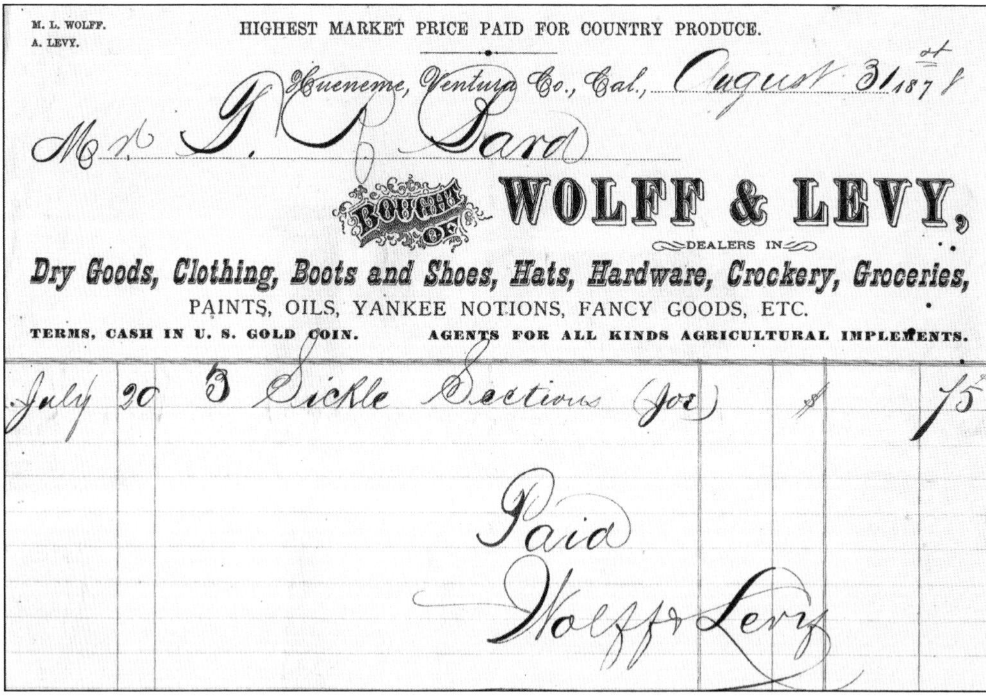
M. L. WOLFF.
A. LEVY.

HIGHEST MARKET PRICE PAID FOR COUNTRY PRODUCE.

Hueneme, Ventura Co., Cal., August 31 1878

Mr. J. R. Bard

BOUGHT OF **WOLFF & LEVY,**

DEALERS IN

Dry Goods, Clothing, Boots and Shoes, Hats, Hardware, Crockery, Groceries,

PAINTS, OILS, YANKEE NOTIONS, FANCY GOODS, ETC.

TERMS, CASH IN U. S. GOLD COIN. AGENTS FOR ALL KINDS AGRICULTURAL IMPLEMENTS.

July 20 3 Sickle Sections (Joe) $ 75

Paid
Wolff & Levy

This 1878 invoice from Wolff and Levy advertises "Everything from Dry Goods & Clothing to Yankee Notions and Fancy goods." The pair were also agents for "All kinds of agricultural implements."

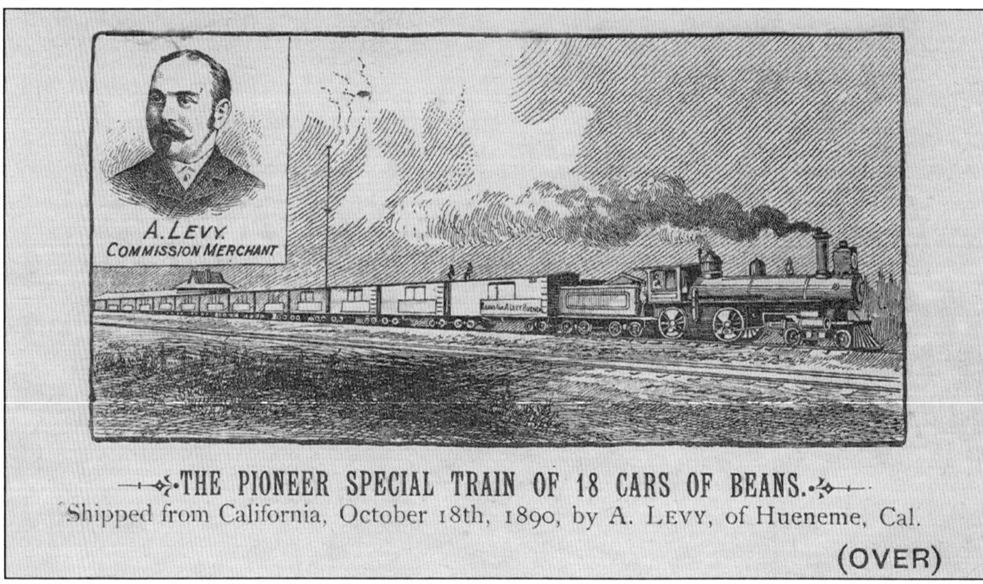

In 1887, Achille Levy formed a cooperative to purchase lima bean seeds. By the next year, 6,000 acres were planted in beans on the south side of the Santa Clara River. To further encourage farmers to plant beans, Levy began shipping the beans via the railroad instead of through the wharf. This lowered the cost of shipping and, thus, increased the profit for Levy and the farmers. Soon, Levy became known as the "Bean King," and up through the 1960s, the Oxnard Plain became known as the "lima bean capital of the world."

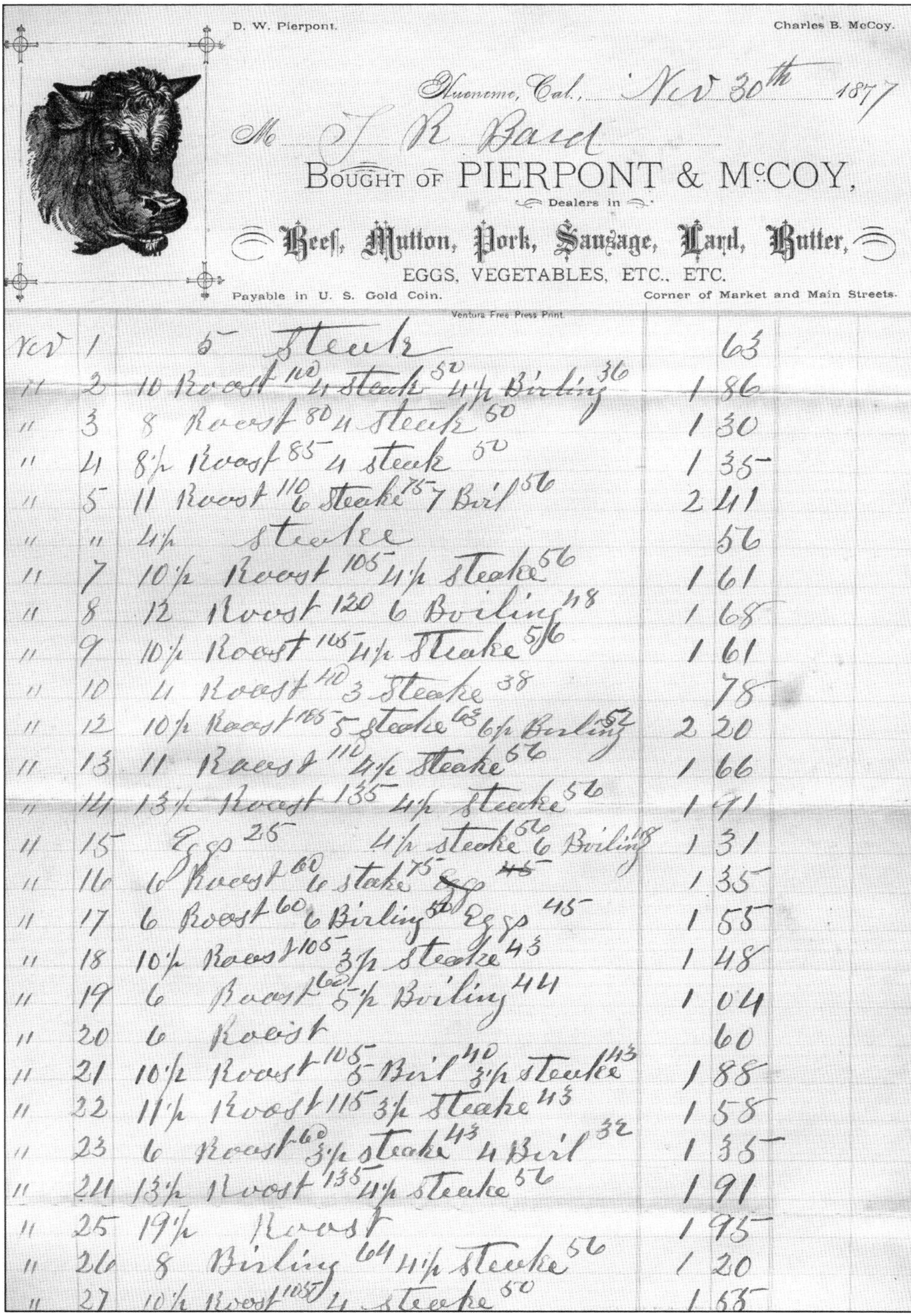

D. W. Pierpont. Charles B. McCoy.

Hueneme, Cal., Nov 30th 1877

Mr T R Bard

BOUGHT OF PIERPONT & McCOY,

Dealers in

Beef, Mutton, Pork, Sausage, Lard, Butter,

EGGS, VEGETABLES, ETC., ETC.

Payable in U. S. Gold Coin. Corner of Market and Main Streets.

Ventura Free Press Print.

Nov	1	5 Steak	63
"	2	10 Roast 110 4 steak 50 4 lb Birling 36	1 86
"	3	8 Roast 80 4 steak 50	1 30
"	4	8 lb Roast 85 4 steak 50	1 35
"	5	11 Roast 110 6 Steake 75 7 Birl 56	2 41
"	"	4 lb Steake	56
"	7	10 lb Roast 105 4 lb steake 56	1 61
"	8	12 Roast 120 6 Boiling 48	1 68
"	9	10 lb Roast 105 4 lb Steake 56	1 61
"	10	4 Roast 40 3 Steake 38	78
"	12	10 lb Roast 105 5 steake 63 6 lb Birling 52	2 20
"	13	11 Roast 110 4 lb Steake 56	1 66
"	14	13 lb Roast 135 4 lb steake 56	1 91
"	15	Eggs 25 4 lb steake 56 6 Boiling 48	1 31
"	16	6 Roast 60 6 stake 75 ~~Eggs 45~~	1 35
"	17	6 Roast 60 6 Birling 50 Eggs 45	1 55
"	18	10 lb Roast 105 3 lb Steake 43	1 48
"	19	6 Roast 60 5 lb Boiling 44	1 04
"	20	6 Roast	60
"	21	10 lb Roast 105 5 Birl 40 3 lb steake 43	1 88
"	22	11 lb Roast 115 3 lb Steake 43	1 58
"	23	6 Roast 60 3 lb steake 43 4 Birl 32	1 35
"	24	13 lb Roast 135 4 lb steake 56	1 91
"	25	19 lb Roast	1 95
"	26	8 Birling 64 4 lb steake 56	1 20
"	27	10 lb Roast 105 4 steake 50	1 55

This November 1877 bill shows Thomas Bard's purchases from the butcher's shop of Pierpont and McCoy. Notice the price for five steaks is just 63¢, while the cost for 25 eggs and 4 steaks was up to $1.31.

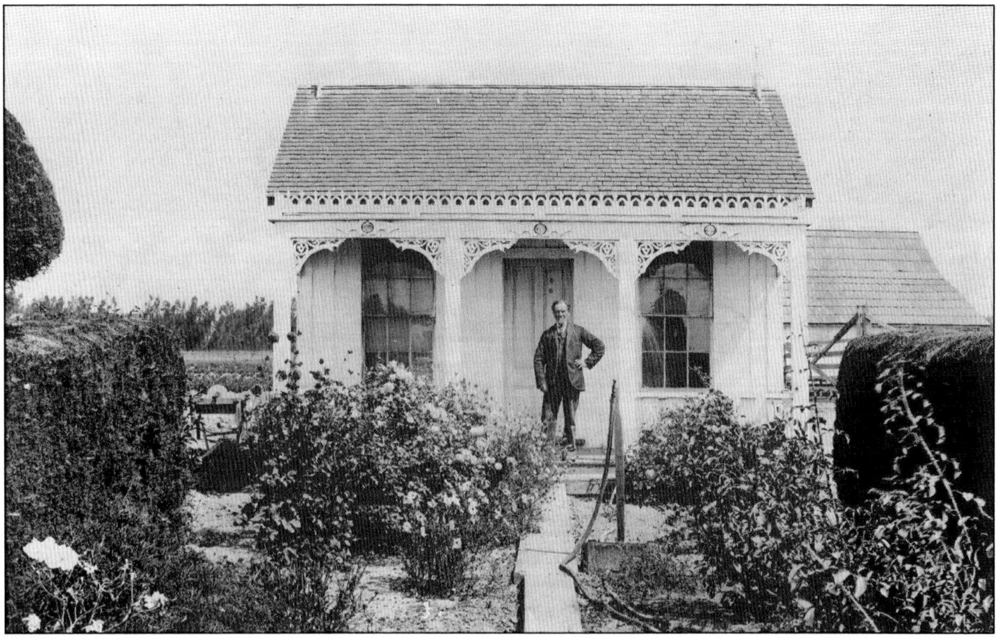

The man standing proudly in front of his 1870s cottage is Christopher M. Robinson, who was listed in the 1897 directory as a farmer, though his name does not appear in an 1898 listing.

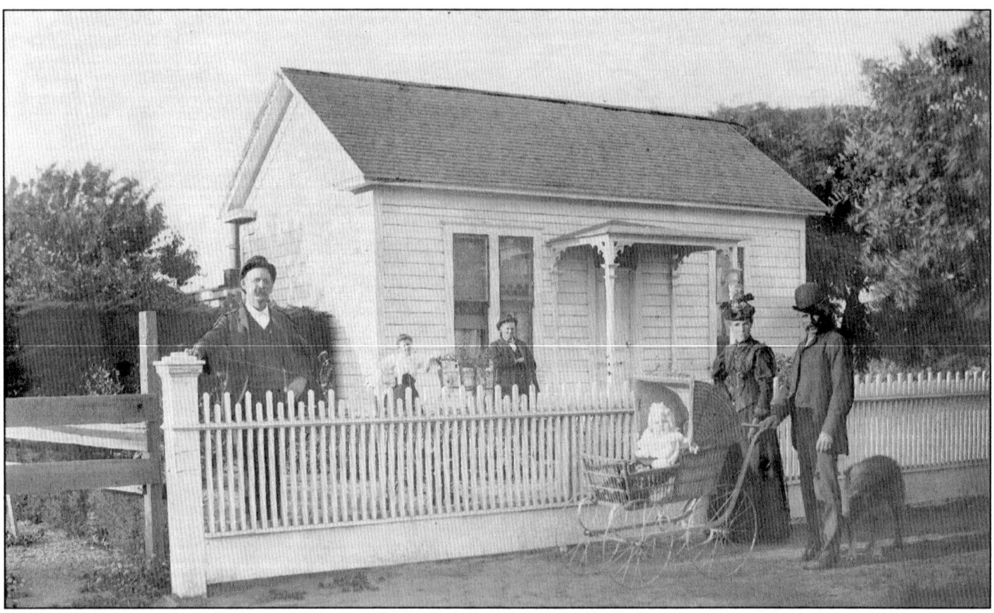

The Woodruff home, pictured in 1893, was located on Broad Street. William B. Woodruff was the postmaster from 1885 to 1889. Both his daughters—Miss Bagey and Miss Wanee—later worked for the Sunset Telephone Company.

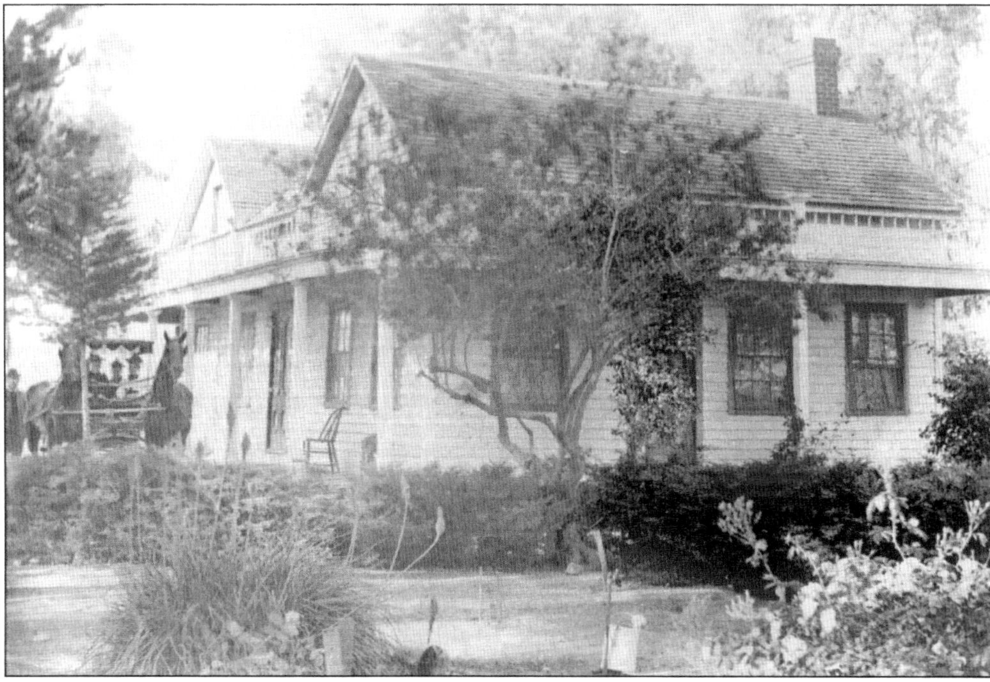

The Peter Donlon home, pictured here in the 1880s, was bounded on the north by the Bard ranch and present-day Ventura Road, on the east by the Albert Maulhardt and, later, Franz Friedrich ranch (with present-day Channel Island running through the southern portion of that ranch), and also by Saviers Road. The Donlon boys, James, Charles, and Joseph, all attended the Hueneme School, where Richard Haydock served as their principal.

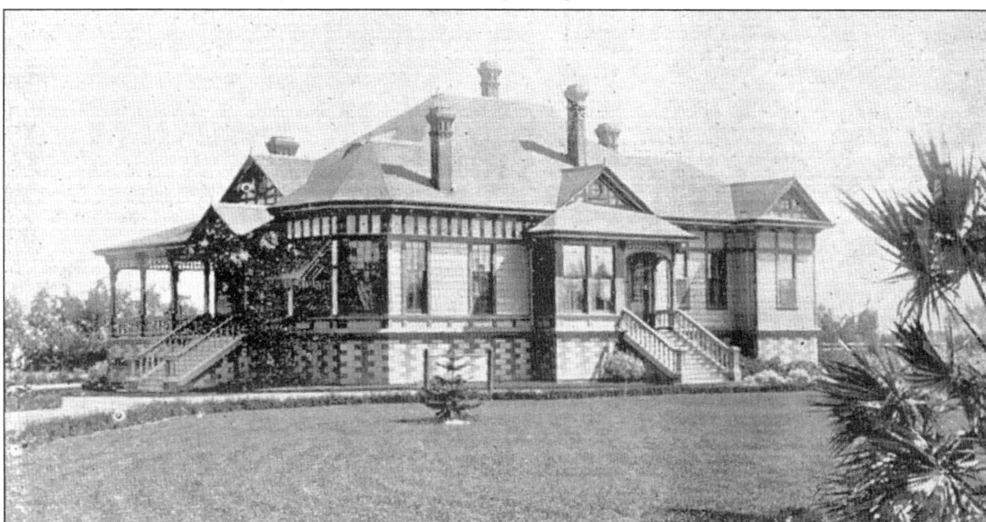

The Perkins Ranch was located to the south of Pleasant Valley Road and across the street from the current Mary Star of the Sea church. David Todd Perkins came to Hueneme in 1880 and raised sheep in partnership with Thomas Bard. He was elected to the state assembly in 1892 and later served as vice president on the board of the Union Oil Company. The residence served as the barbecue grounds for the Giants/White Sox baseball exhibition game in 1913. The home was later moved to Heritage Square in Oxnard.

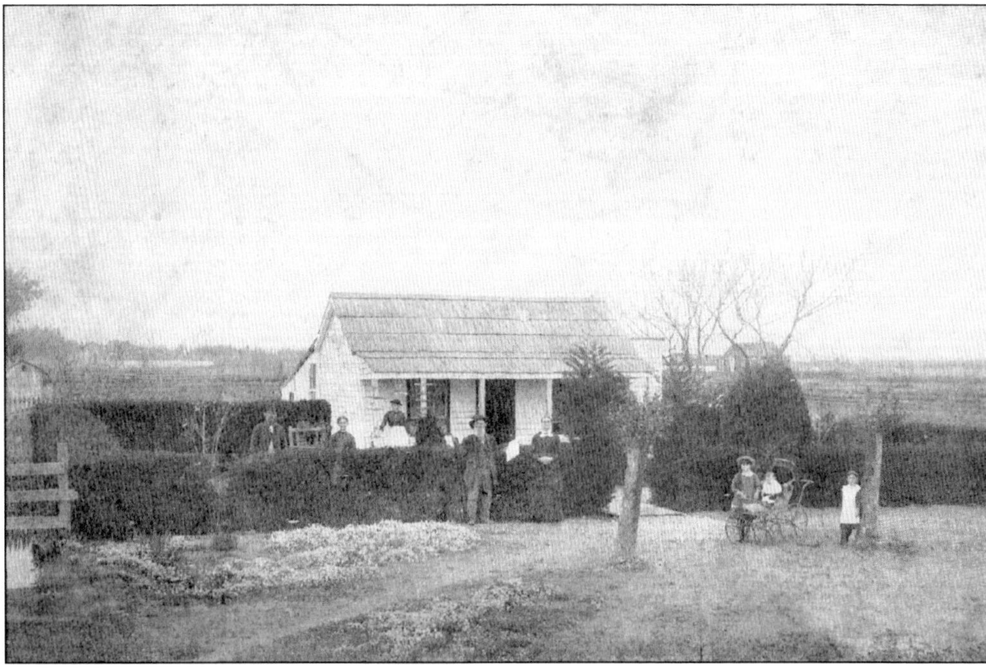

The back of this photograph makes a mention of the residence being off Broad Street, which today is Hueneme Road. The family is not identified, but the beard looks familiar. It may belong to Elijah Fairbanks, who worked as the assistant wharfinger. (Courtesy of the Hueneme Historical Society.)

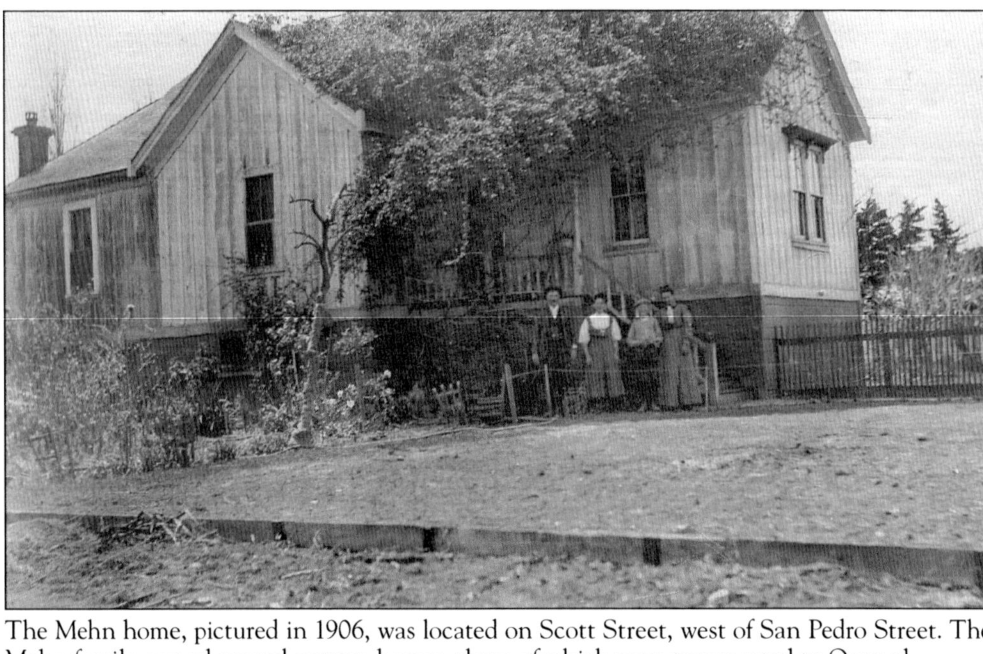

The Mehn home, pictured in 1906, was located on Scott Street, west of San Pedro Street. The Mehn family owned several cottage homes, three of which were transported to Oxnard.

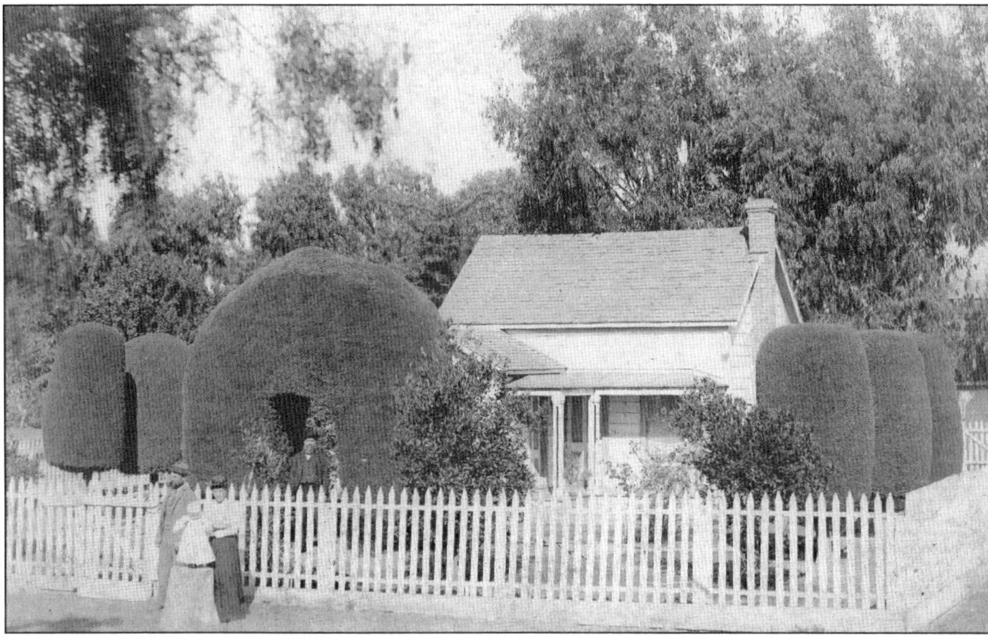

The William Zeller home was located across from the Perkins residence, on the north side of Pleasant Valley Road. Zeller was a cousin of Thomas Bard, and William, along with his father, David, farmed together until David passed away in 1884. William continued farming the 135-acre Pleasant Valley Road ranch until 1903, when he sold it to Franz Friedrich.

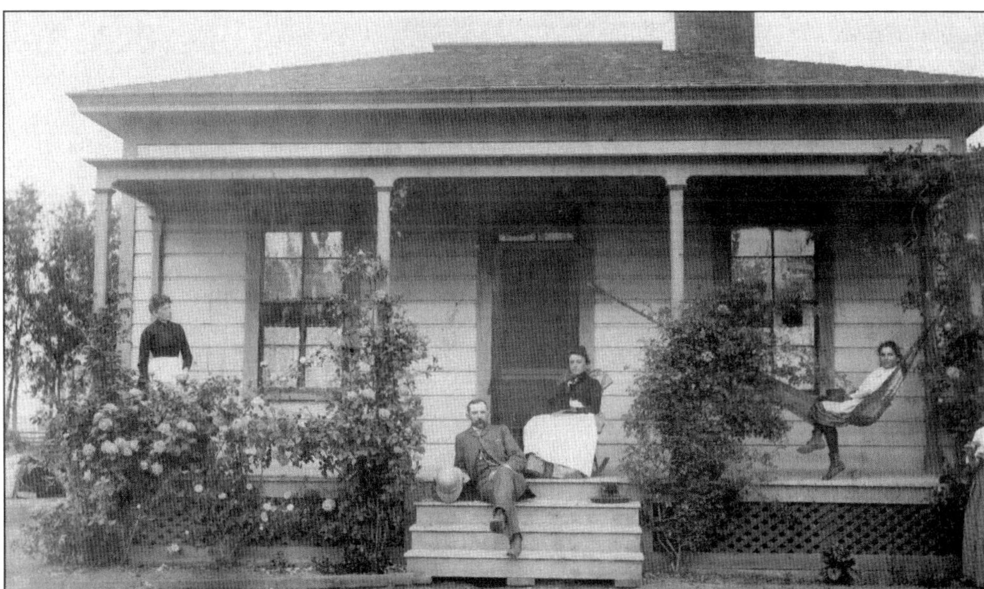

Bart "Dad" Pitts ran the Hueneme Livery and Stageline. The Pitts home, pictured here in the 1880s, tragically burned down in 1913 when Pitts was attending the Giants/White Sox exhibition game.

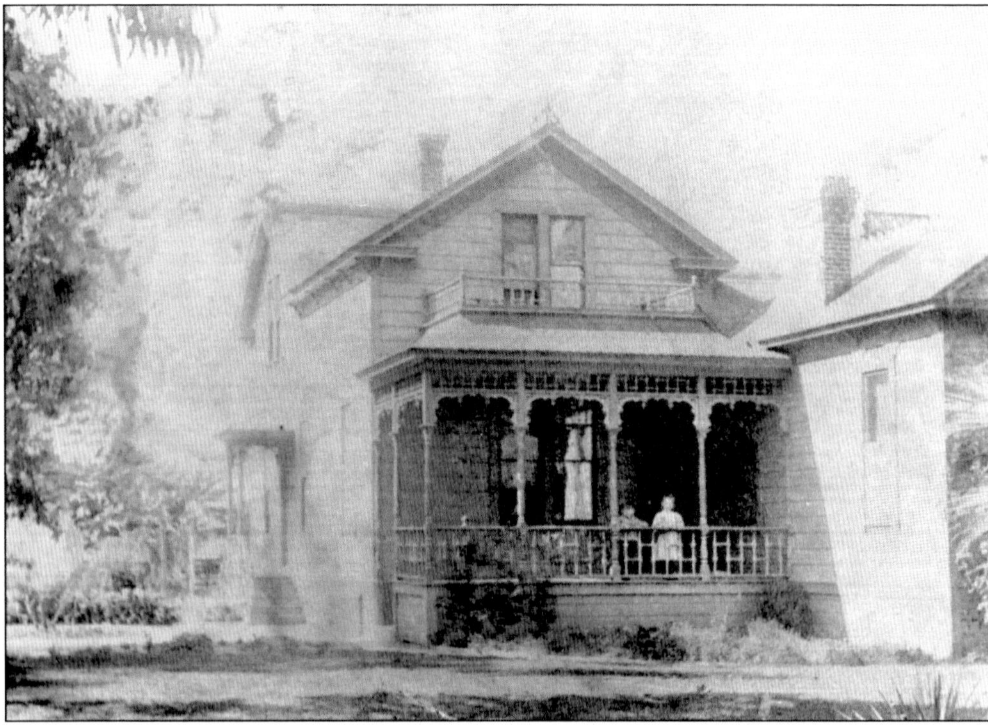

The Gerberding home, located at Third and Clara Streets, was built by Thomas Bard for his brother-in-law, Otto Gerberding. Gerberding was the editor for the *Hueneme Herald* from 1888 to 1906.

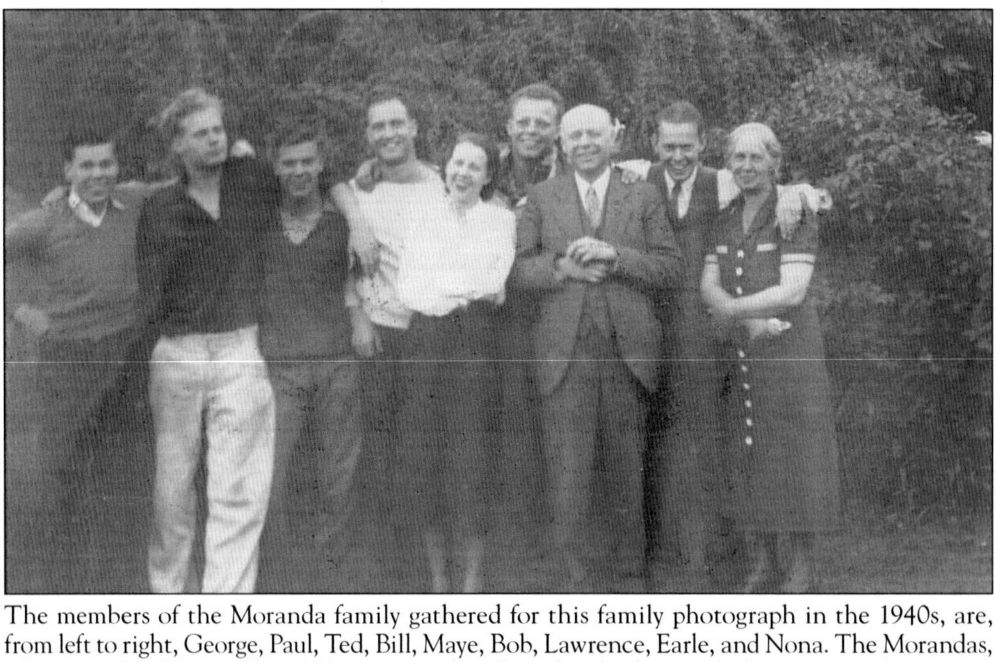

The members of the Moranda family gathered for this family photograph in the 1940s, are, from left to right, George, Paul, Ted, Bill, Maye, Bob, Lawrence, Earle, and Nona. The Morandas, who moved to Hueneme in 1924, were a close-knit family that made lasting contributions to the community.

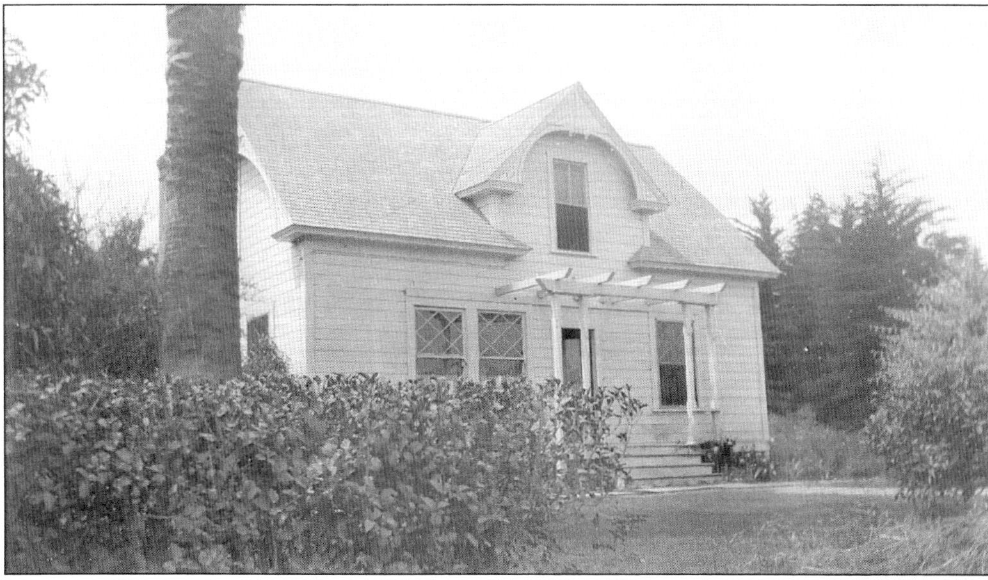

The Moranda family bought the Gerberding home in 1924 and made some modifications to it. Concrete piers were added to stabilize the wooden floor, and the front and living rooms were combined. This move ended the basketball games that the Moranda boys played by using the three-inch decorative ledge over the sliding door as a basket and a tennis ball for a basketball.

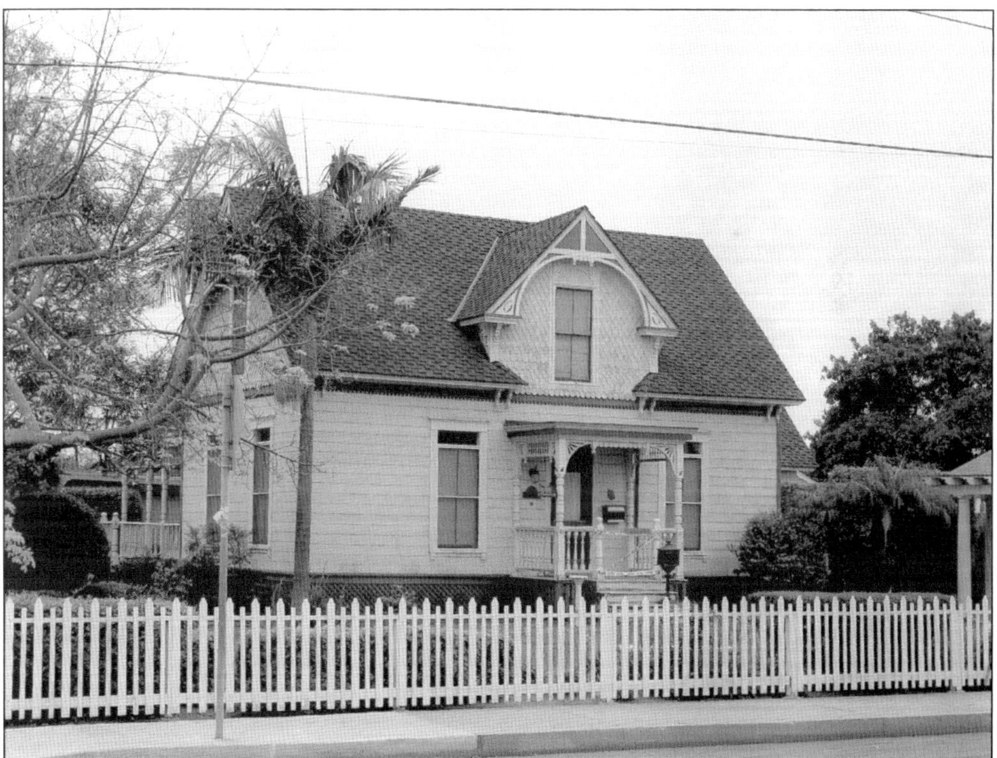

In 1988, Randall, Gladys, and Tristan Richter purchased and moved into the Gerberding/Moranda home, and in 1990, the house was designated Ventura County Landmark No. 86.

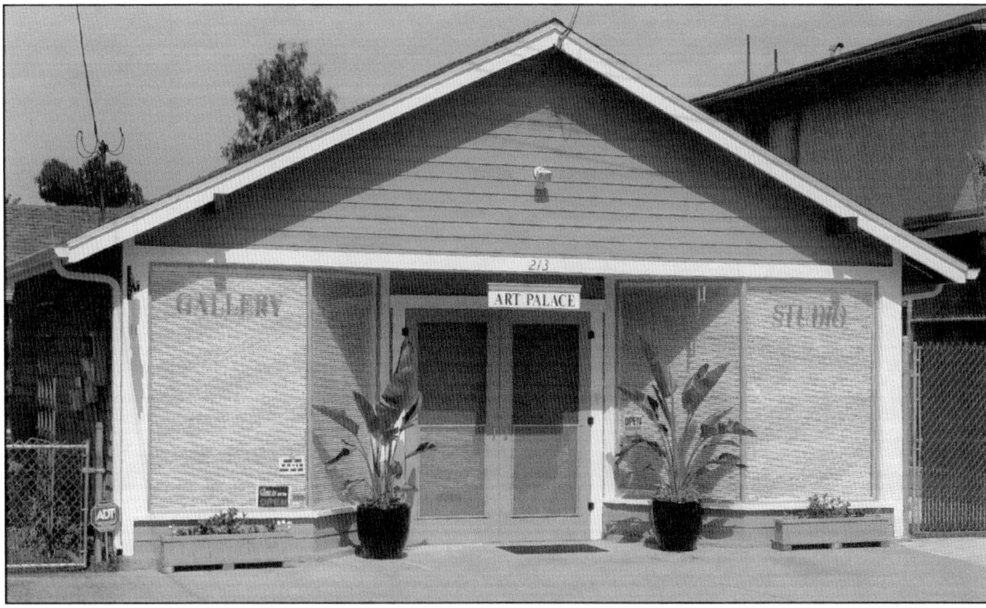

The Bard/Prescott house at 257 East Scott Street was built in 1911 in the Craftsman Bungalow style. On the sidewalk near the house—built for Thomas Bard's wife, Mary, as a beach house—is a marker that reads "Mary Bard, 1911." In 1918, the house was occupied by a Miss Peck, followed by the Snodgrass family, and in 1929, by the Prescott family. In 1995, the residence earned historical landmark status, becoming No. 153 in Ventura County. Also on the site is the original carriage house, pictured above, that was later converted into a storefront market and was next door to the Quonset hut building used as the Melody Theater. The carriage house at 213 North Third Street was painstakingly renovated by current tenant Deborah Findley and her husband, Charlie Barton, and is now home to the Art Palace, selling original paintings, art supplies, and jewelry.

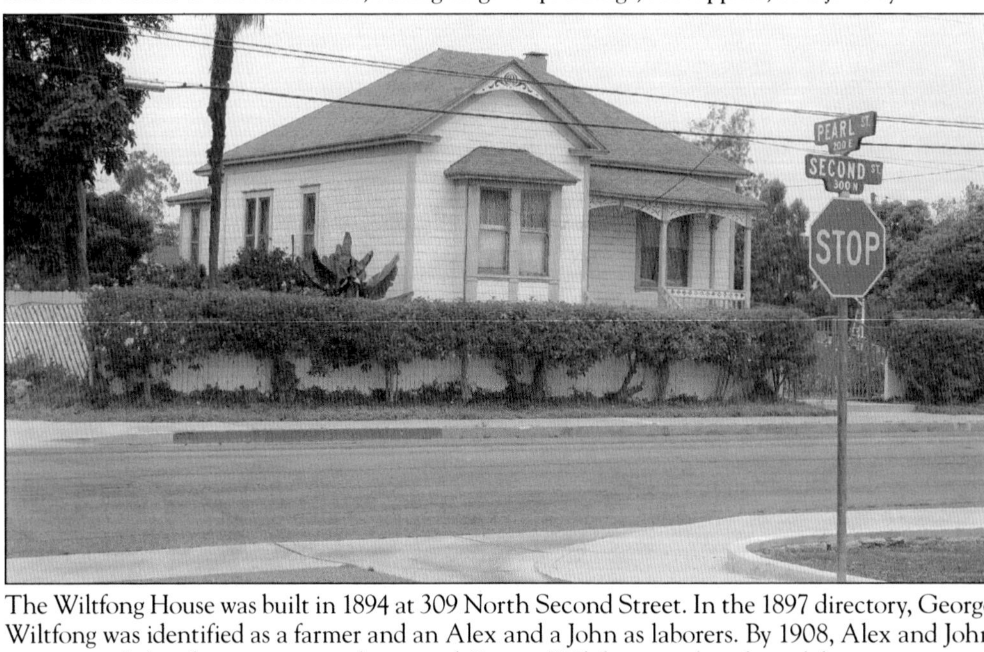

The Wiltfong House was built in 1894 at 309 North Second Street. In the 1897 directory, George Wiltfong was identified as a farmer and an Alex and a John as laborers. By 1908, Alex and John were upgraded to farmer status and a second George Wiltfong was listed as a laborer.

Two

Then Came the Factory

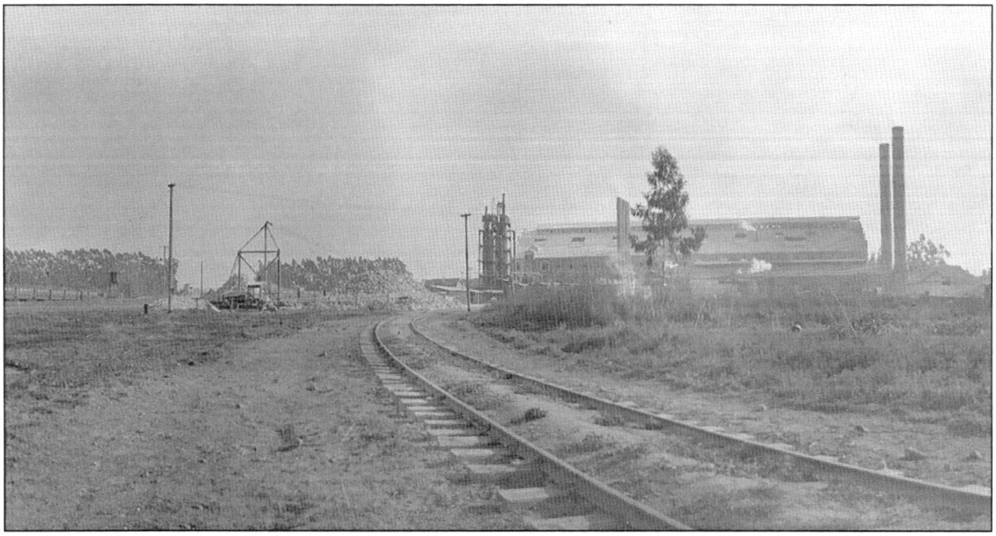

By December 1897, life in Hueneme was about to drastically change with the beginning of construction of the Oxnard Beet Sugar Factory. Things were already slowing down as many farmers had switched to lima beans and were using the rail lines instead of the wharf to ship their goods out.

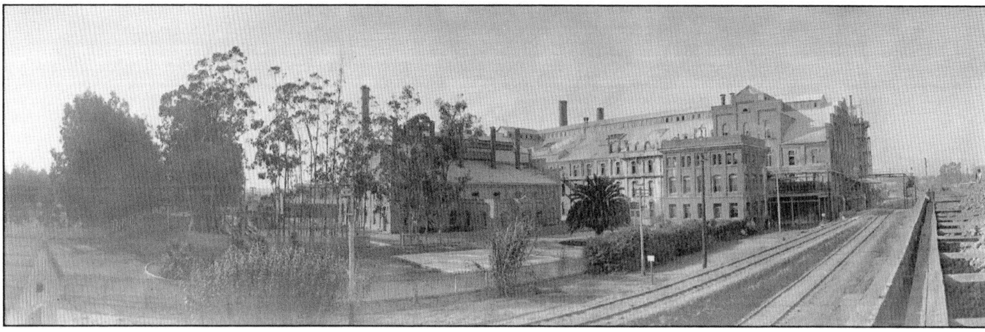

The factory was complete by August 1898. Now, in addition to the lima beans, processed sugar was being shipped out by train. In fact, one of the conditions set by the Oxnard brothers before they built the factory was that there would be a spur line from the factory connected to the mainline in Montalvo. Whole buildings were "rolled" across the fields from Hueneme, Saticoy, and Montalvo. Hueneme lost the businesses of the Wolff and Waterman mercantile store; Steimmillers Harness Shop; Harry Witman's hardware and plumbing business; Jake Dietenbach's tailoring; I. M. Poggi's drugstore; B. F. Korts' butcher shop; Jim Meyers Phoenix Saloon, and the Glenn brothers' livery stables.

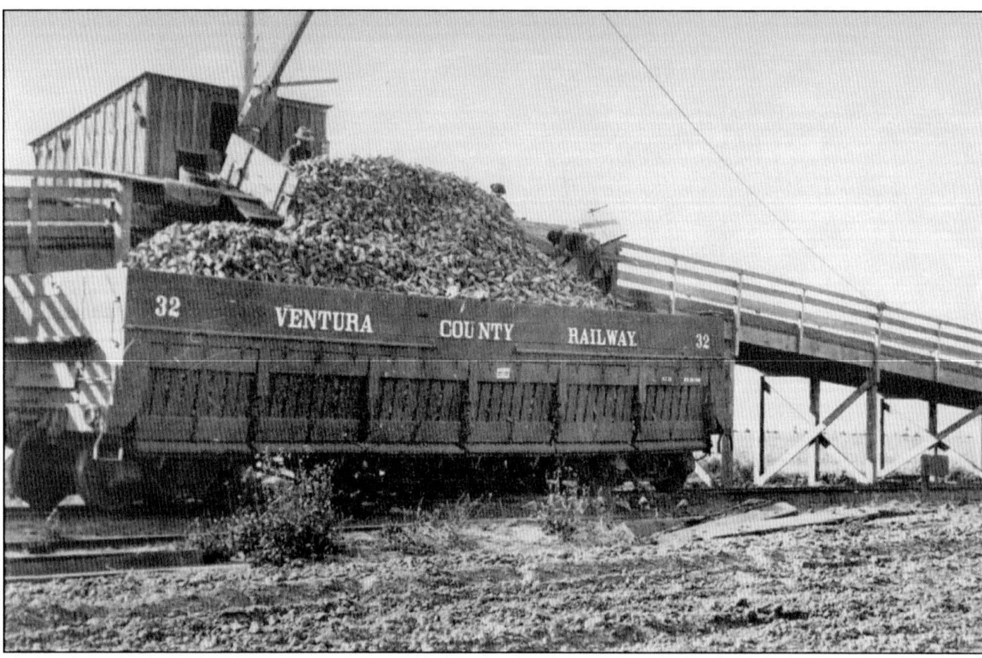

The beet dumps were strategically placed through out the Oxnard Plain so farmers could dump their beets at sites close to their ranches.

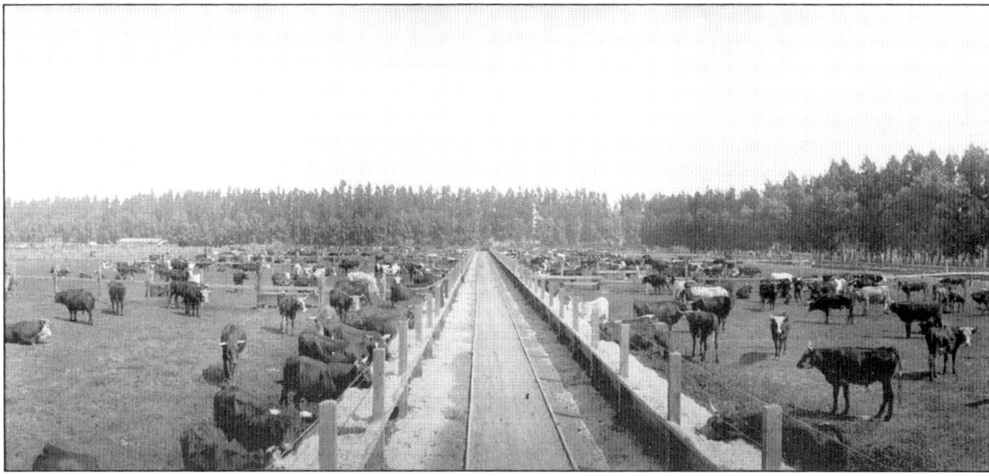

The Patterson ranch was located to the north of the Bard property in Hueneme. Cattle and horses were raised on the nearly 6,000-acre ranch, but after the Oxnard Beet Sugar Factory interests purchased the ranch in 1899, leach lines were laid out for better drainage and sugar beets were planted. The "waste," or unused portion, of the beet was used to feed the livestock.

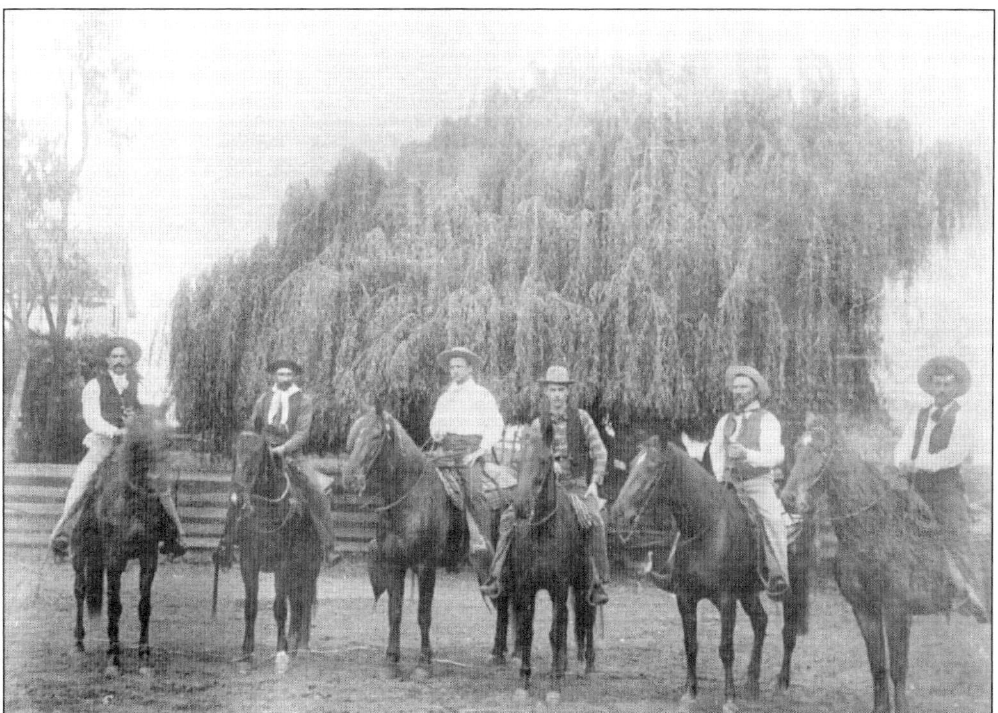

The *vaqueros*, or cowboys, of the Patterson Ranch included some of the top farmers in the area. Charles Daily was sent by J. D. Patterson in New York to the Ventura County ranch in 1885 to take over and manage the property. Daily's father and two brothers eventually followed and became innovative farmers in the Oxnard and Camarillo area. In this c. 1890 photograph are, from left to right, John Machado, Alex Lopez, Ernest Eastwood, Wendell Daily, Frank Olivas, and "Coon" Gonzales.

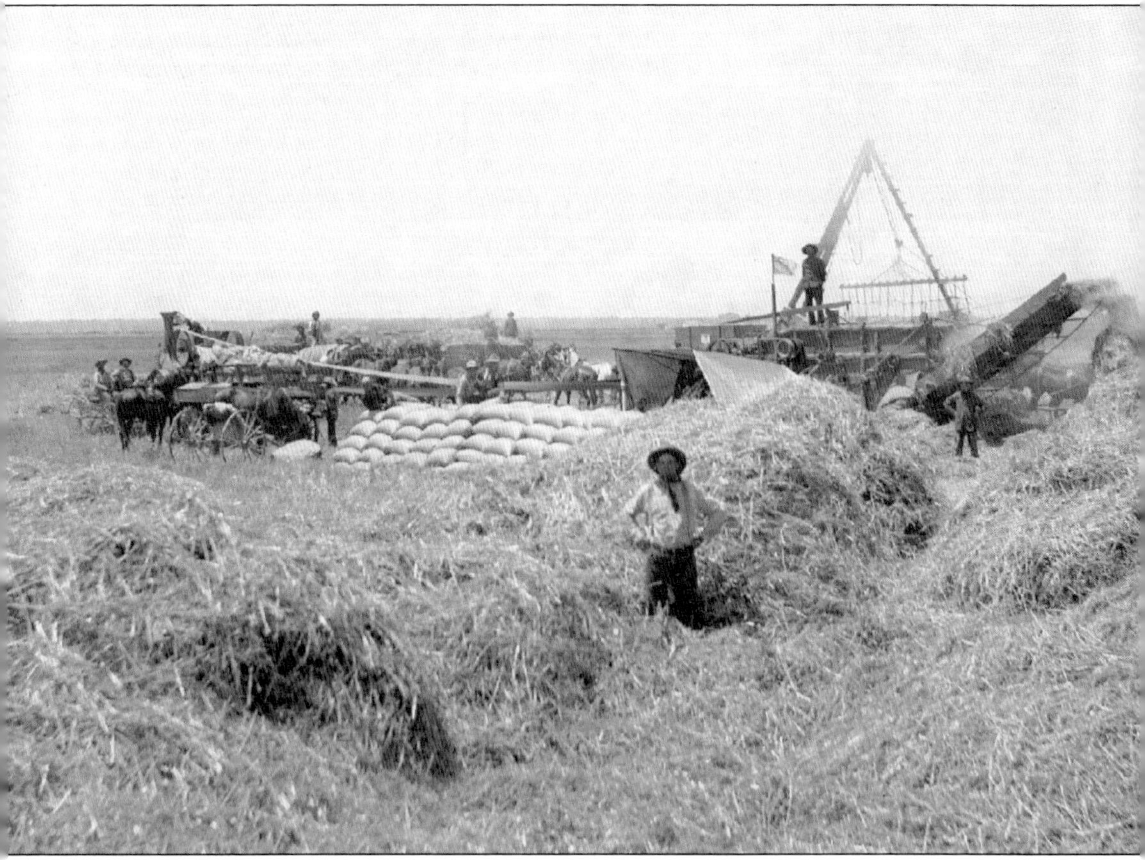

While sugar beets became the area's cash crop once the factory was established in 1898, lima beans also remained a vital crop to local farmers. Because sugar beets are deep-rooted plants, they cause the soil to become depleted of vital nutrients. Successive crops of sugar beets were avoided in favor of planting lima beans or alfalfa, which helped put nitrogen back into the soil. Remy Callens and his crew (pictured) farmed near Hueneme. Lima beans had an advantage over sugar beets because they were a far less labor-intensive crop, and farmers took less of gamble by growing lima beans. The pay off for a good beet crop was much higher, but so was the risk. Some farmers preferred the dry farming of wheat, barley, or lima beans where the only moisture needed was the "June gloom" so prevalent near the coast in the late spring and early summer. Members of the old farming community could often be heard describing the fog as "lima bean weather."

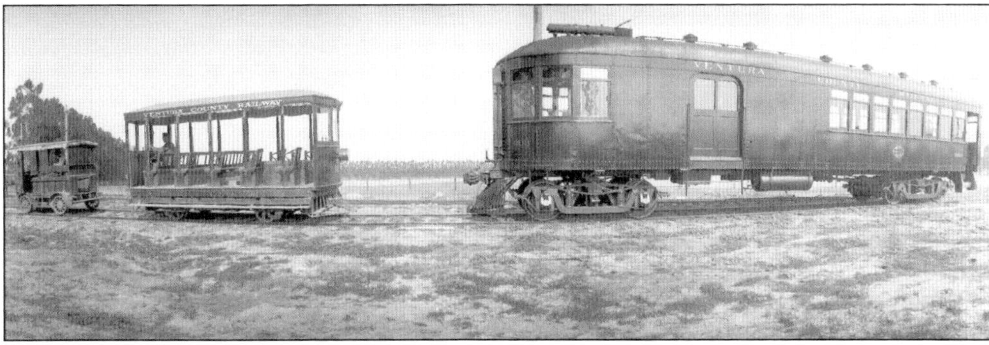

The Bakersfield & Ventura Railway was incorporated in 1905, and a railroad line between Oxnard and Hueneme was complete by July 4 of that year. With this easy transportation to the beach, nearly 9,000 people flocked to the day-long celebration. One of the public's several choices for traveling along the rails was the Seabreeze Flyer, which was a 12-horsepower gasoline car that carried up to 12 passengers. In 1913, the Hall-Scott Motor Car, pictured on the right, was added to the fleet. It had 150-horsepower and a six-cylinder engine. There was even talk as early as 1906 of connecting the Hueneme Wharf with the Malibu & Port of Los Angeles Railway and laying down tracks along the coastline. However, Mrs. Frances Broome objected to having a portion of her land condemned in order to build the rail line, and a protracted legal battle put an end to the project.

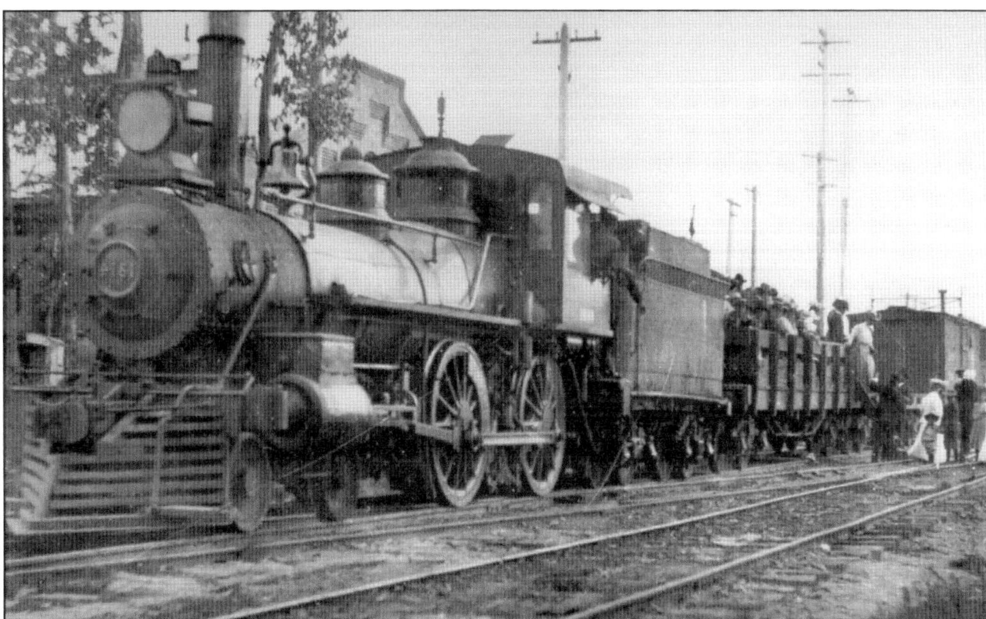

Train service to and from Hueneme was provided in several ways, including open boxcar. Rail service was in demand up to the 1920s, when automobiles eclipsed riding the train in popularity, leading to the end of the rail line completely in 1927.

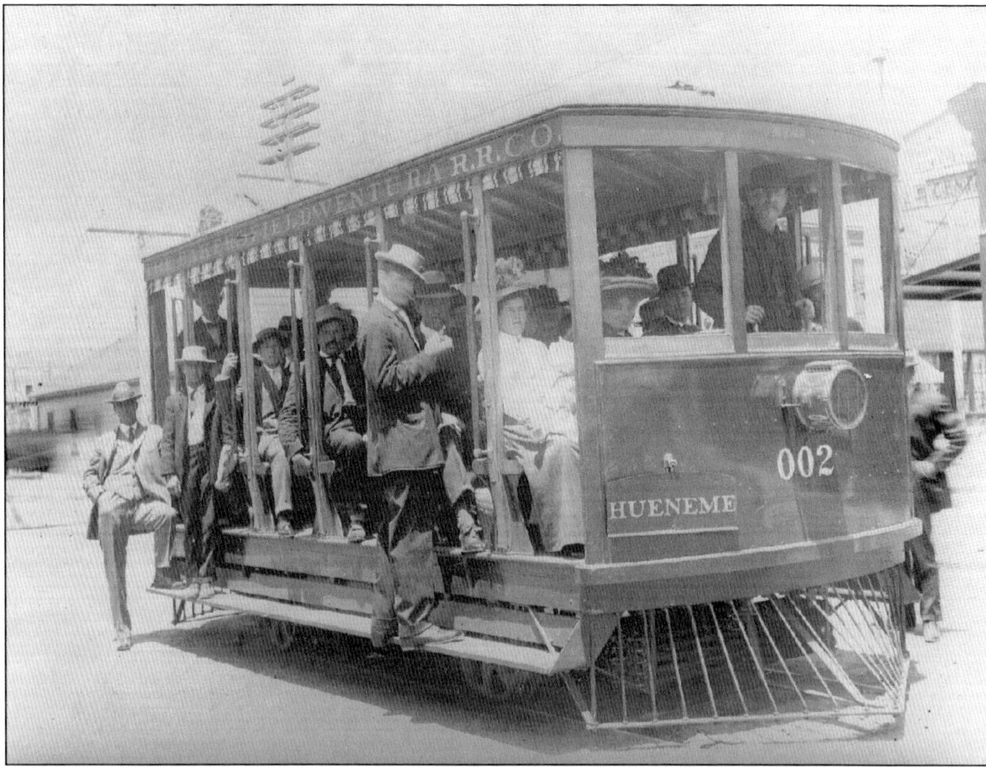

The Bakersfield & Ventura also offered the 25-horsepower "streetcar" with reversible seats. Dennis McKinna was the chief operator for the car. The one-way fare to the beach from Oxnard cost 20¢, or it was just 22¢ for a round-trip.

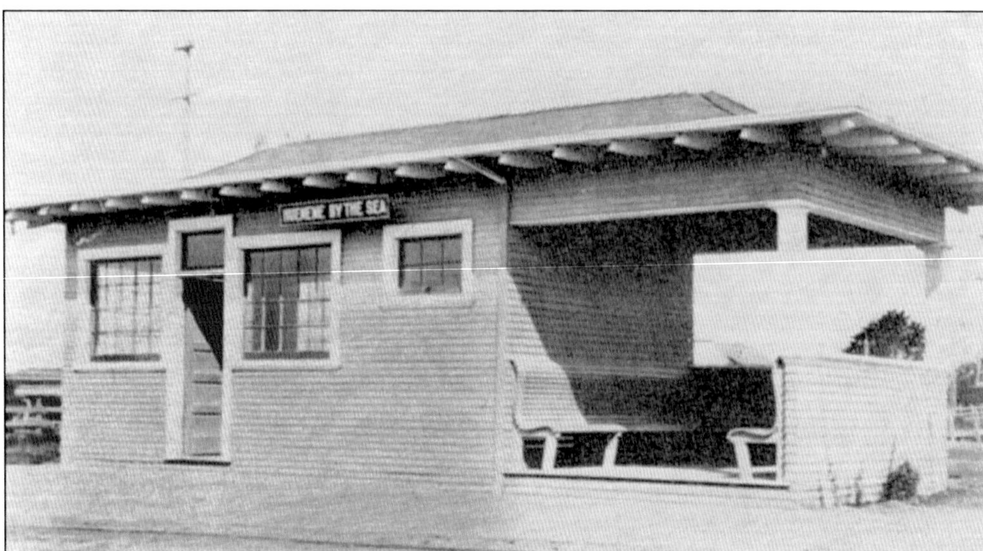

Hueneme by the Sea was the railroad depot of the Bakersfield & Ventura Railroad. It took 15 minutes to travel from A and Magnolia Streets in Oxnard to the beach.

Three

THE BEACH

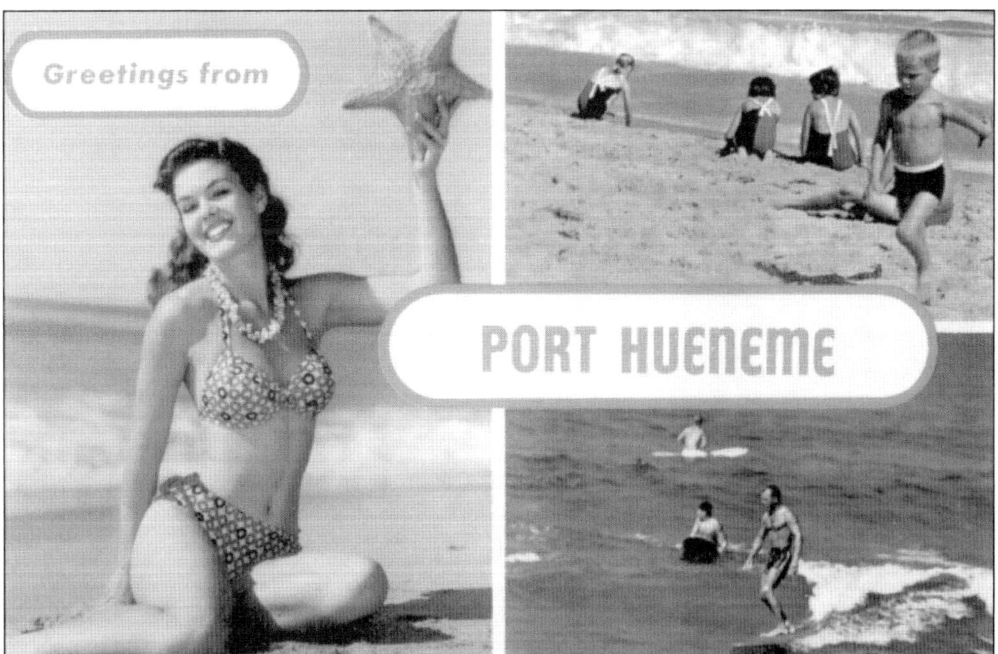

Despite the changes that Hueneme has undergone over the years, the beach has remained a popular destination. This postcard features scenes by the shore from the 1960s.

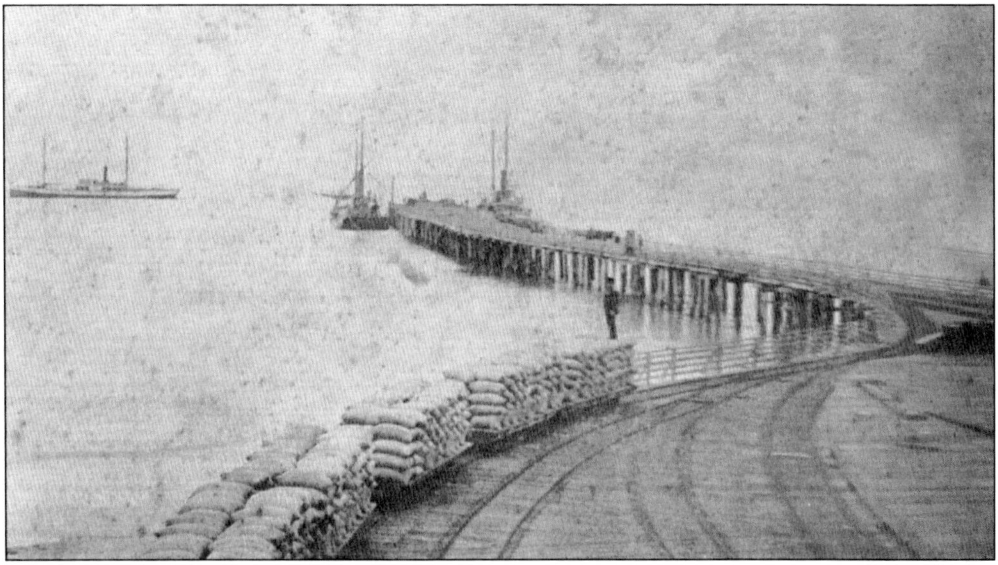

Construction of the original wharf at Wynema was begun in May 1871 by the Hueneme Wharf and Lighter Company, a business that was started by Thomas Bard. The wharf stretched 1,000 feet in length and was completed by August 1871.

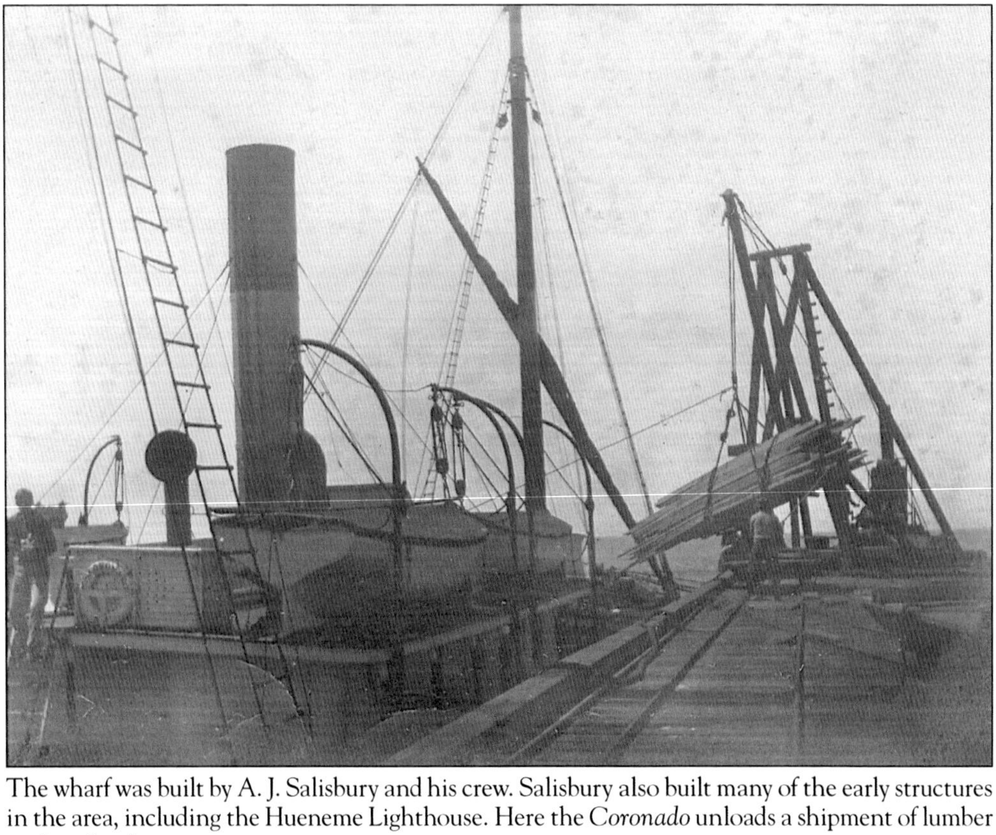

The wharf was built by A. J. Salisbury and his crew. Salisbury also built many of the early structures in the area, including the Hueneme Lighthouse. Here the *Coronado* unloads a shipment of lumber at the wharf.

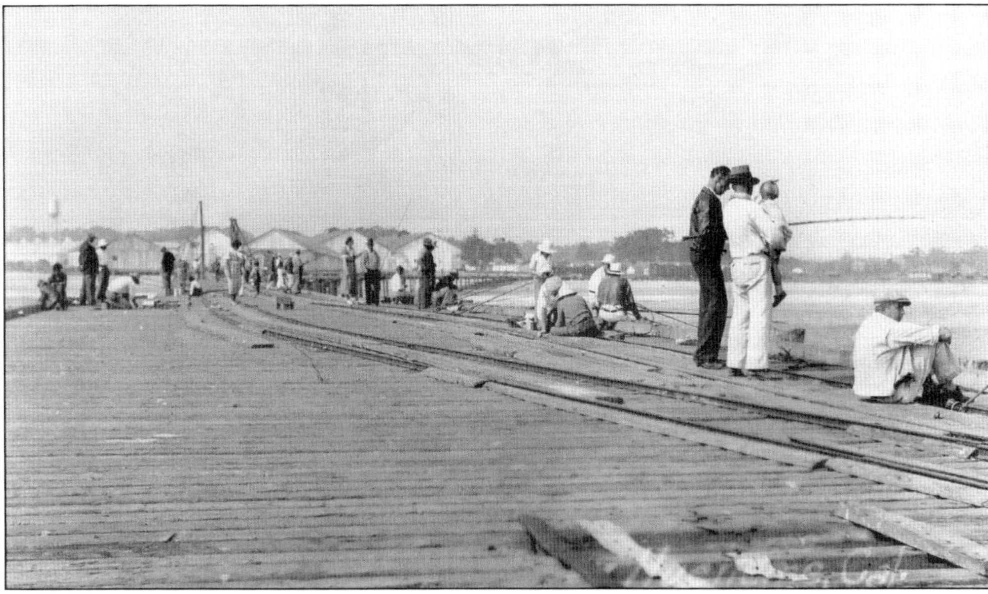

Fishing off the pier was popular up until the tropical storm of 1939 destroyed the wharf. It wasn't until 1956 that another pier was built for the public.

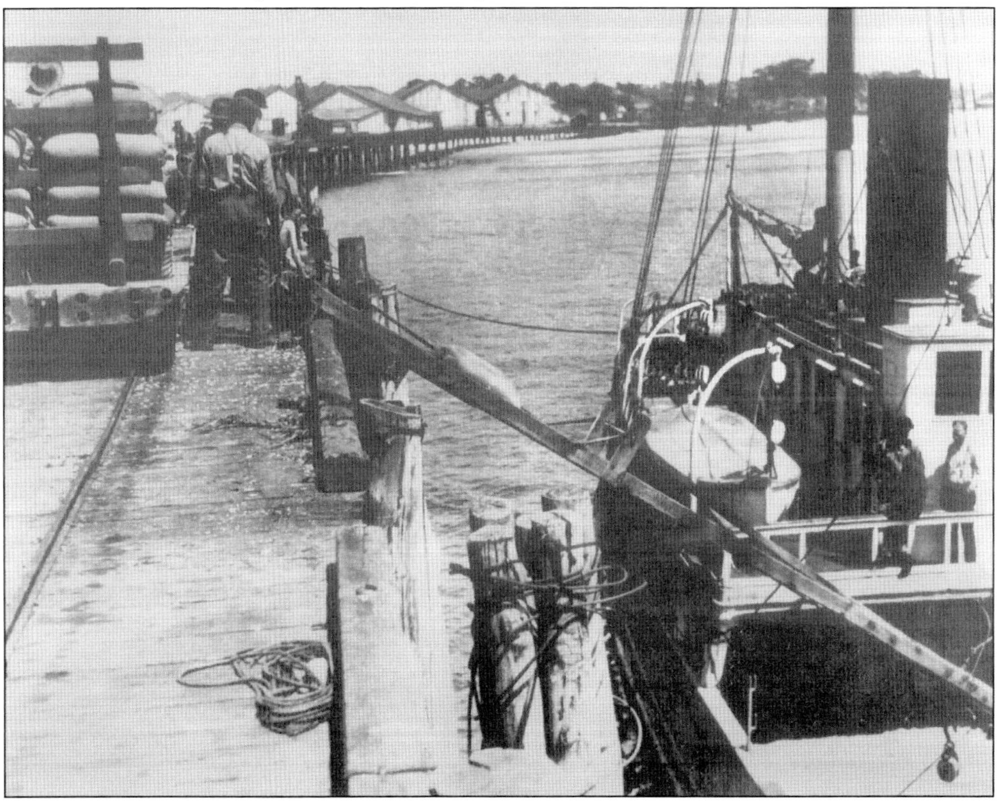

A full-time wharfinger was hired to oversee the 24-hour-a-day activities at the wharf. Thomas Bard set the wharf up as a "free wharf," thus passing on the responsibility of shipping and unloading to the free market.

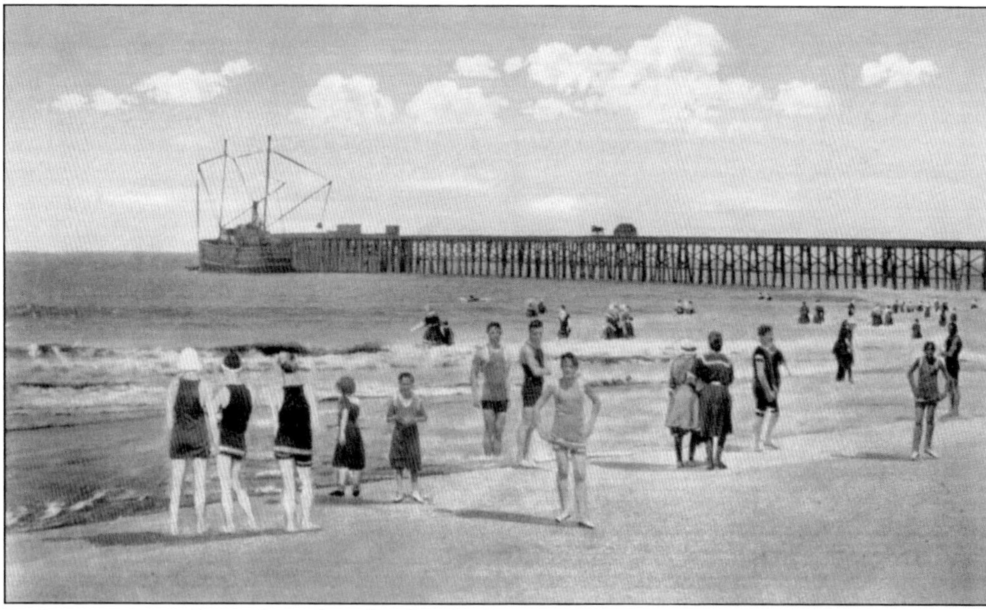

Today many people confuse the wharf with the pier at Port Hueneme. They served not only different purposes but were located at different spots along the beach. The wharf was used to load and unload cargo, while the pier was built almost 85 years later to enhance the beach area and offer a fishing spot.

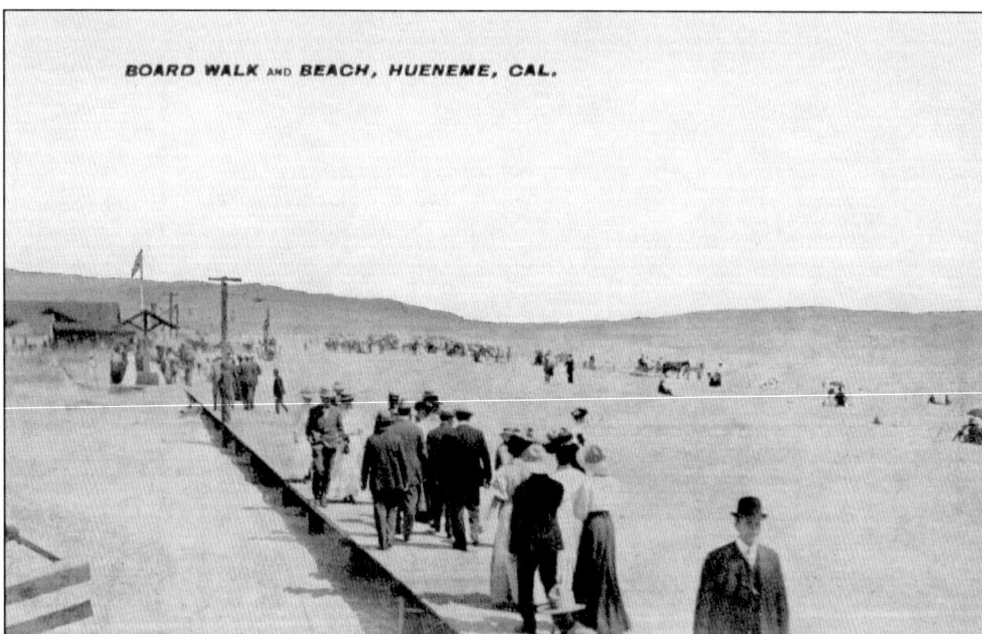

The wharf and, later, the boardwalk were located near the present-day port and Silver Strand Beach. In fact, until the harbor was developed in 1939, the beach communities were linked by a common sandbar.

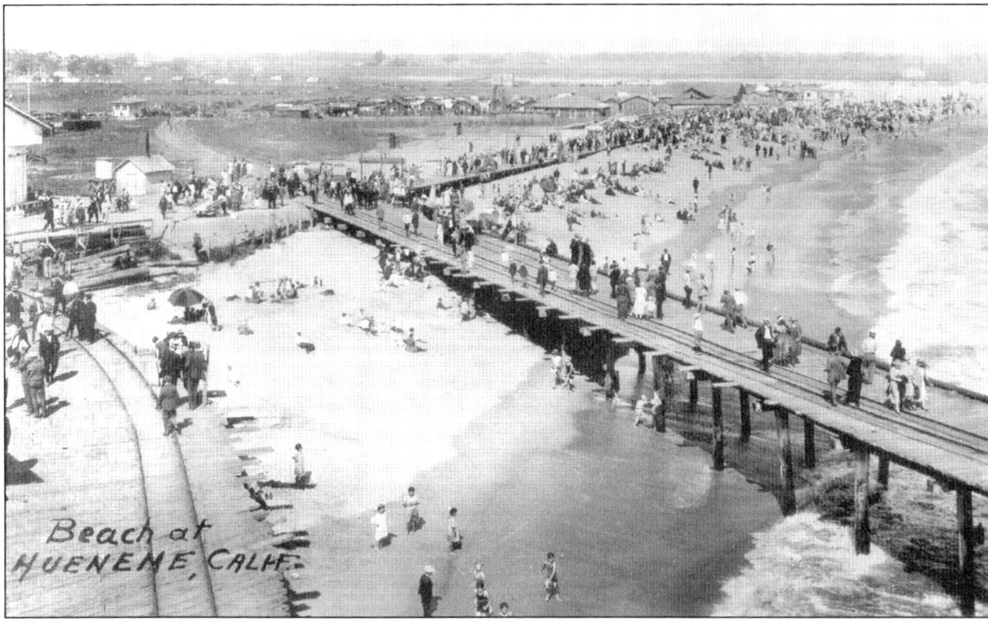

To the north of the wharf were the salt flats that were later dredged to create the harbor in 1939. The discarded sand was disposed to the south to fill in the Hueneme Slough. This image shows the wharf and boardwalk that were destroyed by the 1939 "hurricane."

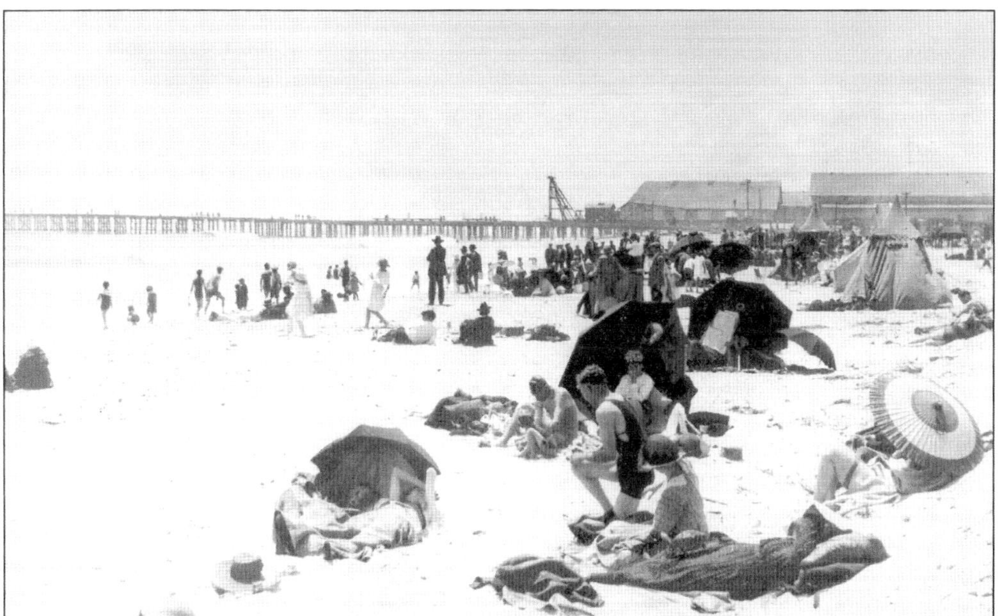

Beachgoers did not have a chance to walk out onto an extended pier until 1967. The pier was located south of the original wharf.

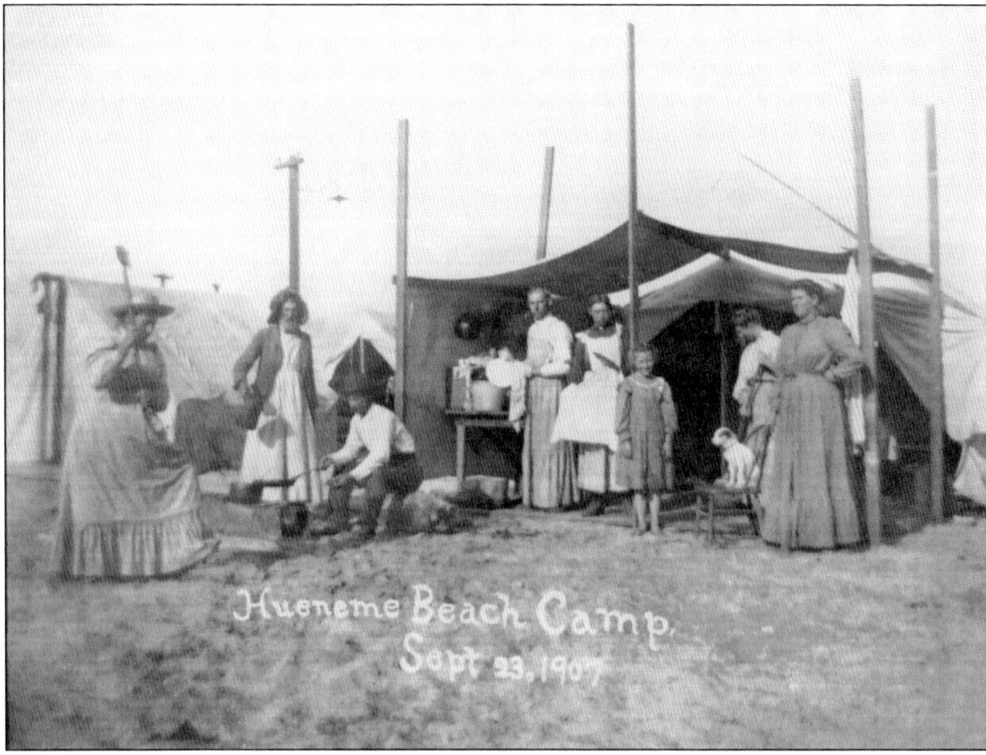

In this picture, taken in September 1907 at the Hueneme beach, the men are dressed in women's clothes and are doing the cooking. It is uncertain whether this photograph inspired the Follies, which began 50 years later at Harbor Days, the annual event that marked the opening of the harbor. (Courtesy of the Ventura County Museum of History and Art.)

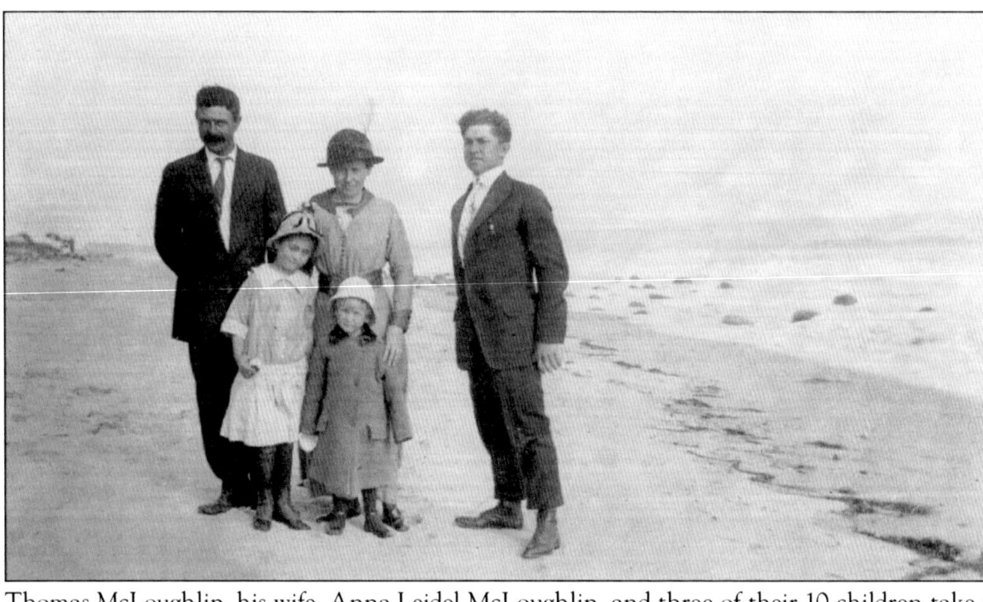

Thomas McLoughlin, his wife, Anna Leidel McLoughlin, and three of their 10 children take a stroll at the beach in their Sunday best, *c.* 1910.

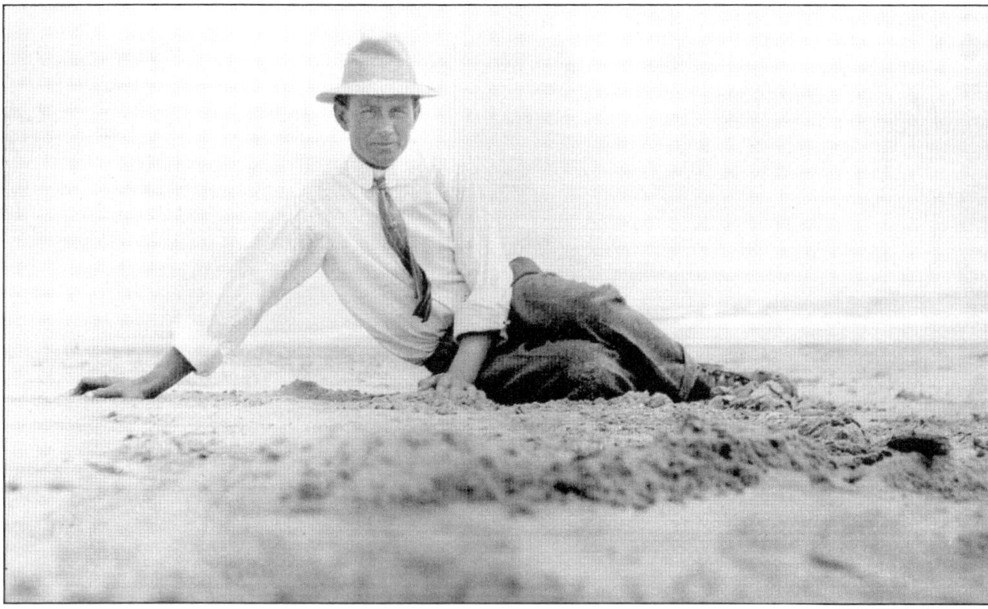

Ed Borchard worked at the sugar beet factory for a few years and then turned to farming in the Newbury Park area. Despite his hat and tie, Borchard appears to be relishing his day away from farming and enjoying stretching out at the beach. The photograph was taken with a Kodak "Brownie" camera, introduced to the public on 1900. For the first time in history, families could document their daily lives. The handheld box camera cost $1.

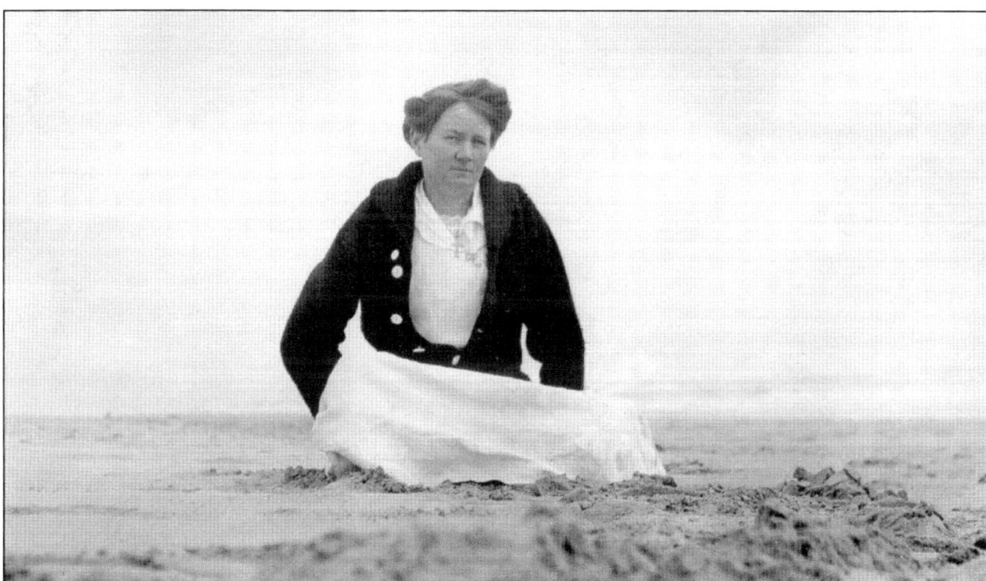

Ed's wife, Teresa, takes a turn sitting on the sand as her husband snaps her picture with a Brownie camera. Brownie camera advertisements appeared in popular magazines, and sales reached 150,000 in the first year. Many valuable moments have been captured by amateur photographers like these.

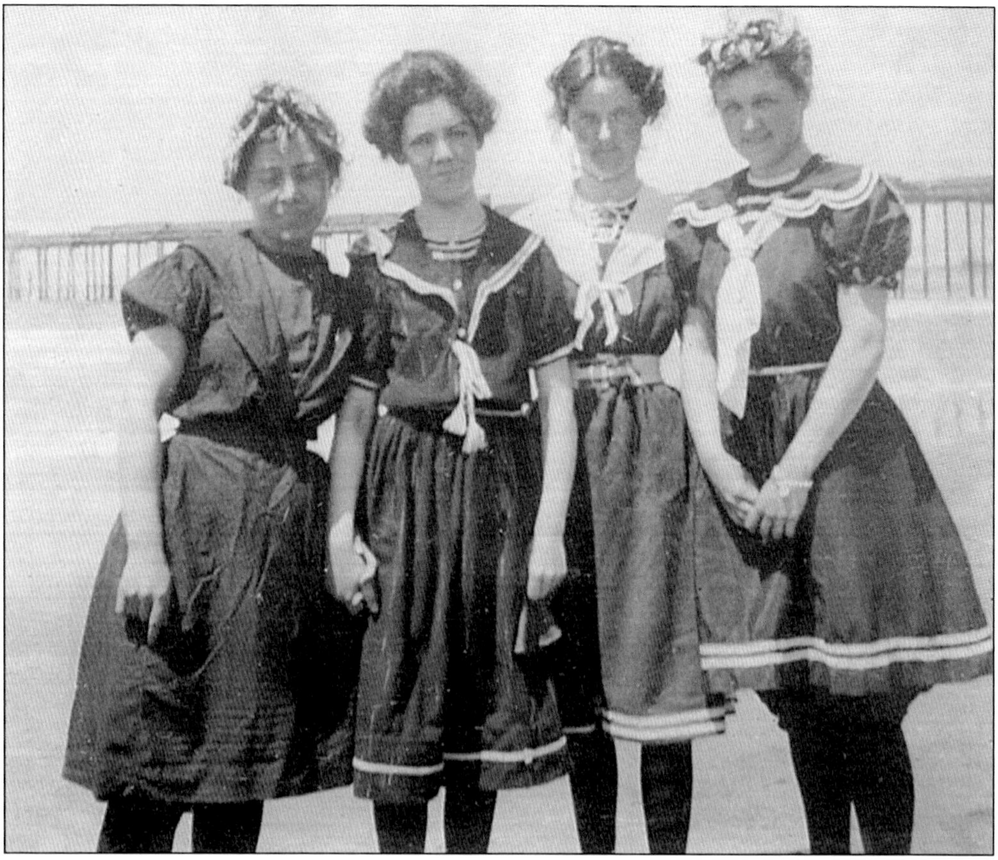

Cecilia McGonigle (second from the left) and her girlfriends strike a turn-of-the-century pose at Ventura Beach, north of Hueneme.

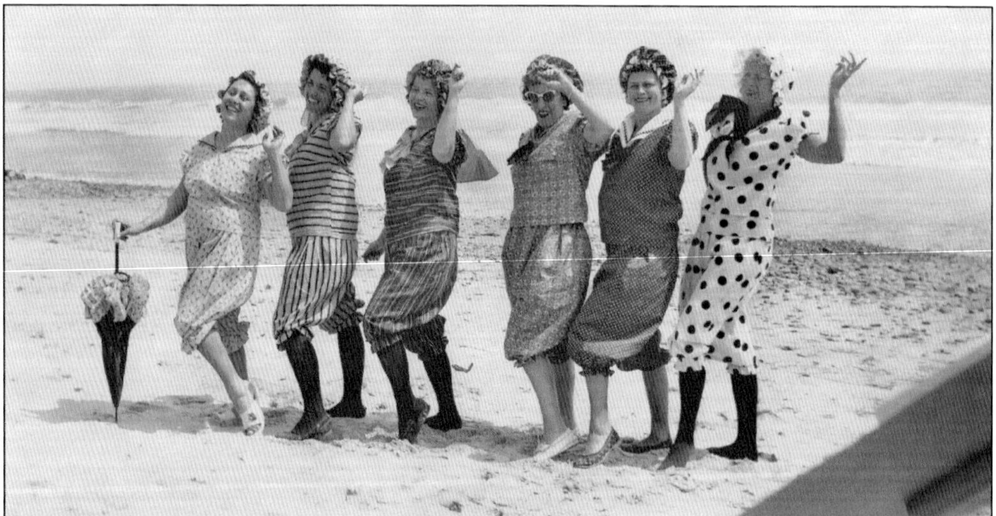

Hueneme locals posed for this costumed picture at the 1959 Harbor Days celebration. From left to right are Dorothy Ramirez, Helen Brant, Laura Prueter, unidentified, Lavern Anderson, and Helen Davis.

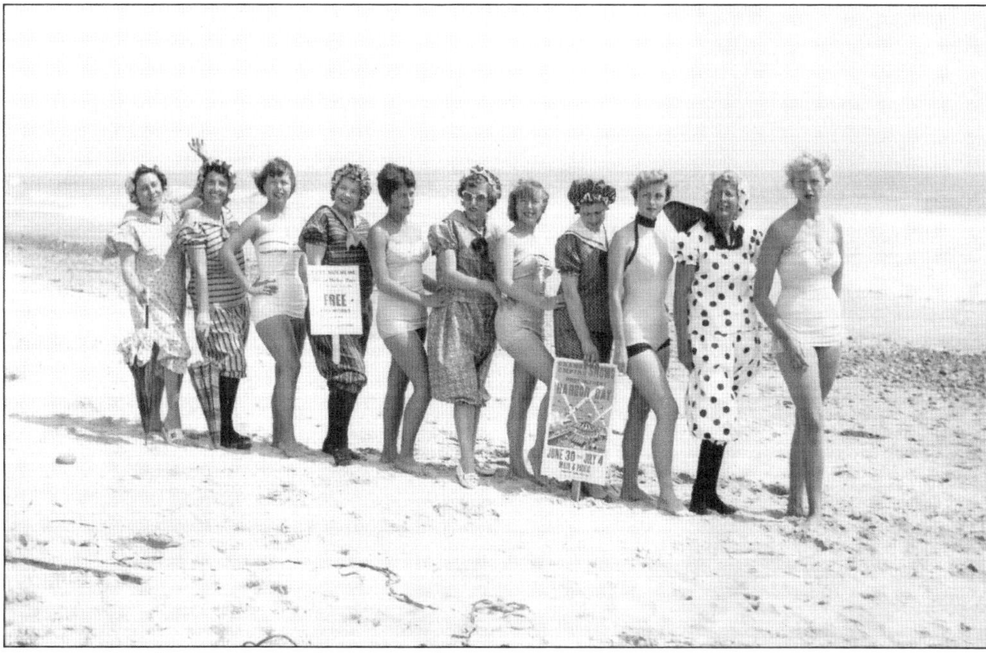

Hueneme locals mixed in with the "modern-day" contestants in 1957. Ladies from across the Southland participated in the annual beauty contest. At the far right, Linda Lee Reitzel of Ventura leads the line of contestants.

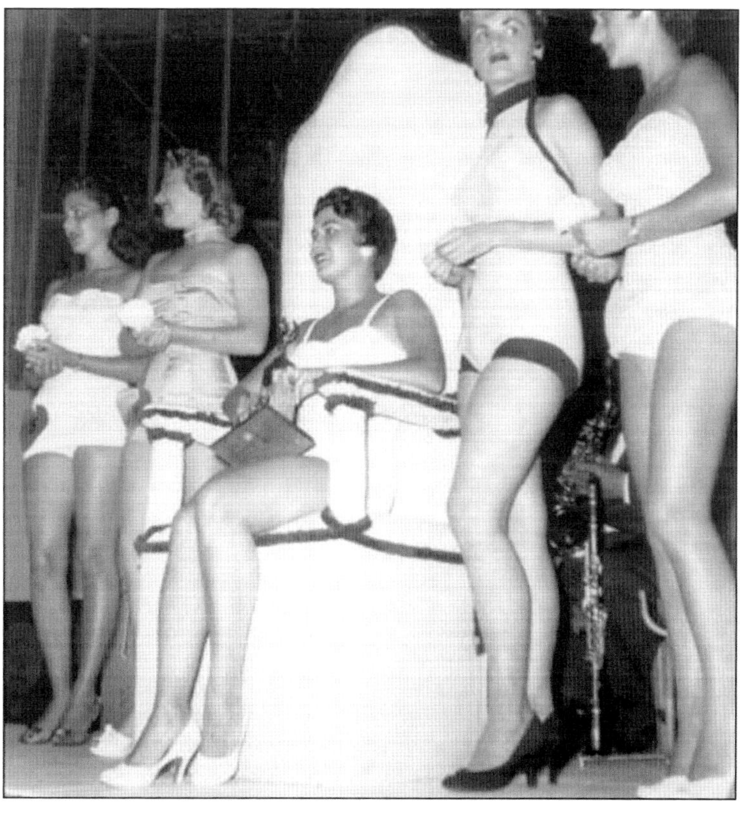

The finals were held at the Oxnard Elks Club, and the winner was awarded a diamond ring from Hueneme Jewelers. The 1956 Harbor Days queen, Judie Garret (seated), hailed from Ojai. The 1958 Harbor Days queen title went to Patricia Lapp, and the 1959 title to Barbara Beer.

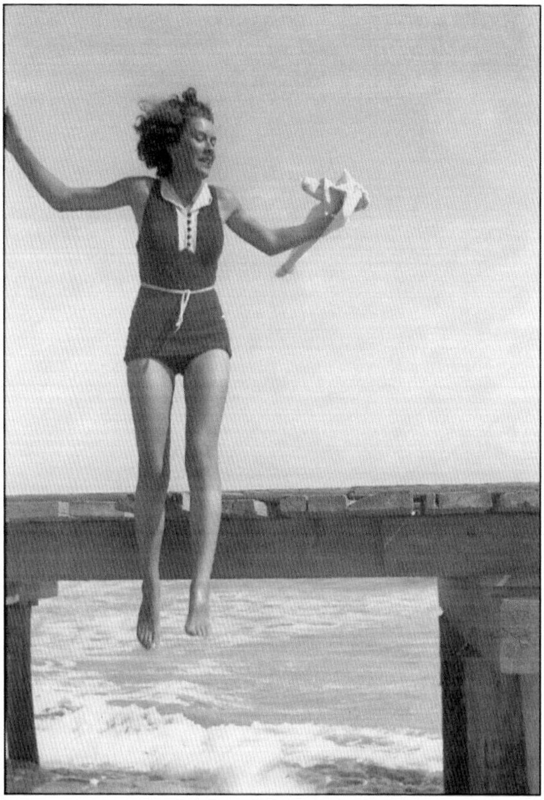

June Robinette takes a jump off the boardwalk at Hueneme in the 1930s. Bathing suits were still several threads away from the styles in the 21st century but yards away from turn-of-the-century swimming costumes.

Paul Moranda, pictured here in the 1930s doing a backwards flip off the boardwalk, was featured in a 1999 book, written by his brother Ted, entitled *Me and Paul and Old Hueneme*. The book chronicles the adventures of the two brothers during the sleepy years in Hueneme from the 1920s to the 1940s. In addition to the beach activities, there was a tennis court behind the Women's Improvement Club, the mysteries of the Hueneme Slough, and there was always time for a game of baseball.

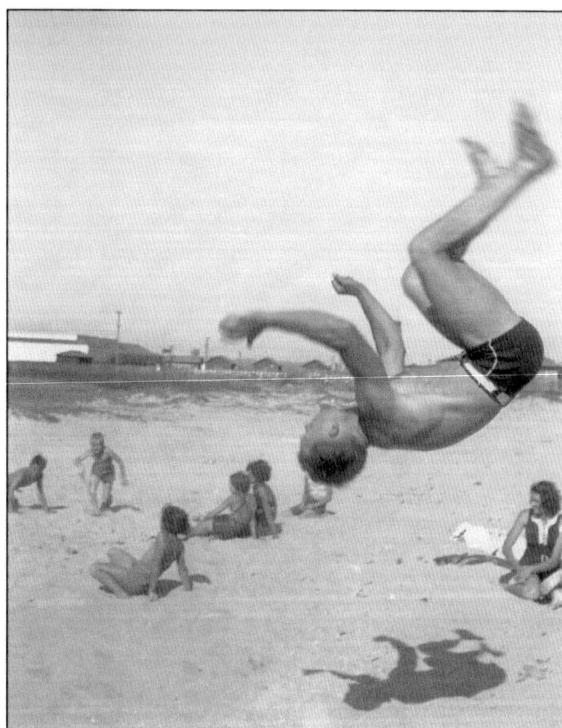

The boardwalk was used for everything from practicing flips and dives to just strolling or enjoying a game of catch.

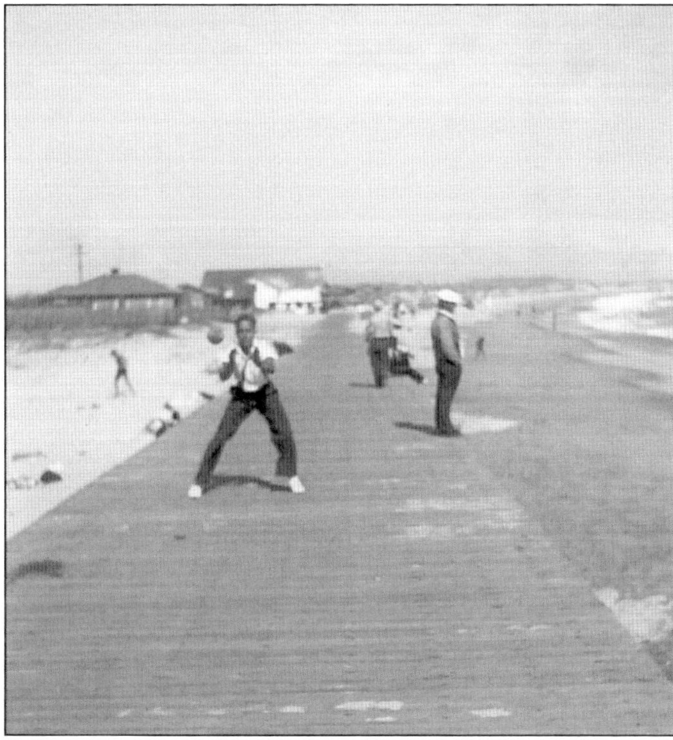

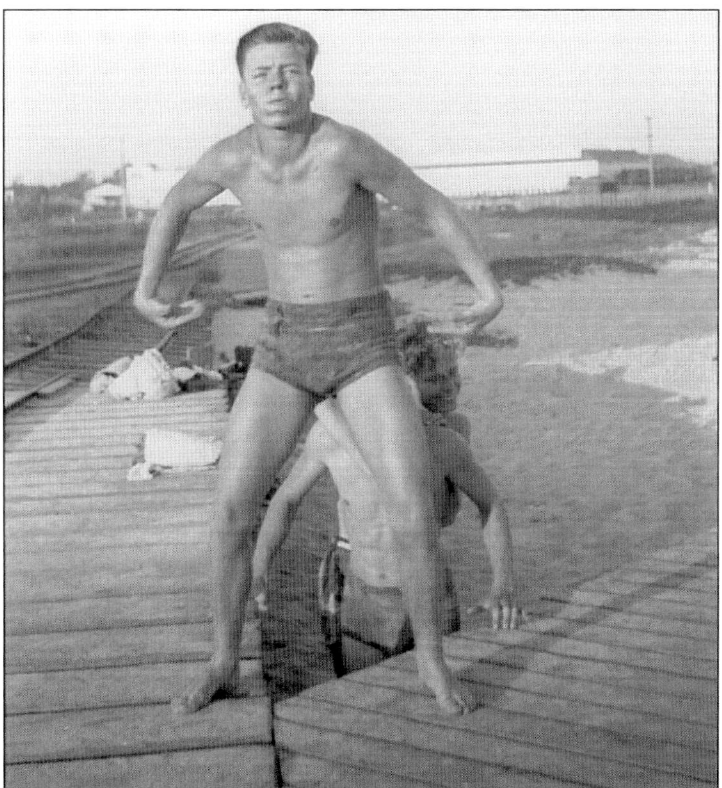

Ted Moranda does his best Mr. Universe flex. Moranda went on to a distinguished career as a history professor at Fresno City College.

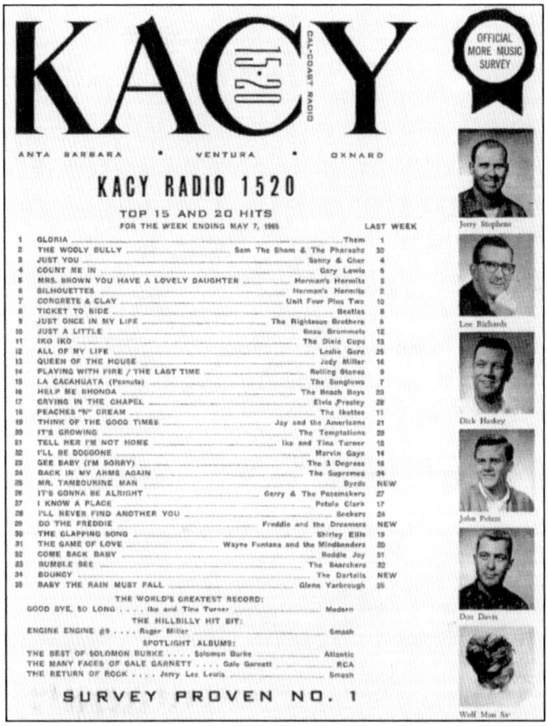

KACY 1520 CAL-COAST RADIO

OFFICIAL MORE MUSIC SURVEY

ANTA BARBARA • VENTURA • OXNARD

KACY RADIO 1520

TOP 15 AND 20 HITS

FOR THE WEEK ENDING MAY 7, 1965

			LAST WEEK
1	GLORIA	Them	1
2	THE WOOLY BULLY	Sam The Sham & The Pharaohs	30
3	JUST YOU	Sonny & Cher	4
4	COUNT ME IN	Gary Lewis	5
5	MRS. BROWN YOU HAVE A LOVELY DAUGHTER	Herman's Hermits	3
6	SILHOUETTES	Herman's Hermits	2
7	CONCRETE & CLAY	Unit Four Plus Two	10
8	TICKET TO RIDE	Beatles	8
9	JUST ONCE IN MY LIFE	The Righteous Brothers	6
10	JUST A LITTLE	Beau Brummels	12
11	IKO IKO	The Dixie Cups	13
12	ALL OF MY LIFE	Leslie Gore	25
13	QUEEN OF THE HOUSE	Jody Miller	16
14	PLAYING WITH FIRE / THE LAST TIME	Rolling Stones	9
15	LA CACAHUATA (Peanuts)	The Sunglows	7
16	HELP ME RHONDA	The Beach Boys	23
17	CRYING IN THE CHAPEL	Elvis Presley	28
18	PEACHES "N" CREAM	The Ikettes	11
19	THINK OF THE GOOD TIMES	Jay and the Americans	21
20	IT'S GROWING	The Temptations	29
21	TELL HER I'M NOT HOME	Ike and Tina Turner	18
22	I'LL BE DOGGONE	Marvin Gaye	14
23	GEE BABY (I'M SORRY)	The 3 Degrees	16
24	BACK IN MY ARMS AGAIN	The Supremes	34
25	MR. TAMBOURINE MAN	Byrds	NEW
26	IT'S GONNA BE ALRIGHT	Gerry & The Pacemakers	27
27	I KNOW A PLACE	Petula Clark	17
28	I'LL NEVER FIND ANOTHER YOU	Seekers	24
29	DO THE FREDDIE	Freddie and the Dreamers	NEW
30	THE CLAPPING SONG	Shirley Ellis	19
31	THE GAME OF LOVE	Wayne Fontana and the Mindbenders	20
32	COME BACK BABY	Roddie Joy	31
33	BUMBLE BEE	The Searchers	32
34	BOUNCY	The Dartells	NEW
35	BABY THE RAIN MUST FALL	Glenn Yarbrough	35

THE WORLD'S GREATEST RECORD:

GOOD BYE, SO LONG . . . . Ike and Tina Turner — Modern

THE HILLBILLY HIT BIT:

ENGINE ENGINE #9 . . . . Roger Miller — Smash

SPOTLIGHT ALBUMS:

THE BEST OF SOLOMON BURKE . . . . Solomon Burke — Atlantic

THE MANY FACES OF GALE GARNETT . . . . Gale Garnett — RCA

THE RETURN OF ROCK . . . . Jerry Lee Lewis — Smash

SURVEY PROVEN NO. 1

Jerry Stephens

Lee Richards

Dick Haskey

John Peters

Don Davis

Wolf Man Sa

Radio station KCAY was the "Boss of the Beach" in the 1960s. In the days before FM radio and decades before satellite systems, AM radio served as the soundtrack for the summer. It was not uncommon to walk down the beach at Hueneme and hear the Beatles, the Beach Boys, the Supremes, or a one-hit wonder.

As soon as Little League was over in June, every day was a beach day. From left to right are Ed Maulhardt (with a glove over his face), Paul Thomas, Frank Thomas, Tim Maulhardt, John Griggs, Craig "Moe" Maulhardt, David Thomas, and future author Jeff Maulhardt.

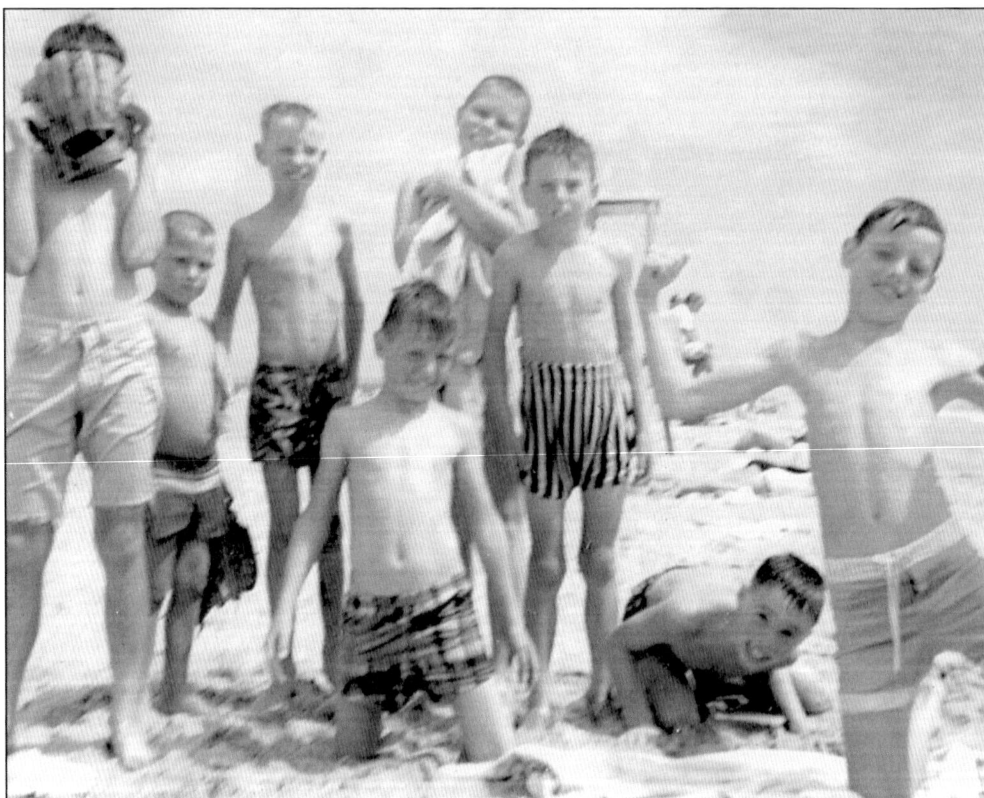

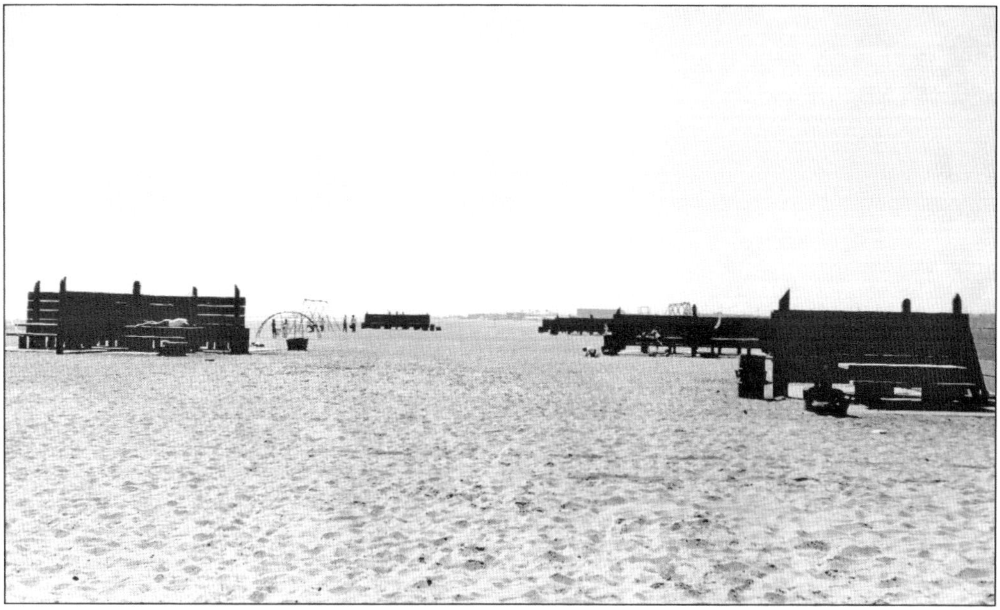

By the late 1970s, picnic tables and wind blocks were added to the Hueneme beach.

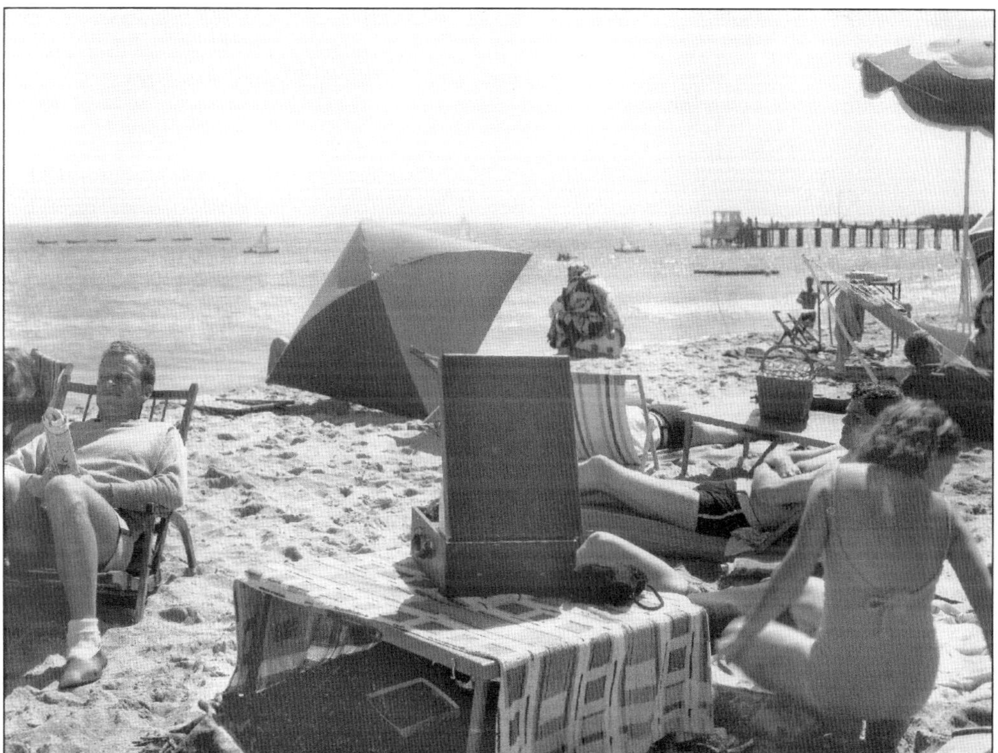

The Hueneme pier, visible in the background, was first constructed in 1956. Fishing from the pier was not possible until 1967, when a 1,000-foot, T-shaped extension was added at a cost of $250,000. Offshore oil money paid for $70,000 of the cost, and a bond was passed to pay the remainder of the cost.

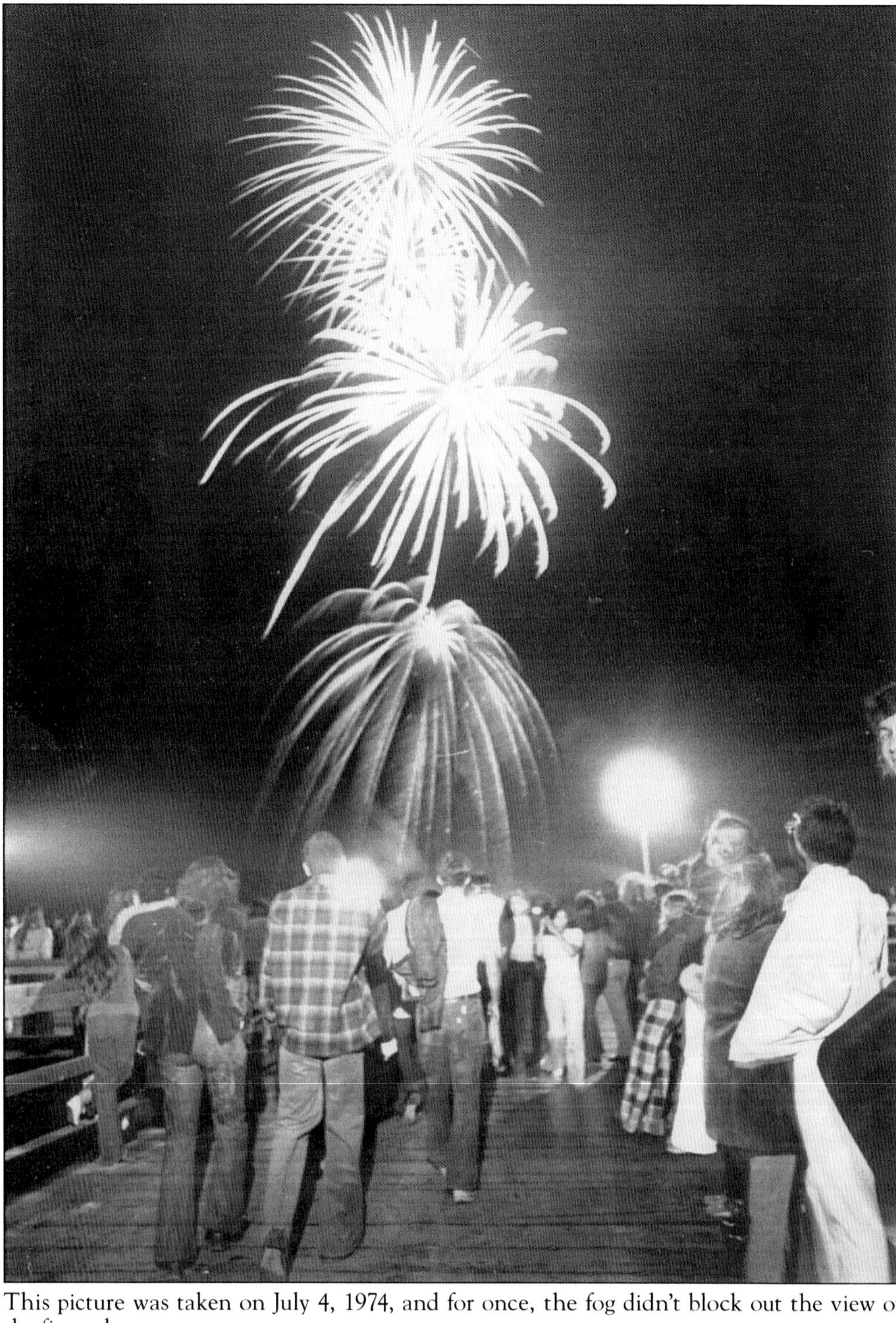

This picture was taken on July 4, 1974, and for once, the fog didn't block out the view of the fireworks.

Four

More Water

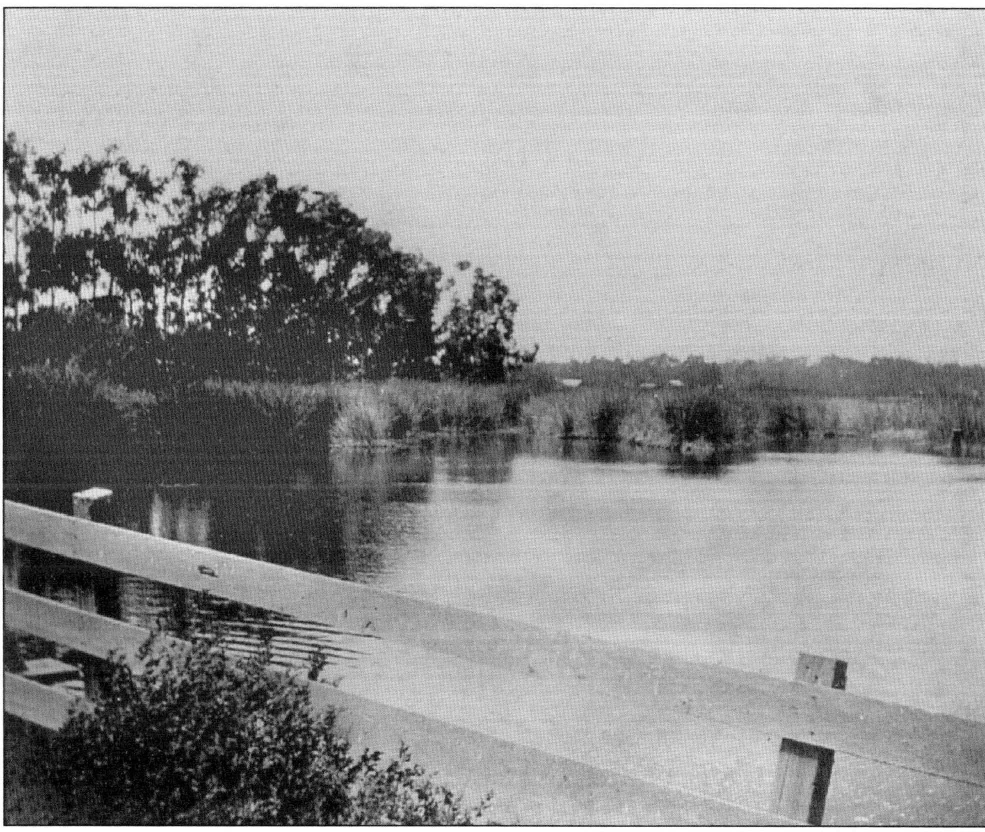

An inland lake replenished by the tidal action of the Pacific Ocean, the Hueneme Slough was located at Hueneme Road and Fifth Street, extending to the shoreline. A canal stretched from the Bard and Donlon properties and emptied into the slough, thus preserving the life of the "water hole." The site of the former eight-acre body of water, now Moranda Park, was designated Historical Landmark No. 37 in 1977.

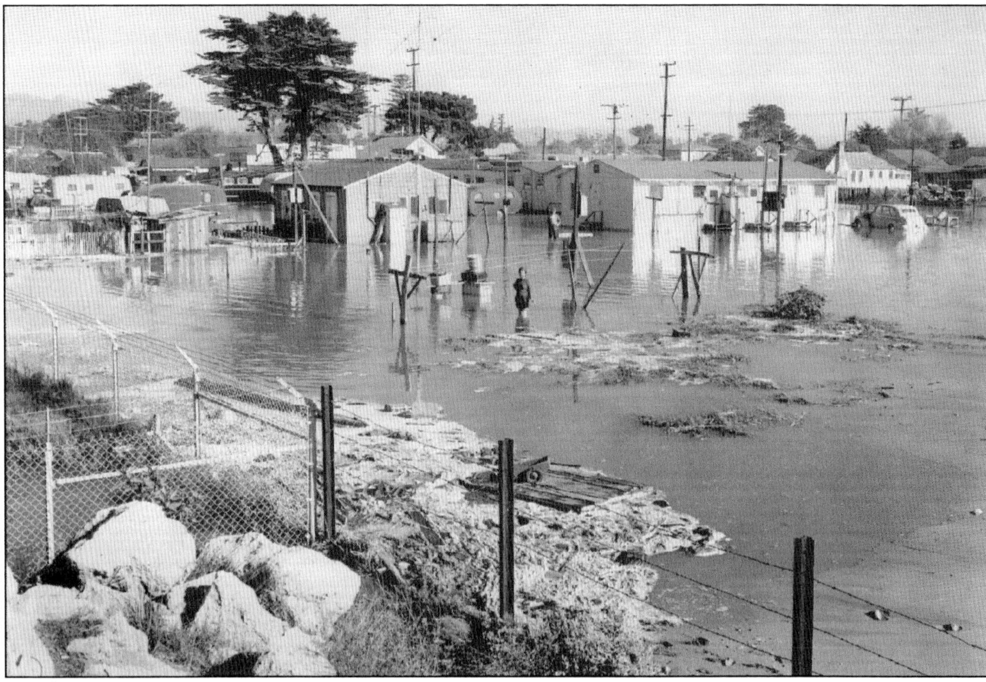

During the rainy season and high tides, the area near the beach would sometimes overflow into the neighborhoods. In January 1951, one of the worse floods occurred, bringing several feet of water to the streets of Hueneme.

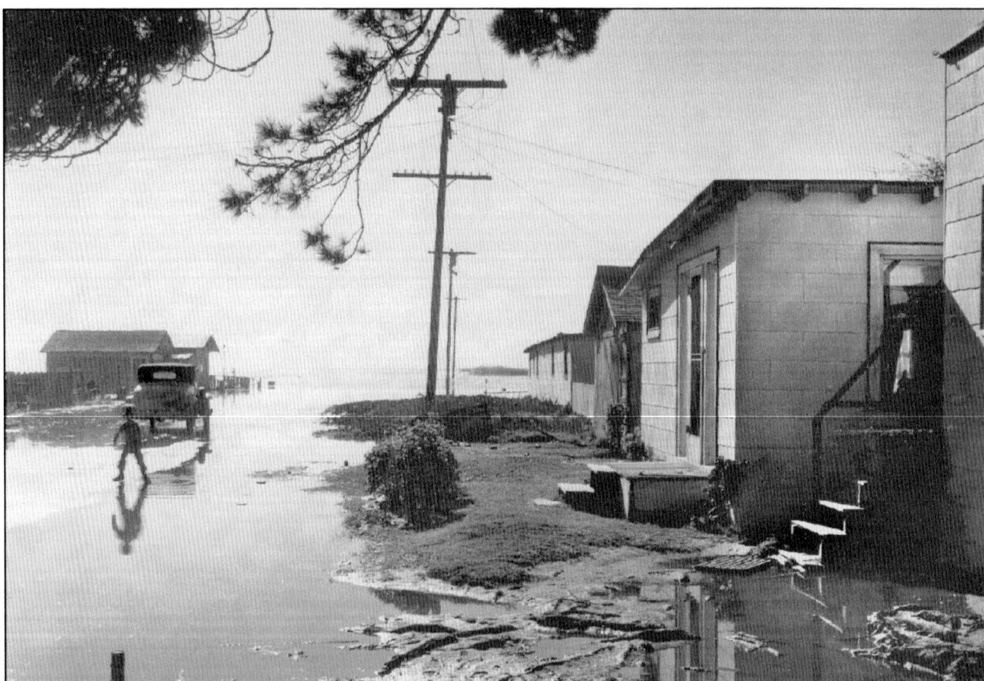

The shoreline went through drastic changes when the port was expanded. It would take many years to manage the eroding shoreline.

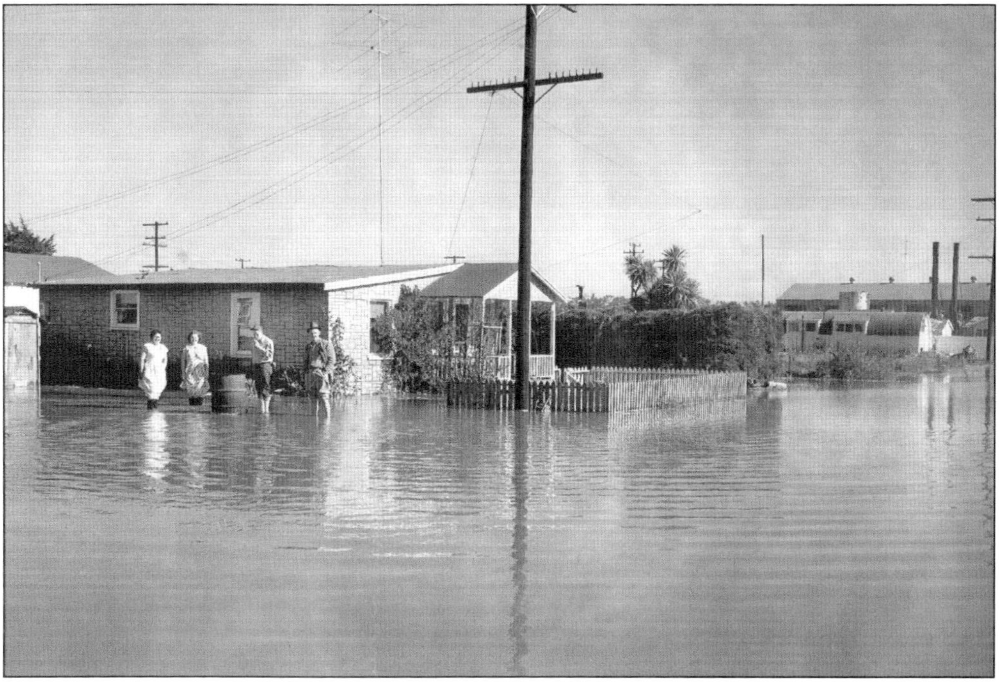

The Siebert Trailer Park was hit hard by rising waters in January 1951. The park became part of the redevelopment area and is now part of Anacapa View.

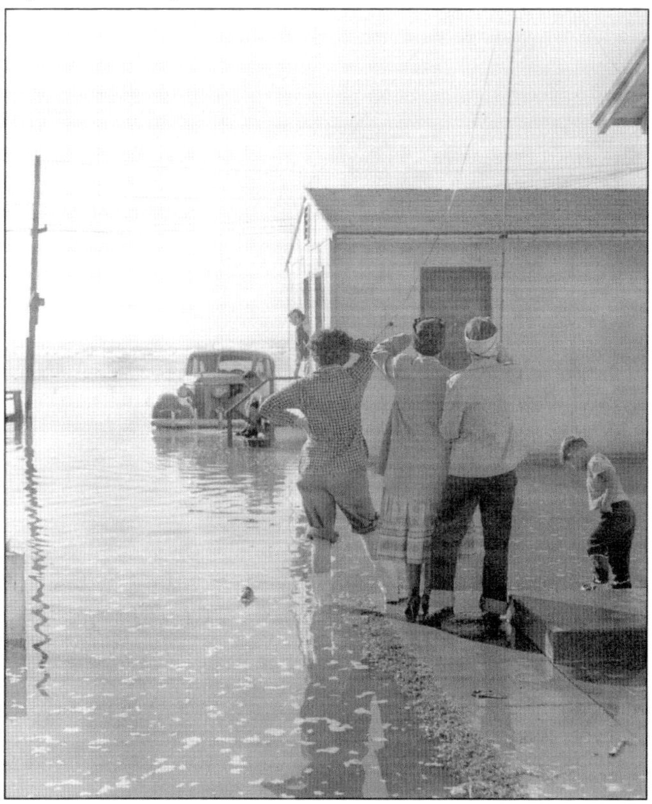

By 1953, Hueneme hired engineer R. A. Wilson to tackle some of the reoccurring problems the city faced, including beach erosion. Sand from Silver Strand beach, northwest of the city, was pumped to the beaches of Hueneme and down along the coast to Point Mugu.

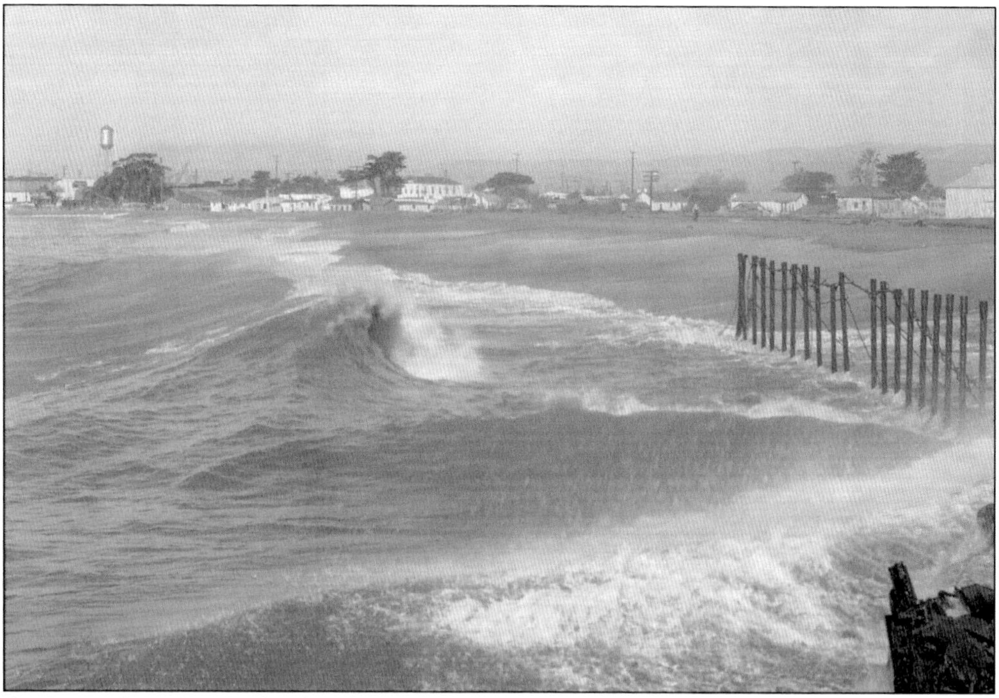

On September 25, 1939, the shoreline of Hueneme and the surrounding areas was bombarded by heavy rains and 50-mile-per-hour winds, causing devastation that had never been seen before or since. At least 45 people were killed between Los Angeles and Santa Barbara.

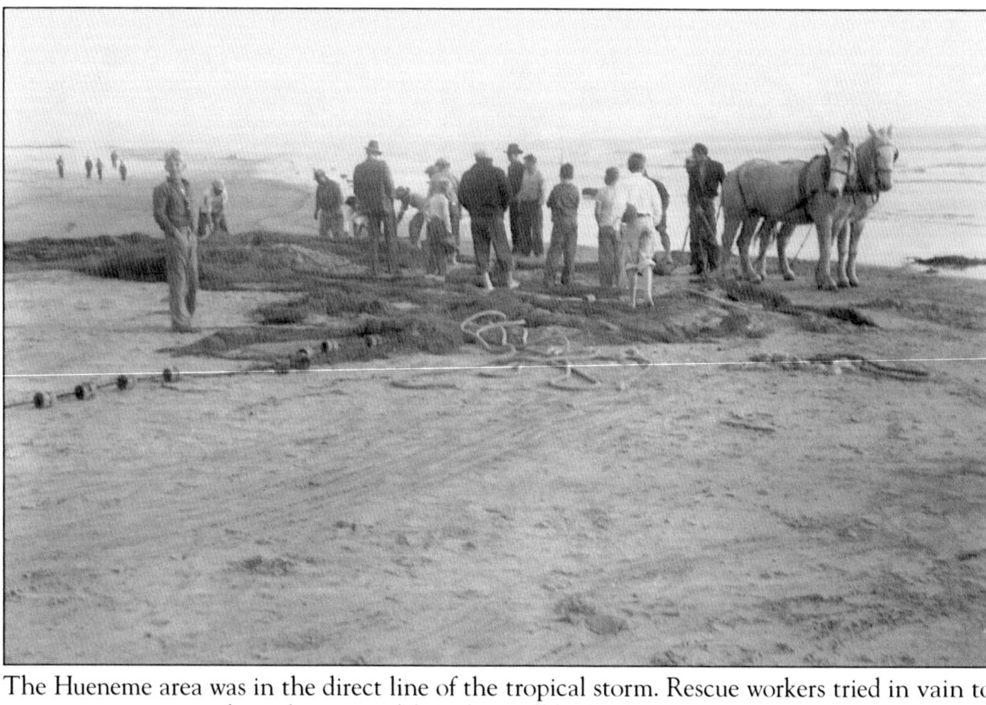

The Hueneme area was in the direct line of the tropical storm. Rescue workers tried in vain to save any survivors and to salvage any debris that still had value.

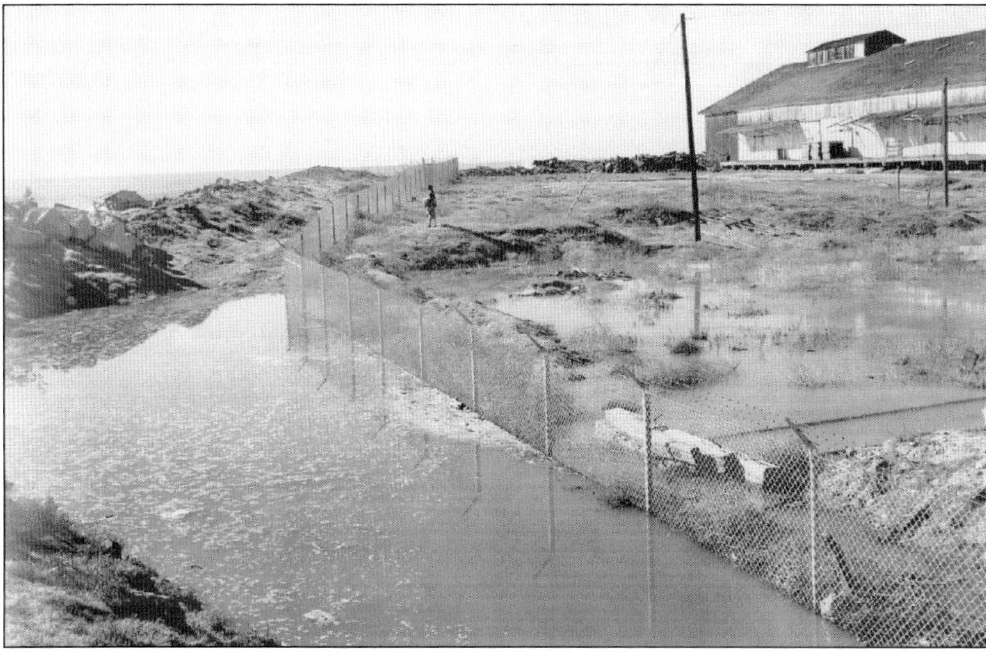

The lemon warehouse survived, but flooding caused a delay in every part of production. Eventually four wells were drilled to alleviate the flooding beneath the building.

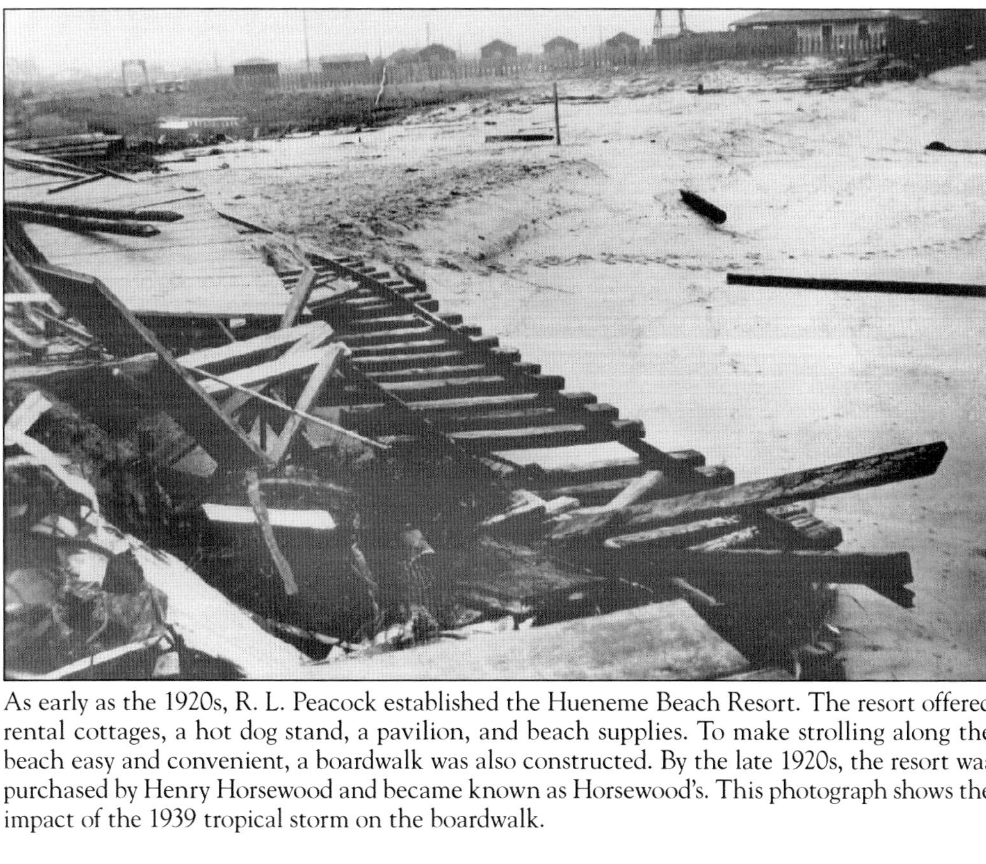

As early as the 1920s, R. L. Peacock established the Hueneme Beach Resort. The resort offered rental cottages, a hot dog stand, a pavilion, and beach supplies. To make strolling along the beach easy and convenient, a boardwalk was also constructed. By the late 1920s, the resort was purchased by Henry Horsewood and became known as Horsewood's. This photograph shows the impact of the 1939 tropical storm on the boardwalk.

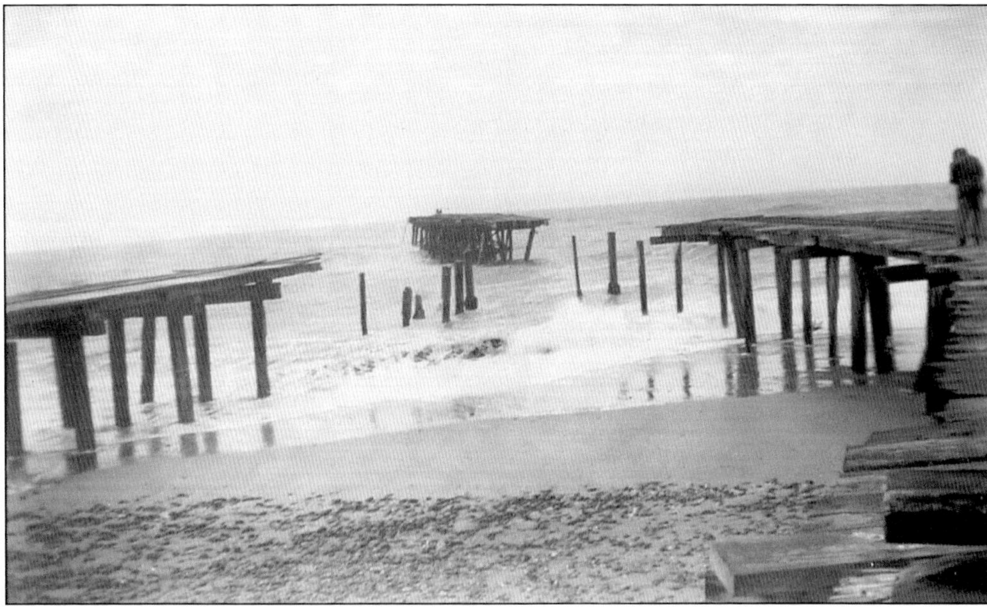

The wharf suffered the worst damage when a barge that was being used in the construction of the breakwater rammed into the wharf and broke apart the 68-year-old structure. For the next 18 years, Hueneme was without a pier, and it would be another 10 years, in 1967, before the community had a pier long enough to cast a line for fishing.

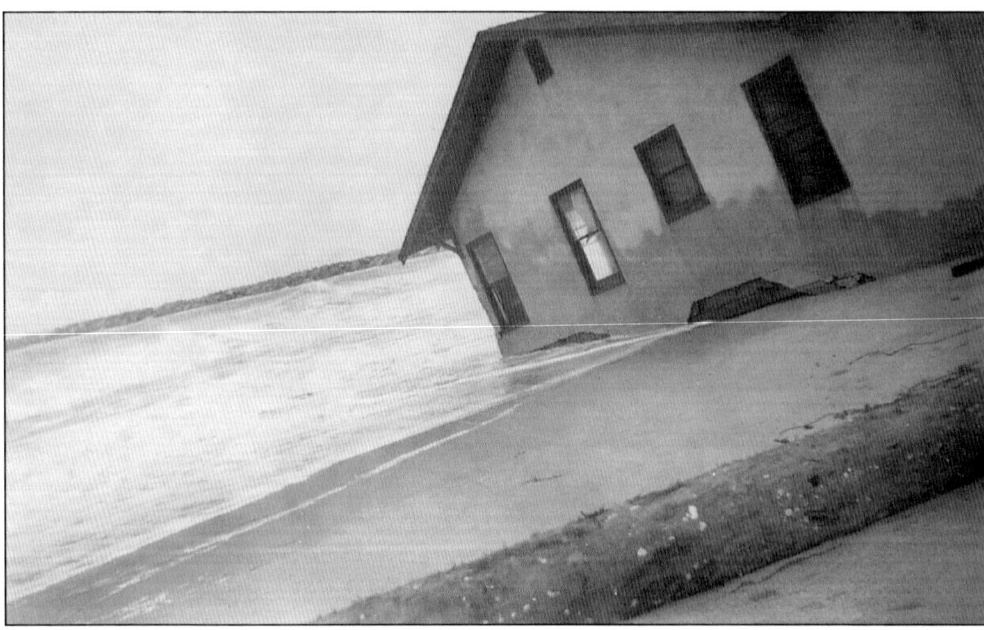

Another victim of the hurricane was this house, which was torn from its foundation and relocated along the beach.

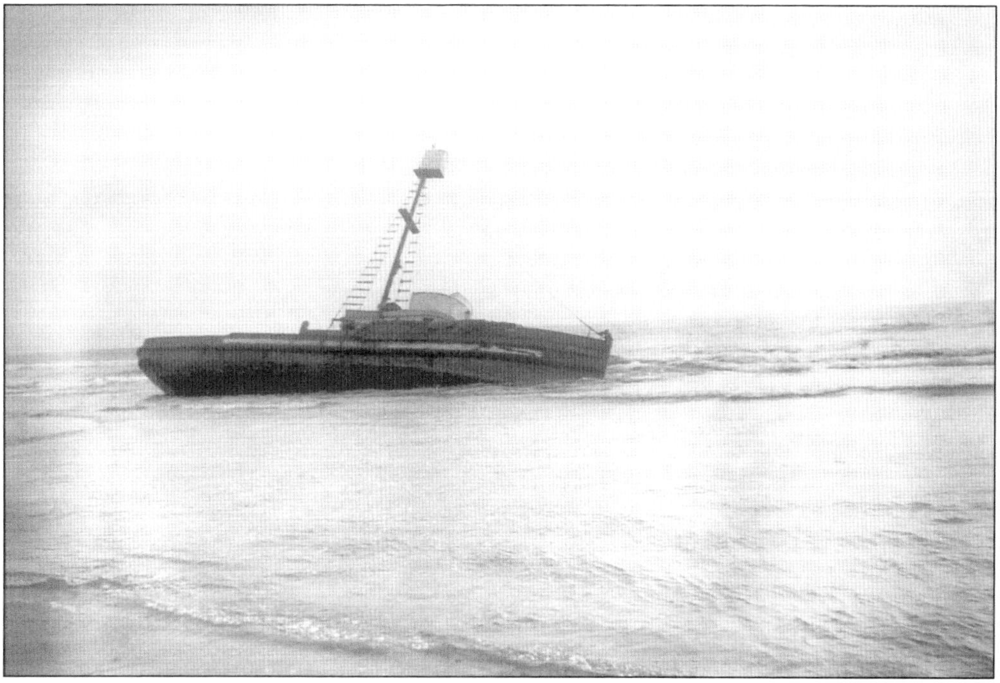

No boat was safe from the brutal winds and crashing waves.

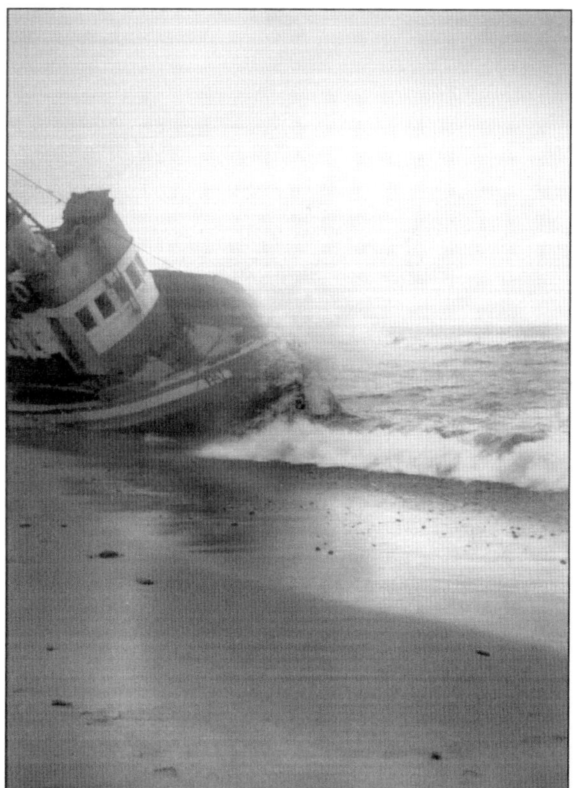

The Hueneme tugboat was a favorite of the citizens, and the sight of her grounding caused much grief. Fortunately she was brought back to life.

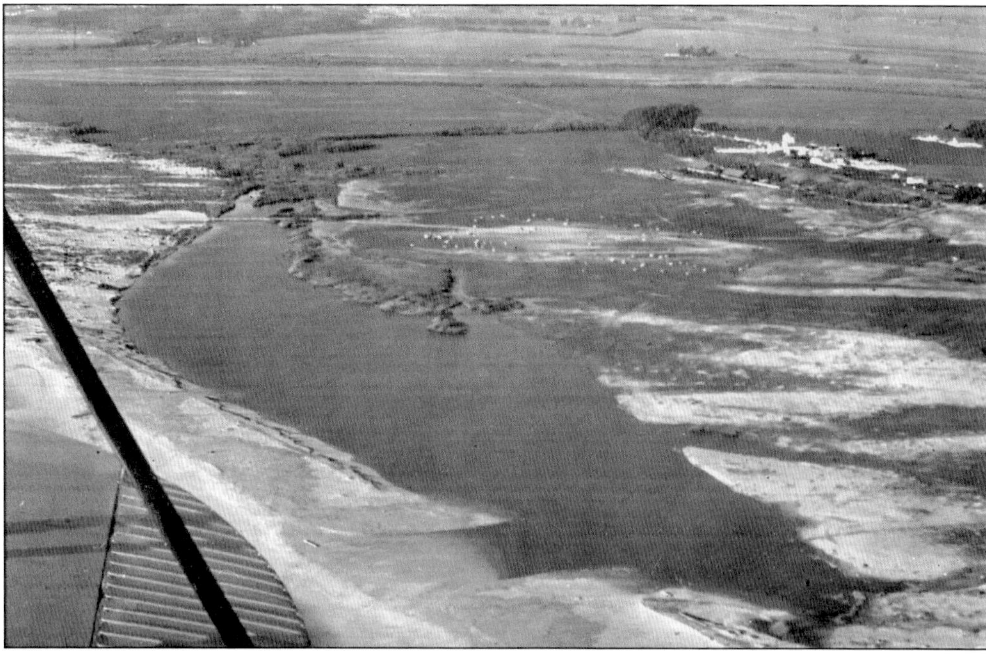

The flat lands of the plains were dotted with a variety of sloughs. In his self-published memoirs, *Me and Paul and Old Hueneme*, Ted Moranda called the Hueneme Slough "our Walden Pond."

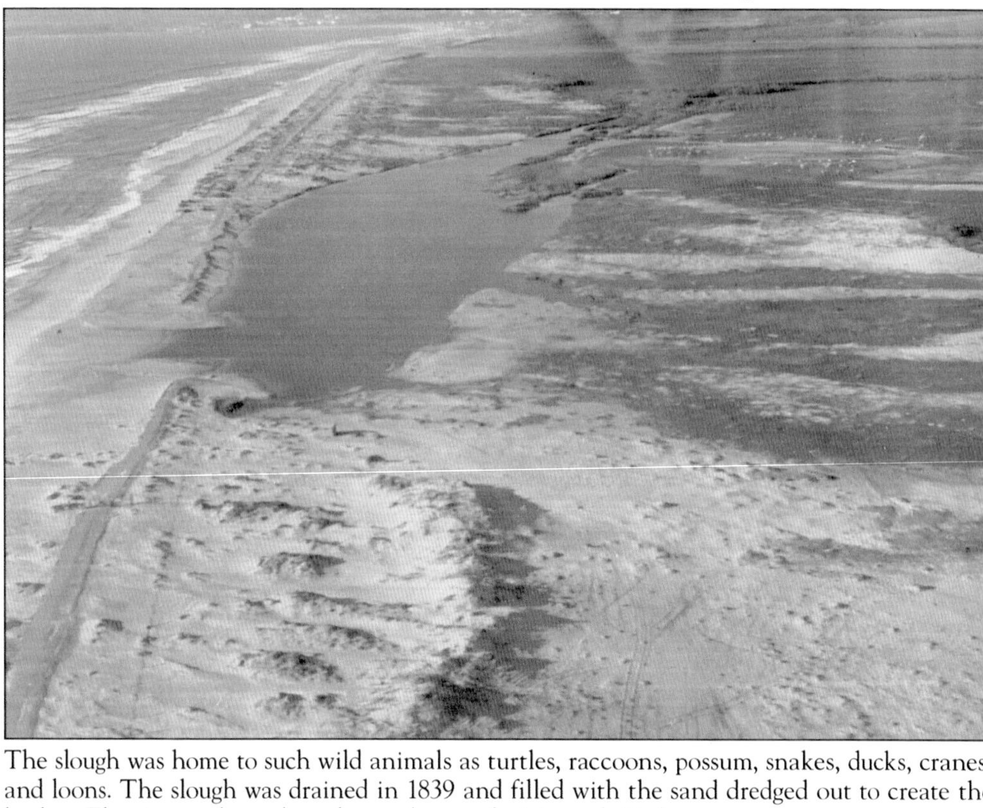

The slough was home to such wild animals as turtles, raccoons, possum, snakes, ducks, cranes, and loons. The slough was drained in 1839 and filled with the sand dredged out to create the harbor. The site was later cleared to make way for Moranda Park.

Five

The Harbor

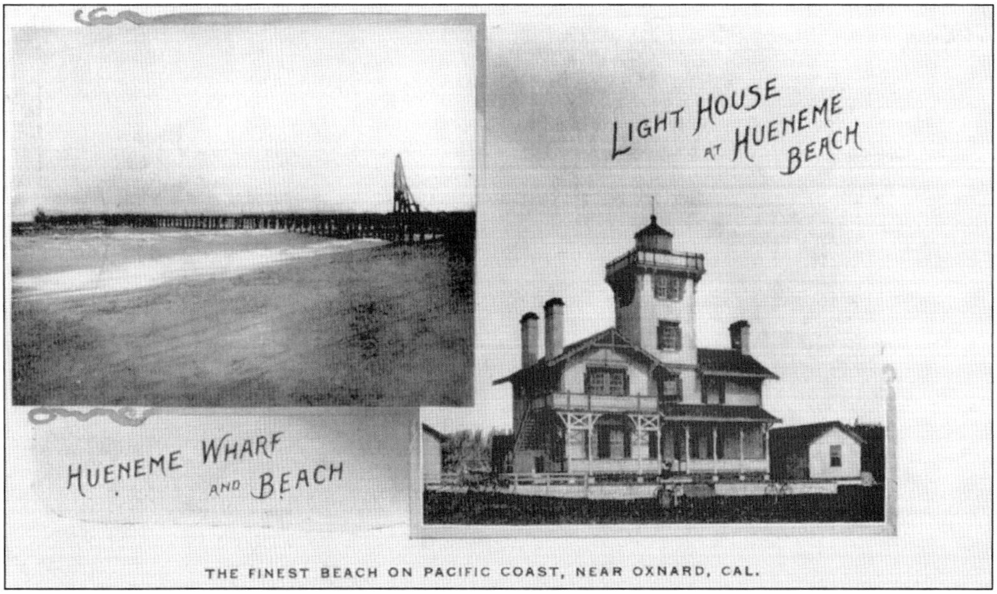

The original lighthouse at Point Hueneme, built in 1872, was located one mile west of the wharf. The structure was built by A. J. Salisbury and his crew, the same group of men who built the wharf. The Italianate building was constructed of oak and contained 10 rooms.

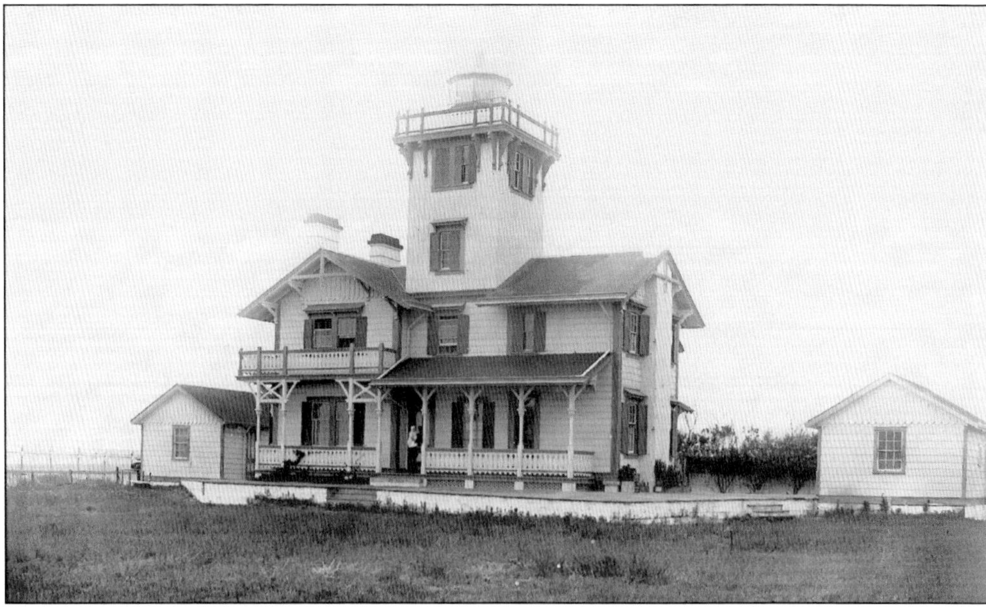

This c. 1875 cabinet card view is one of the earliest pictures of the lighthouse. The light tower reached a height of 65 feet. The first keeper was Samuel Ensien, who lived on the first floor; B. H. Korts offered assistance as needed.

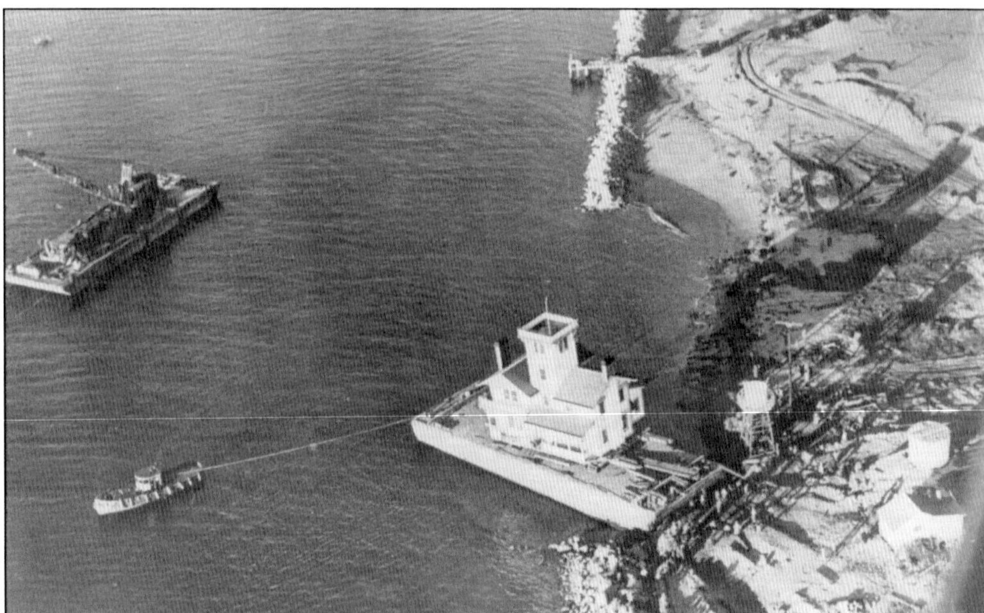

In 1939, the Oxnard Harbor District made plans to move the building 300 feet to the east to allow entrance to the channel, which was to be widened 700 feet. John Brakey, who was in charge of moving many of the buildings out of Hueneme when Oxnard sprang up as a town in 1898, was again in charge of the historic move.

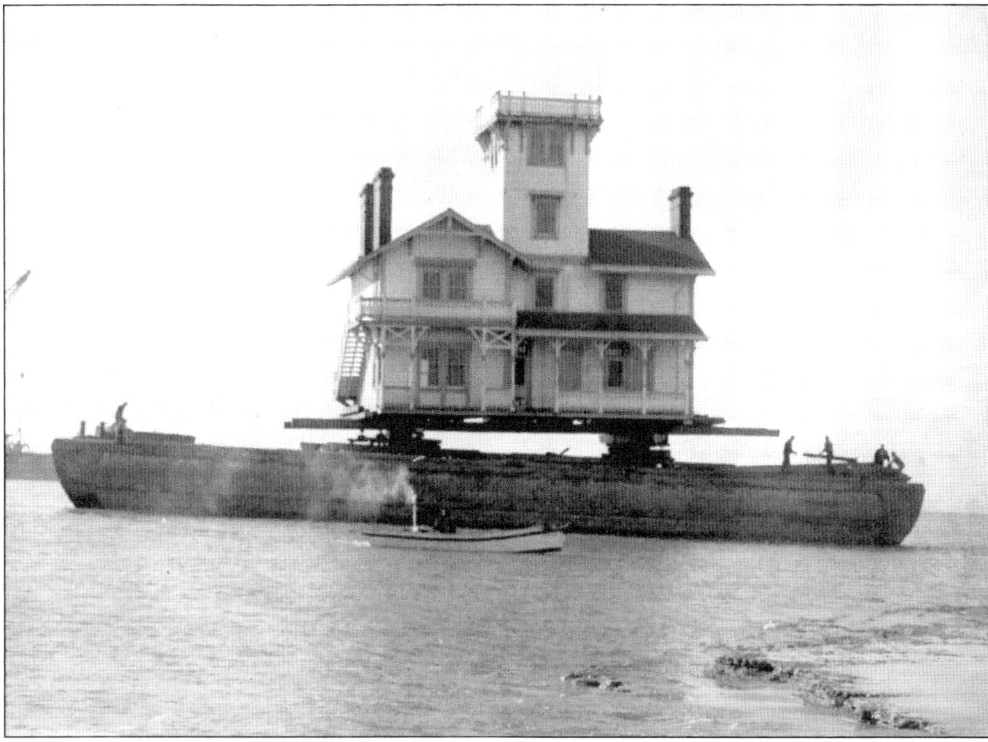

The Hueneme Yacht Club took charge of the 104-ton building and made plans to renovate the old structure. With the lighthouse placed on a barge, the move began on February 10, 1940, and ended on February 18, 1940. Before plans to renovate the lighthouse could be realized, World War II erupted. With the necessary manpower off helping in the war effort and because of the scarcity of materials during this time, the original lighthouse was torn down only two years after the move.

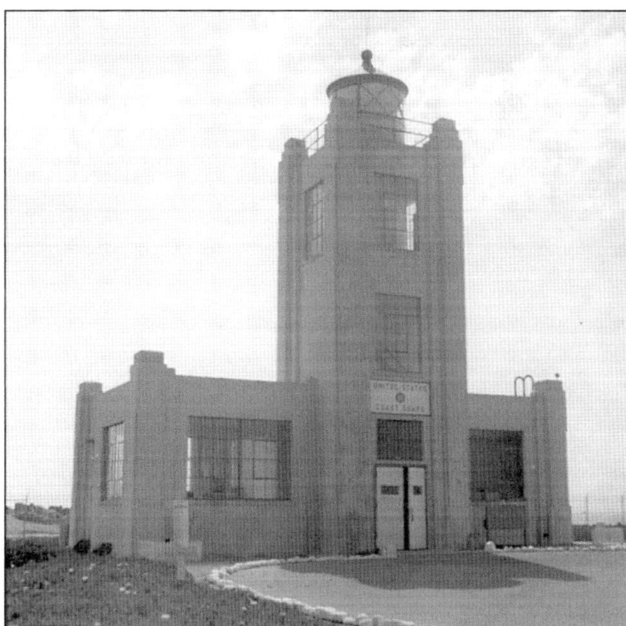

The new lighthouse was built soon after the old one was moved. A temporary light shown across the Pacific Ocean at night time, while during the day, a new 52-foot-high tower was constructed to house the 1,000-watt, six-panel light. The light could make two revolutions per minute, and the foghorn could be heard as far as Anacapa Island, 10.5 miles away.

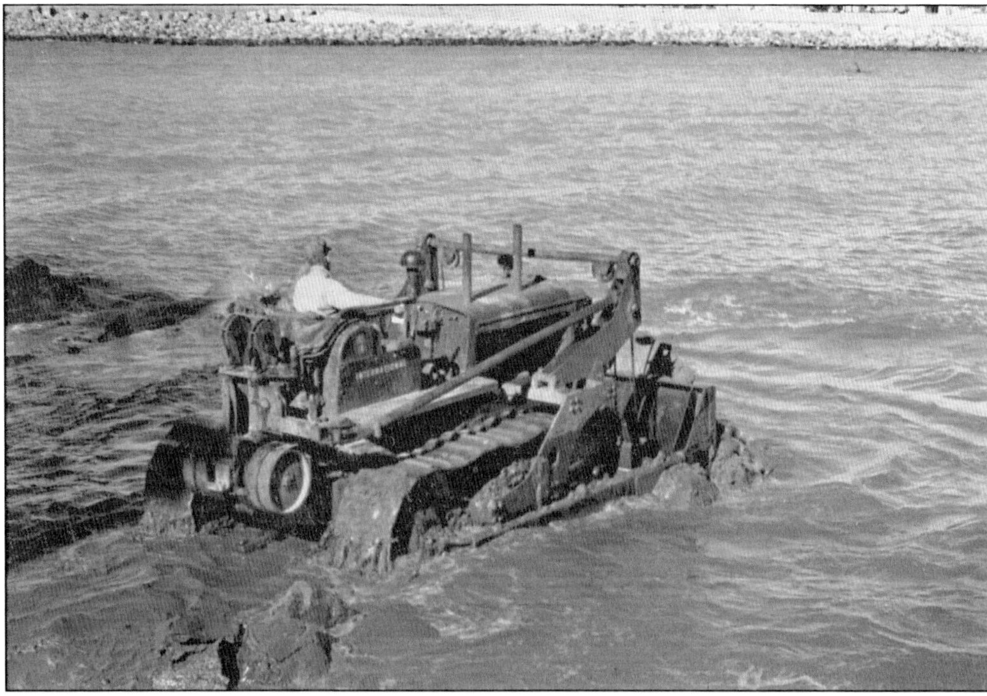

The area's first yacht club, the Ventura County Regatta Association was organized in 1939 with the first races taking place on November 12. The dredging of a yacht basin, as seen in this picture, was part of a $100,000 project that also included adding fishing facilities, a boat yard, and mooring slips.

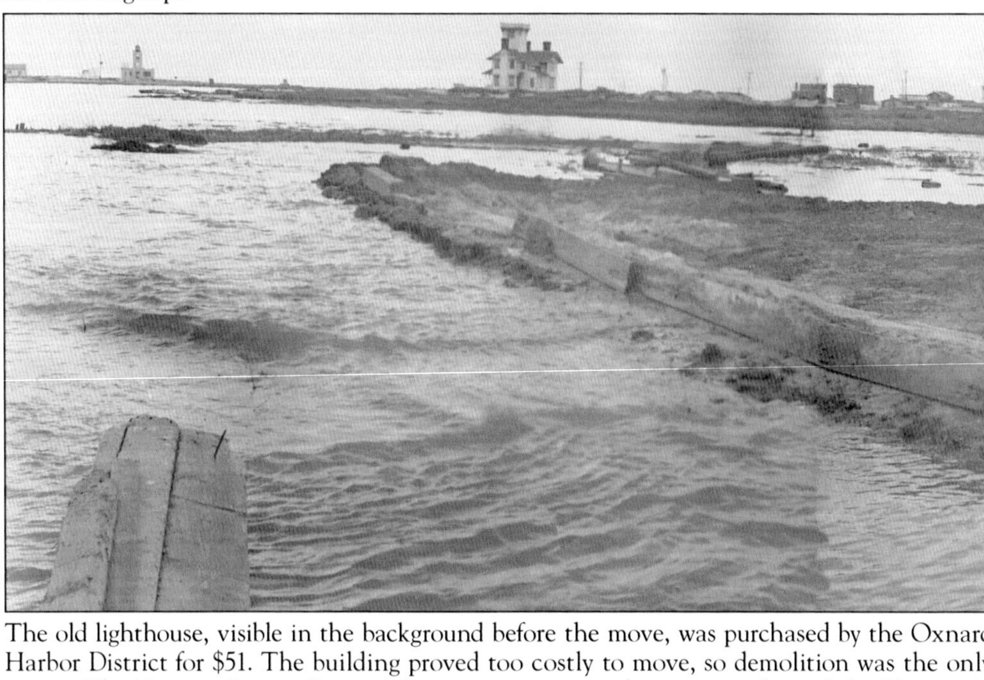

The old lighthouse, visible in the background before the move, was purchased by the Oxnard Harbor District for $51. The building proved too costly to move, so demolition was the only option. The Ventura County Regatta Association came to the rescue and saved the 65-year-old building but only for a few years.

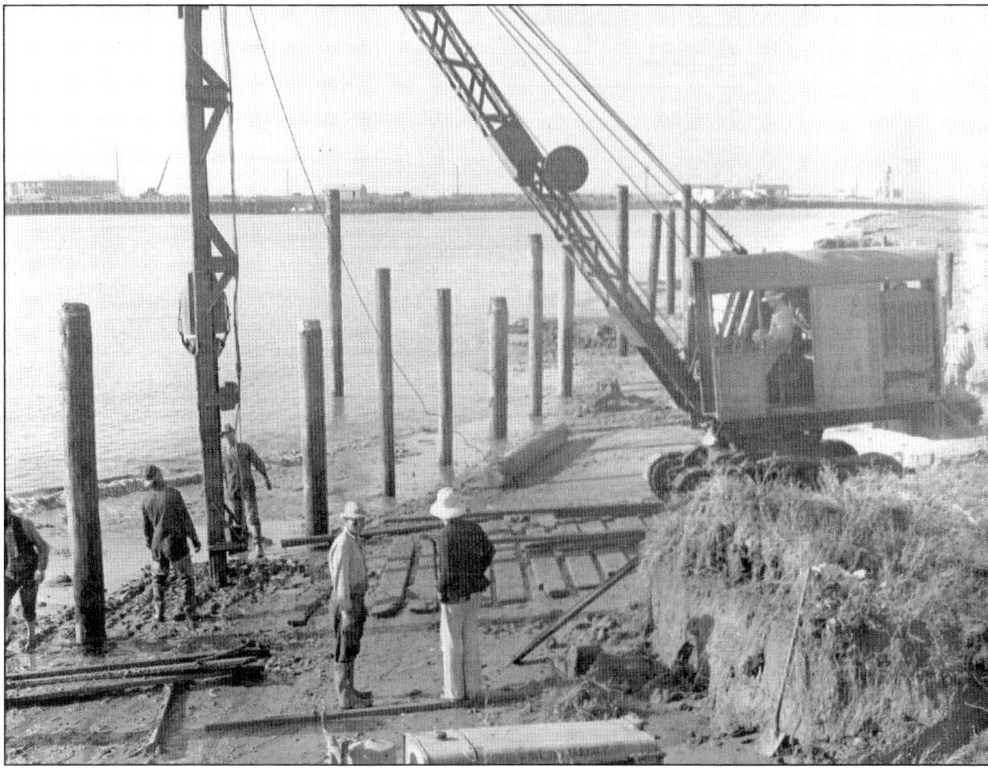

The Ventura County Boat Club was an outgrowth of the original Regatta Club. The commodore was Dr. Howard Taylor. Among the members were Bob Pfeiler, H. C. Dawley, Fay Overton, Dick Pidduck, Dick Maulhardt, Earl Davis, and Ray Johnson, all from Oxnard.

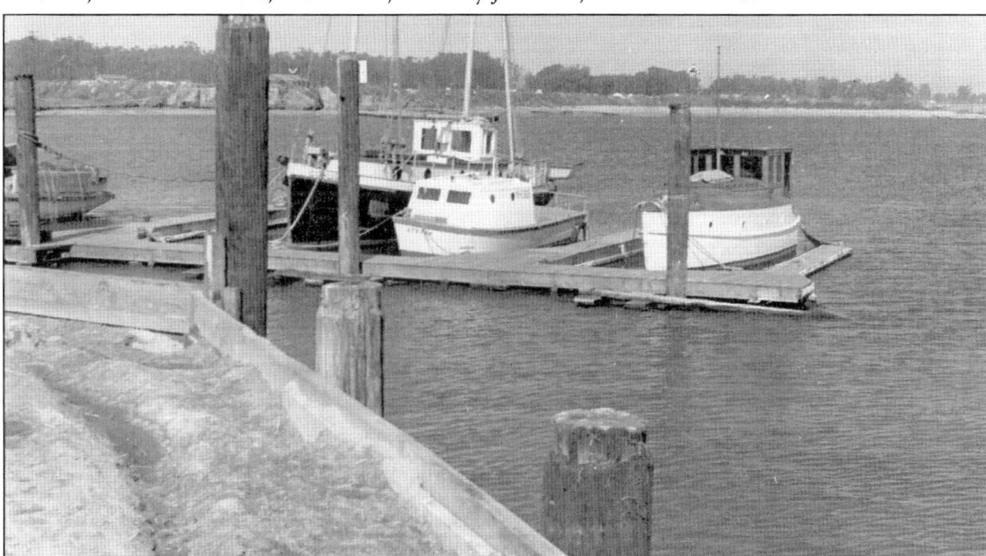

The Ventura Boat Club members from Ventura who docked at the harbor included Robert Fournier, Tom Beal, Carlton Beal, Joe Bircaw, George Brokaw, Dick Lundsford, Forest Fix, Don and Bob Hunter, and Bill Merrill. Other members from the surrounding area included Albert Vanoni, Walter and Philip Bell, Dick Underwood, Urban Underwood, and Don Nisbet.

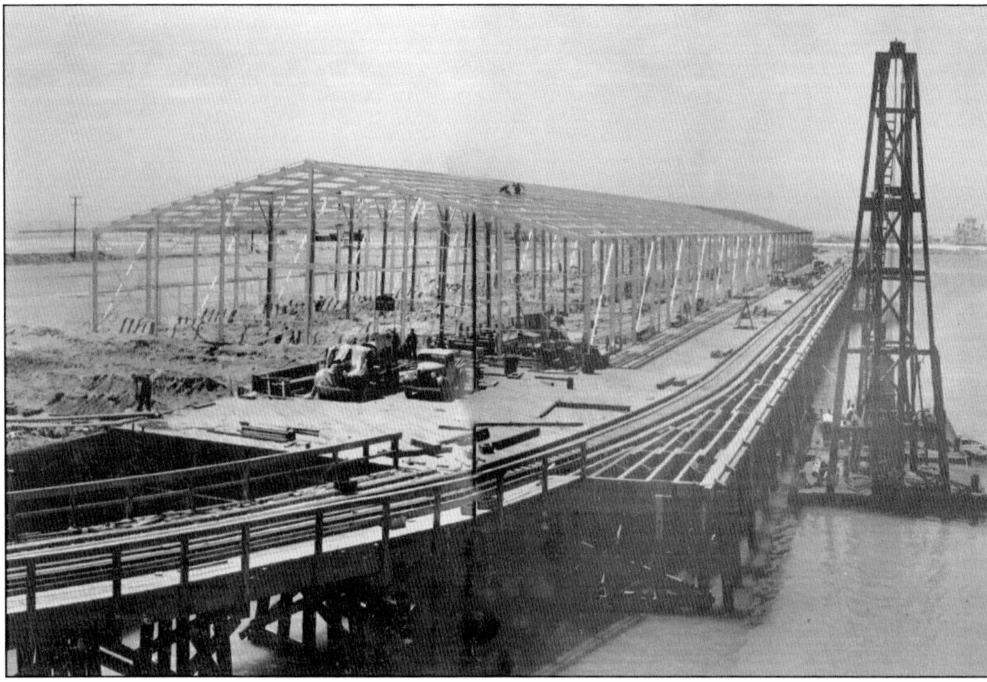

The construction of the galvanized iron transit shed was captured in this 1940 photograph by Bob Pfeiler.

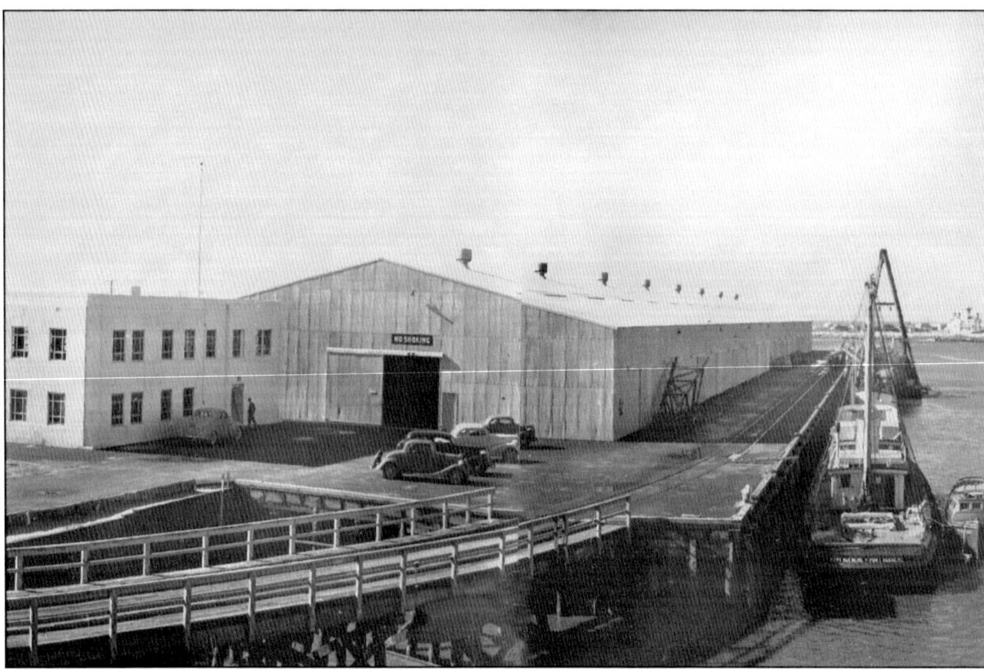

The completed shed featured sliding doors that opened onto the wharf. The shed was 600 feet long and 200 feet wide with a storage area of 27,000 square feet.

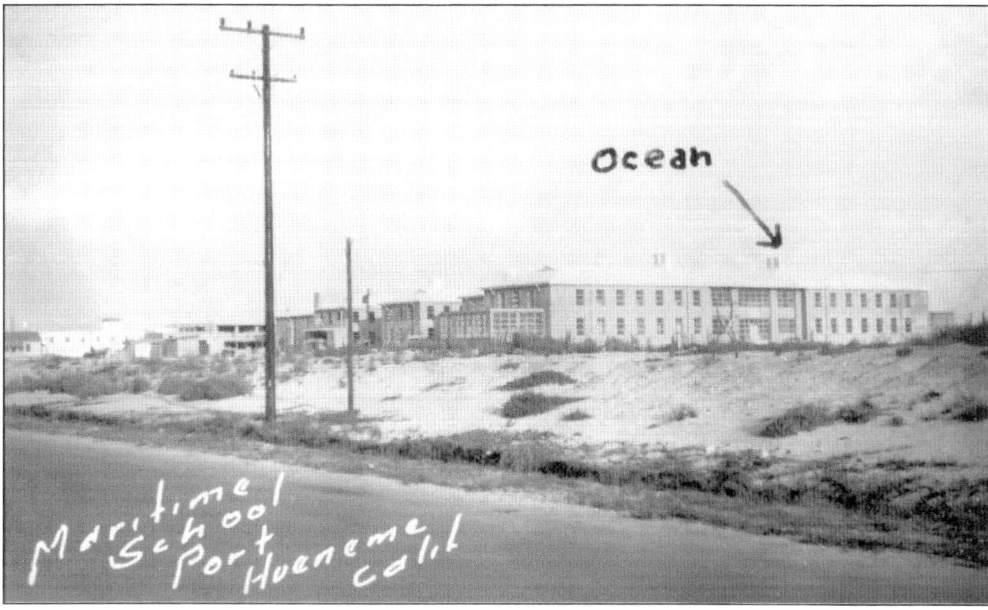

The Maritime School was built shortly after the completion of the Navy's takeover of the port. The building contained eight 40-by-50-foot dormitories, an auditorium, a hospital, administrative offices, recreation rooms, officers' quarters, a mess hall, and kitchens. The school, designed to accommodate 250 apprentice seamen, trained some of the top Navy officers in the country.

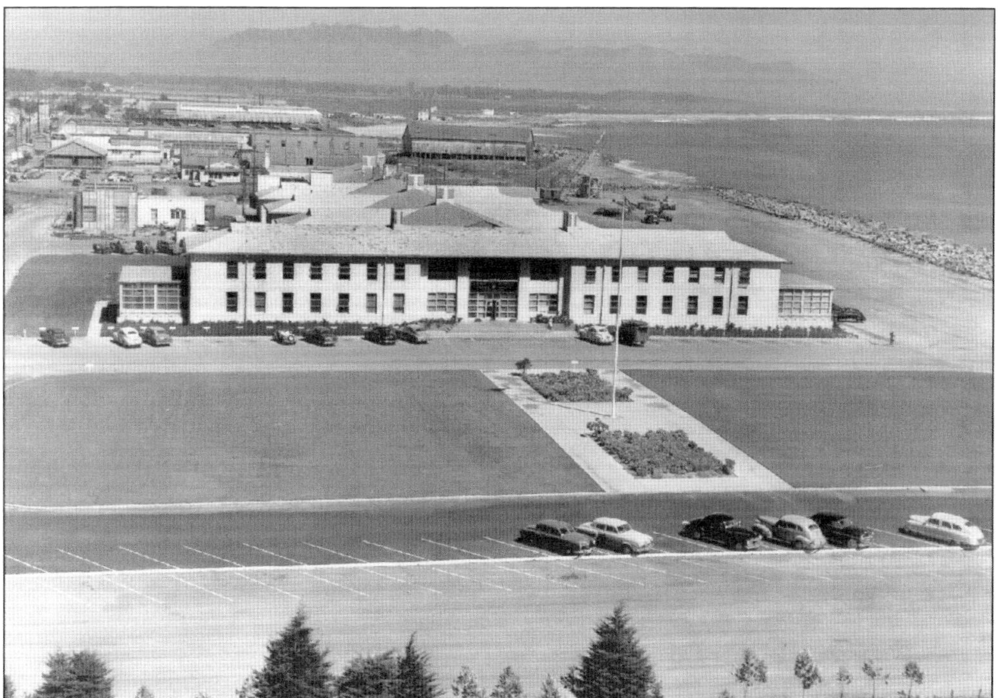

The Naval Engineering Laboratory, founded in 1950, is used as a research and testing facility. The scientists there work on a variety of activities, including electronics, nuclear physics, deep-water systems, atomic defenses, floating dry-docks, and waterfront structures.

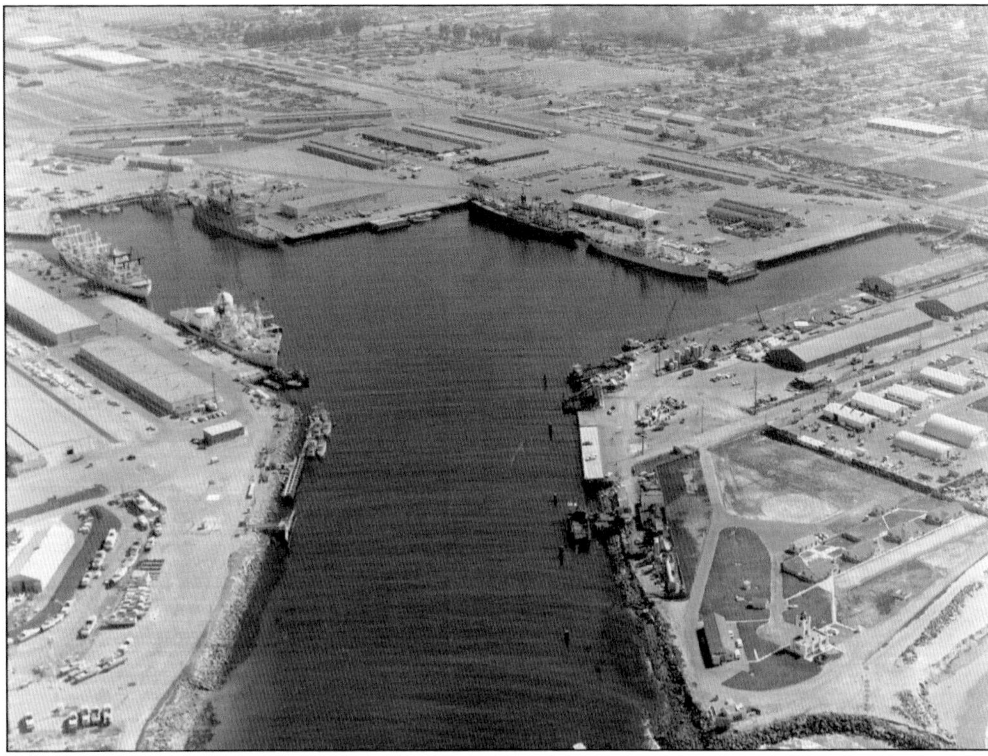

As early as 1926, Richard Bard, the son of Thomas Bard, began setting the stage for the development of the harbor. Eleven years later, in 1937, the Oxnard Harbor District was formed. By January 1939, the Standard Dredging Company began dredging, and by 1940, the harbor was 400 feet wide and 30 feet deep.

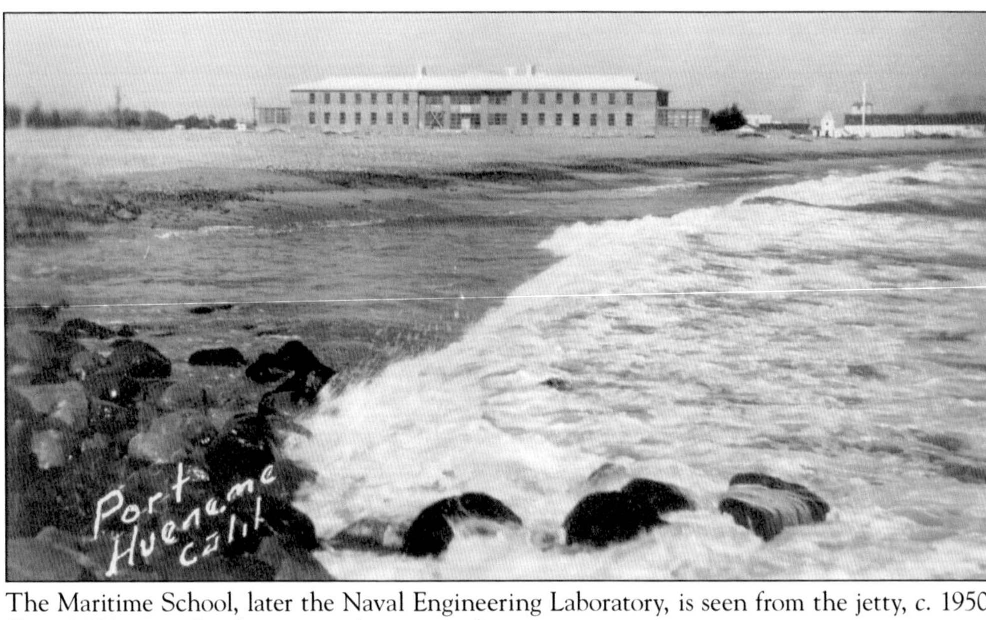

The Maritime School, later the Naval Engineering Laboratory, is seen from the jetty, c. 1950. Over 1,400 tons of rocks were used to create the jetties.

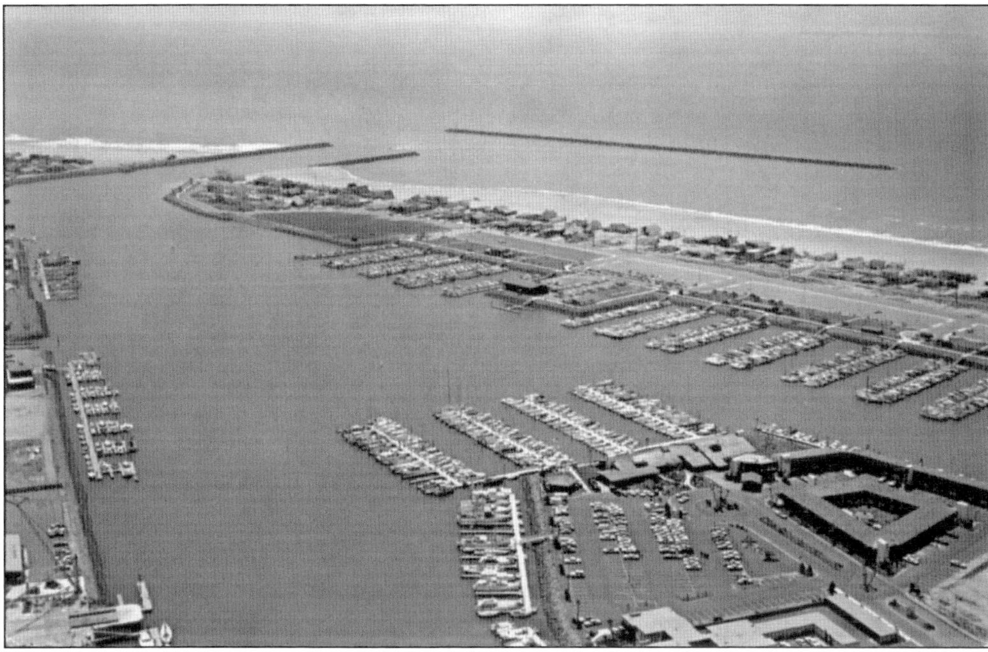

Like the Port Hueneme Harbor, the Channel Island Harbor came about through the early efforts of Richard Bard, who realized that the erosion of the beach was caused by the expansion of the Hueneme port. Bard's solution was to dredge a second harbor, which, in addition to easing the erosion problem, would give small-craft owners a place to dock their boats. After Bard was unsuccessful in his attempts to get financing, the Army Corps of Engineers began digging the new harbor in 1960.

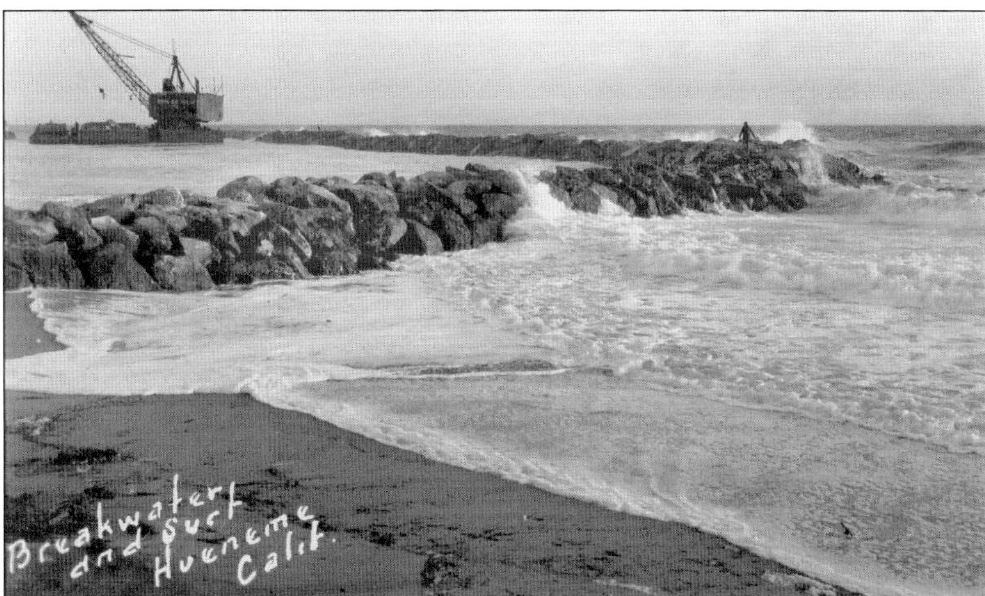

The breakwater near the port was built to keep the harbor from silt accumulation and to keep the waters calm.

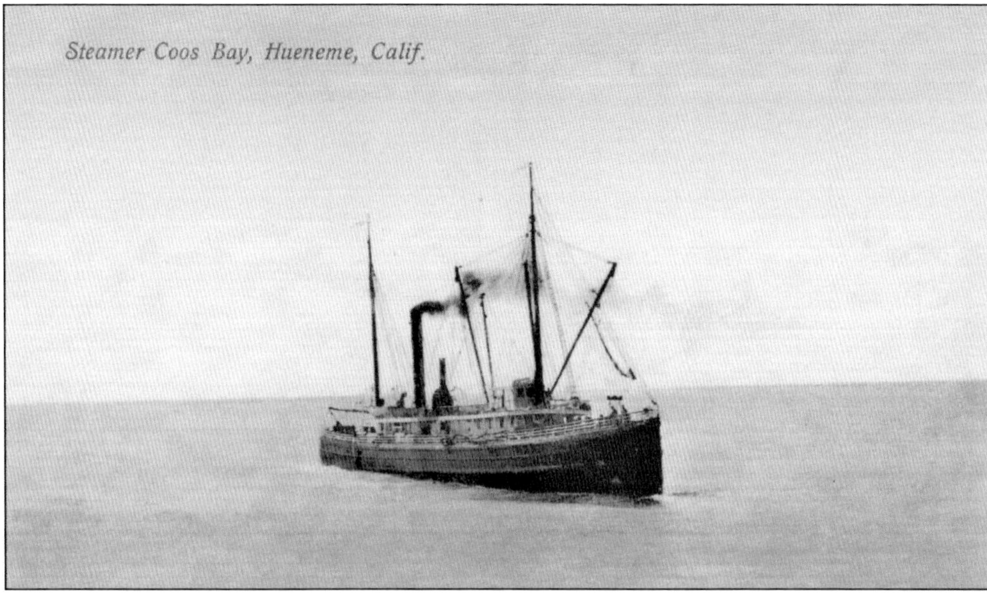

The *Coos Bay* made frequent visits the wharf. In 1897, the vessel brought 250 400-pound barrels of cement that were used to build the future of Oxnard, the Oxnard sugar factory. Years later, the *Coos Bay* struck a sandbar at the foot of Figueroa Street. The ship was eventually rescued but, not long after, was wrecked during a storm.

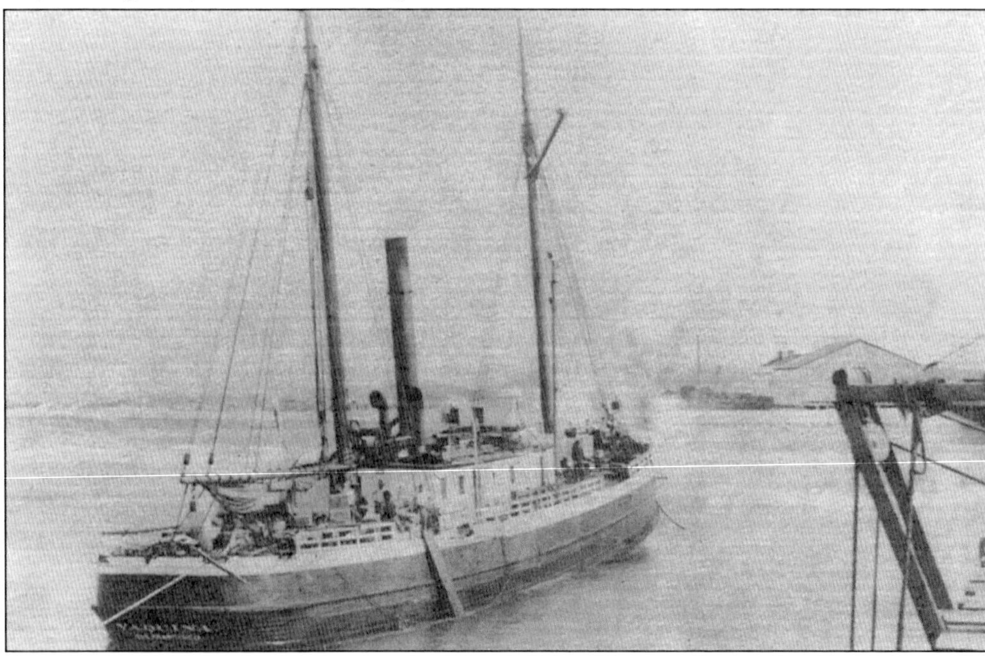

The *Yaquina* was a steamship from of San Francisco. In April 1897, the deep-hulled steamer struck a sandbar while trying to coast up to the wharf, which had recently been extended to 1,500 feet to accommodate larger vessels. Once the ship lost its propeller shaft, the waves took over. The *Yaquina* was quickly unloaded, and the waves pounded the ship to pieces over the next several years. Other famous shipwrecks in the area include the *Kalorama* in Ventura in 1886 and the *Winfield Scott*, wrecked on rocks off Anacapa Island in 1883.

Dock No. 1 was leased by the Navy for commercial purposes starting in 1942, shortly after the government took over the harbor. Shown here at Dock No. 1 is the boat owned by Ford Davis, who also owned Davis Furniture and Appliance at 241 East Broad Street in Port Hueneme.

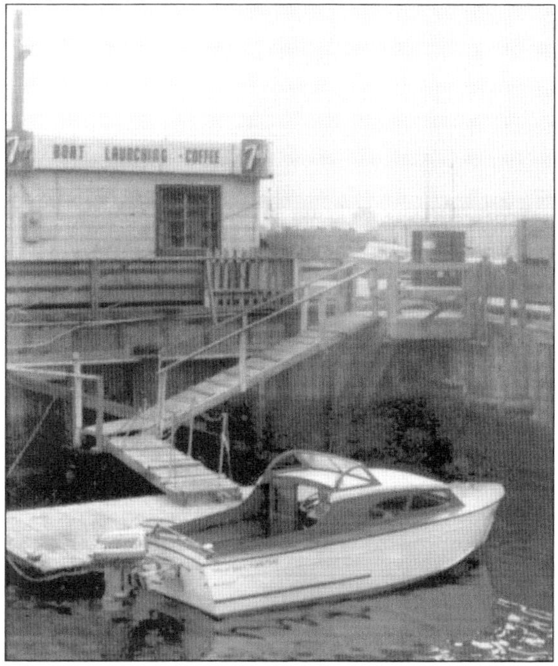

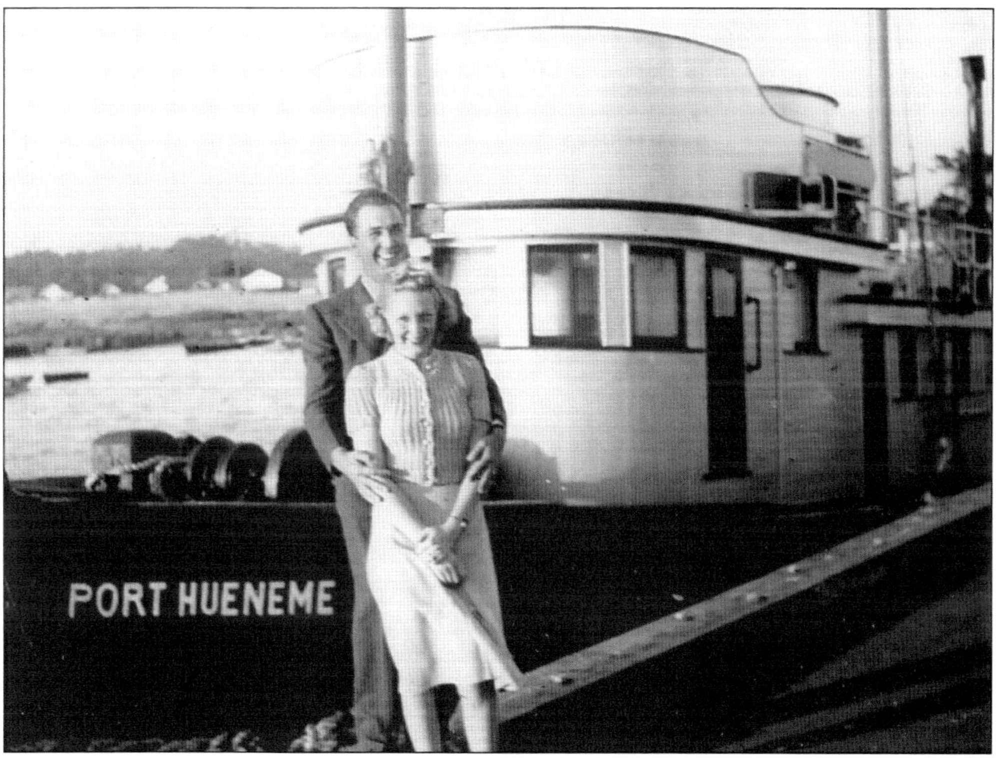

John and Marge Bott pose in front of the *Hueneme* tugboat. The Botts were sentimental towards the old boat since it sailed into the harbor for the first time on their wedding day. The tugboat was 92 feet long and was powered by a 350-horsepower diesel engine. The winch and boom could handle up to two tons.

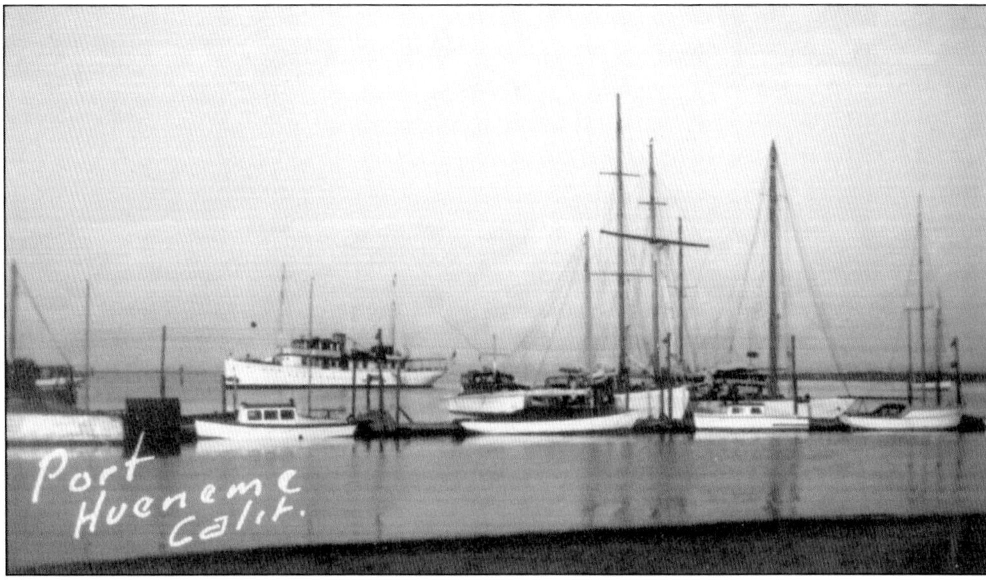

When the harbor was completed in 1940, over 300 boat owners signed up for a space, while 150 others were put on a waiting list. With the outbreak of World War II, the government took over the harbor in December 1941. Boat enthusiasts would have to wait.

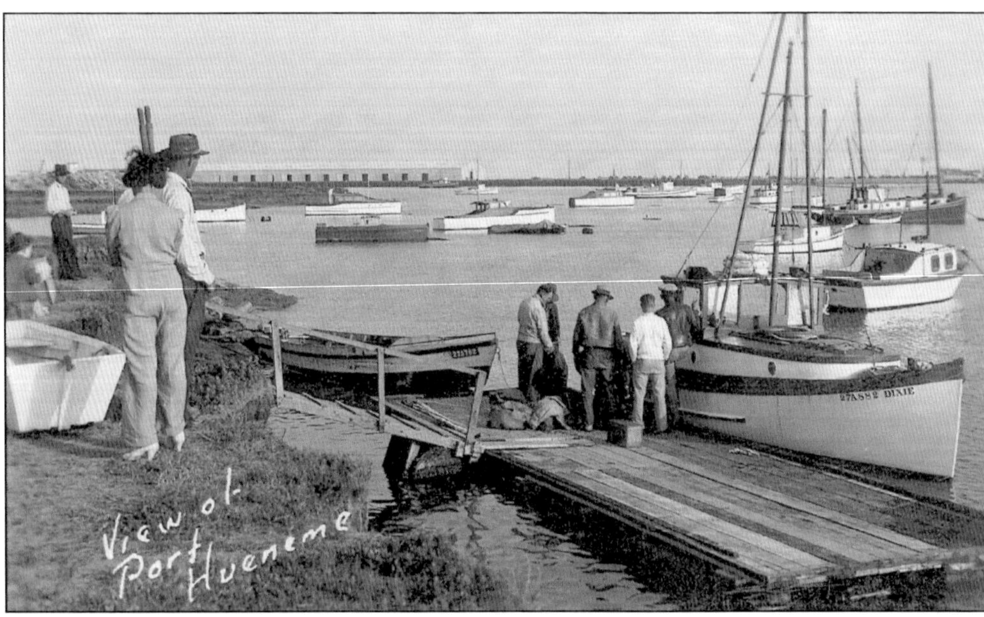

When the Navy took over the site, the boats had to be dry-docked.

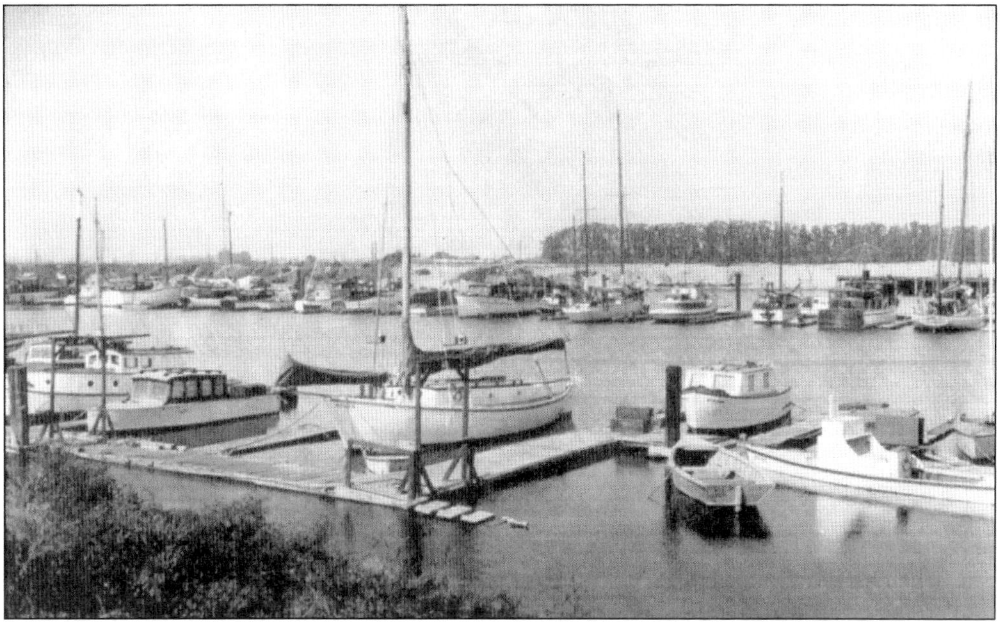

A portion of the harbor was leased back to the community for commercial purposes. The ship Margaret Schafer was the first commercial vessel to enter the port. By 1947, the Navy announced that they would lease back 1800 lineal feet of berthing space.

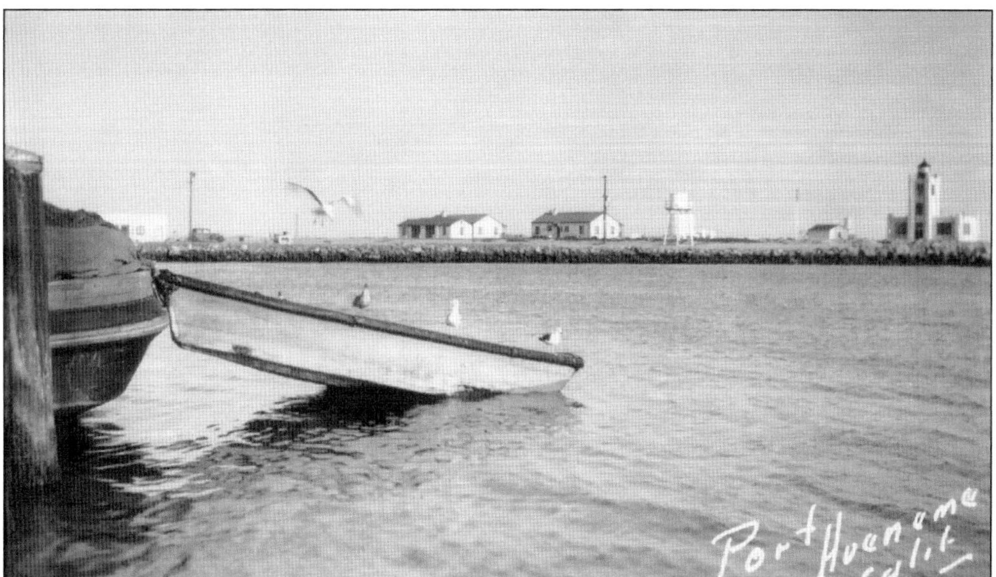

Notice the "new" lighthouse in the distance. It was built in 1942 using some of the old lighthouse equipment.

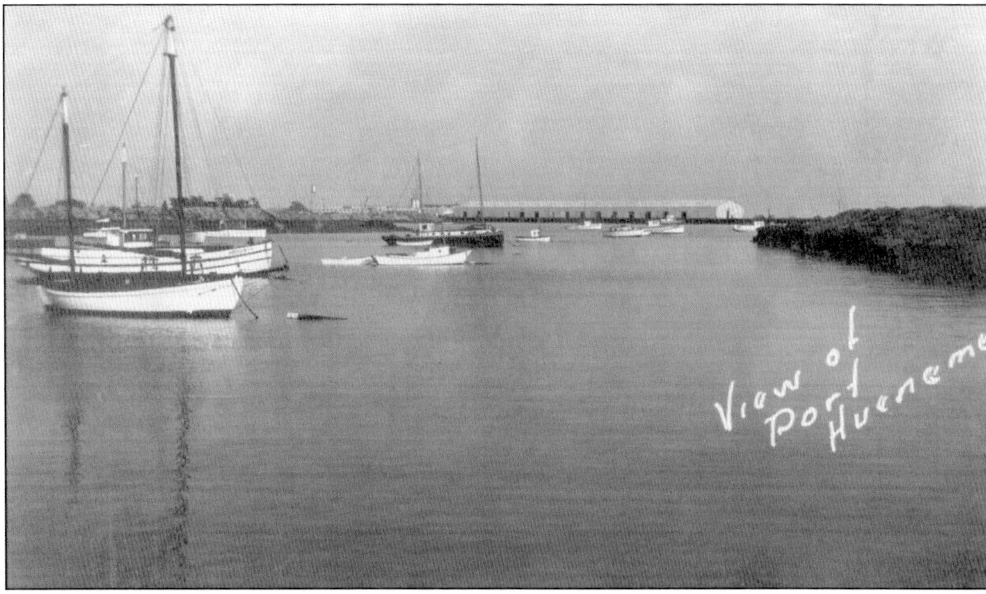

The Lamia Boat Works was created to take care of small-craft needs and repairs. The Port Hueneme Boat Works constructed the Yacht Club and Boathouse to build small sport craft, similar to the boats pictured here.

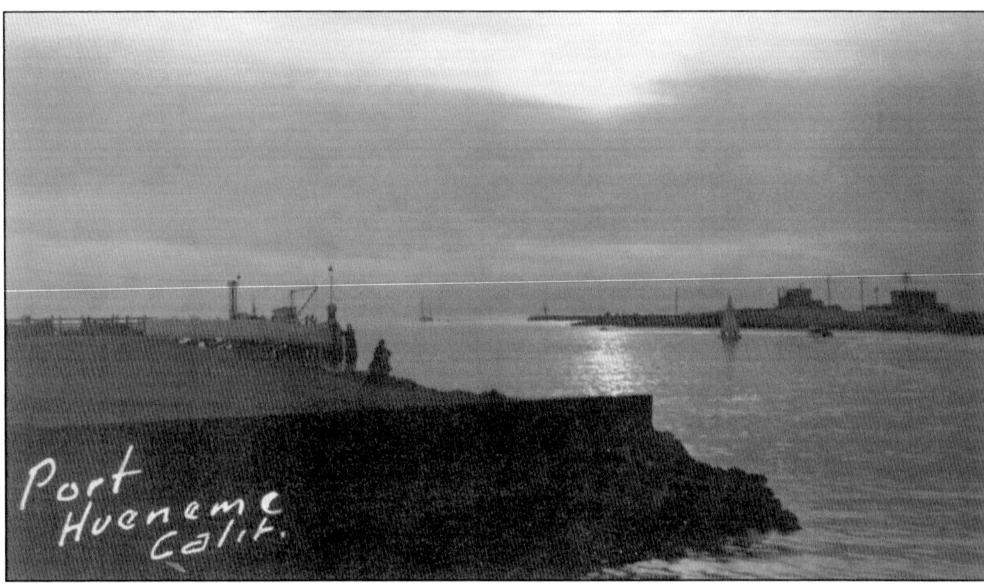

During Prohibition, rumrunners anchored off the shore, floating 10-gallon cans of alcohol to the shoreline. Years later, a sunset cruise becomes more commonplace.

Six

GHOST TOWN

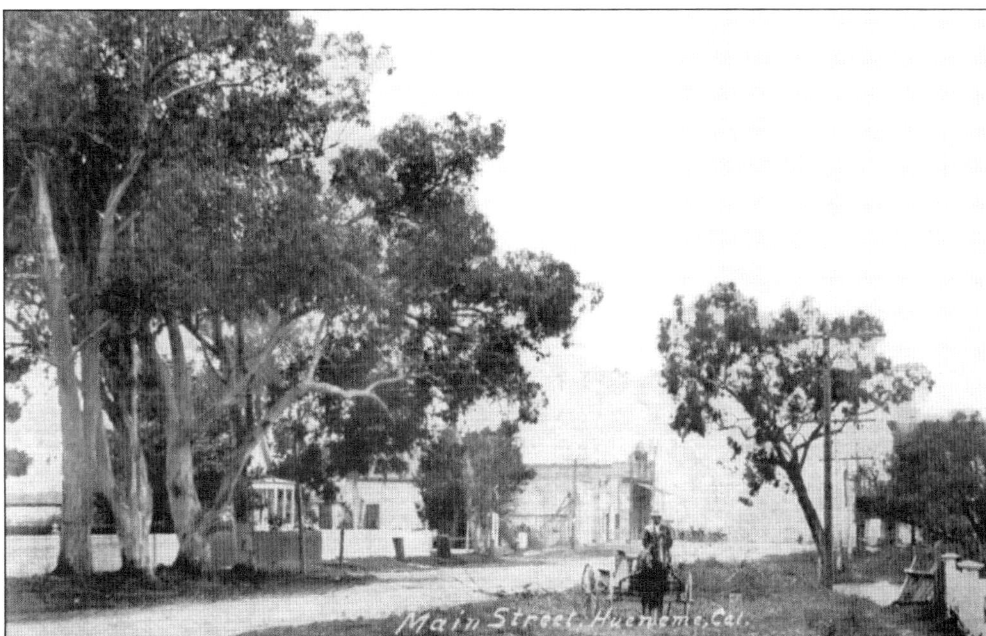

Business on Main Street, like all the streets of Hueneme, was slow for much of the first part of the century. Main Street was the closest street to the beach and was eventually abandoned. Today the area is covered with condominiums overlooking the Pacific.

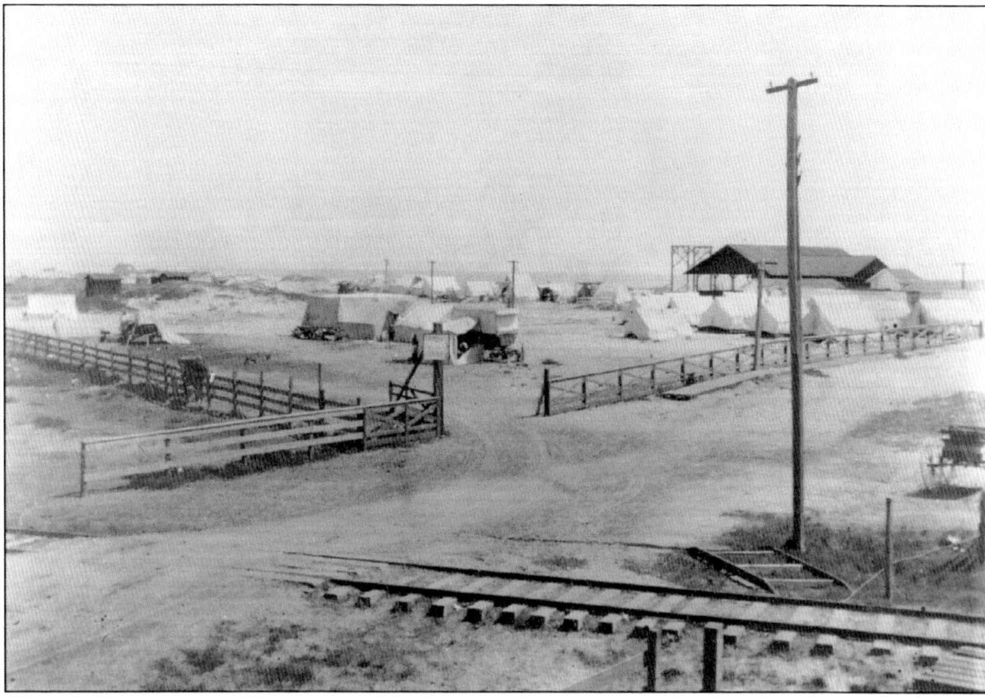

Though the majority of businesses left the area, creating a nearly abandoned town, the beach area was a popular spot for summer camping.

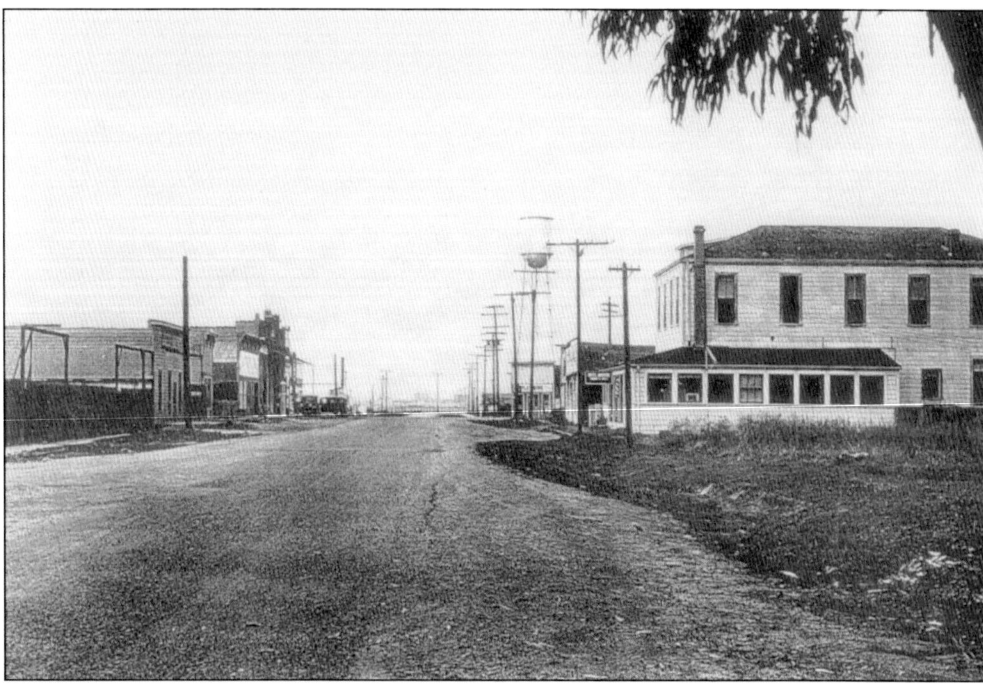

This 1930s view of downtown Hueneme shows little activity compared to the bustling days of the 1890s. Hueneme was even described during this time by a Pasadena newspaper as "set down in a quiet spot that seems to have no excuse for a town."

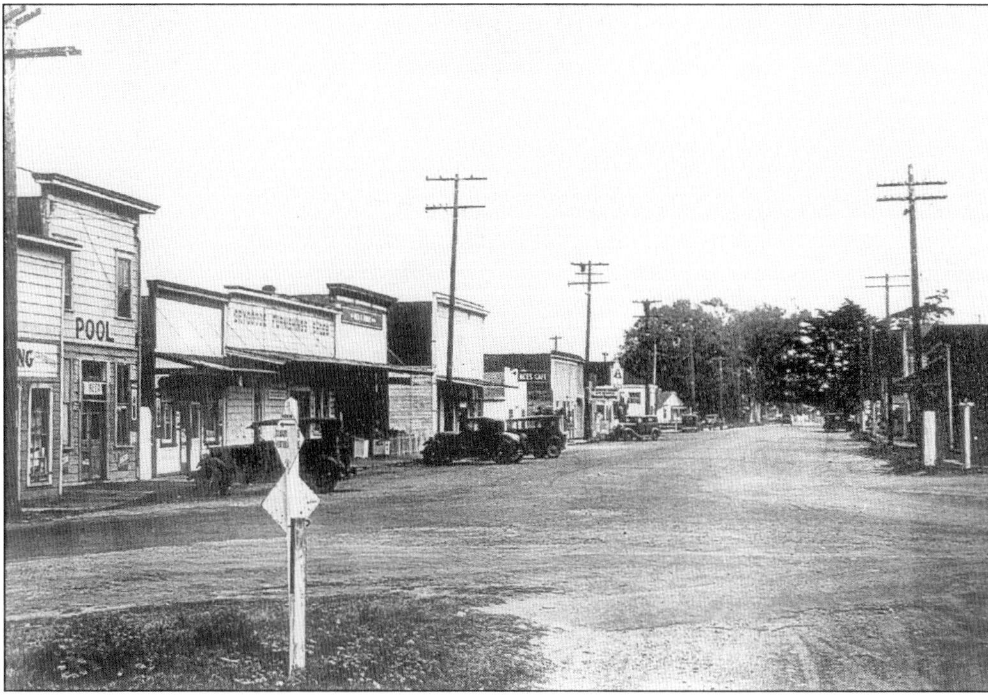

During this time, Hueneme was surrounded by the ocean, salt flats, a lagoon, and miles of farms—and the Great Depression.

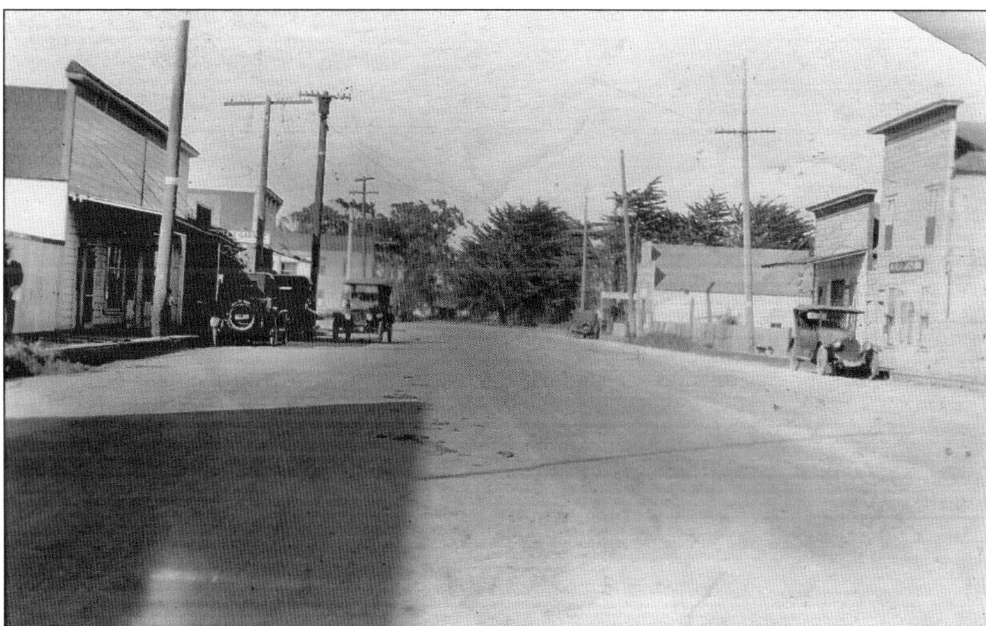

Walter Bill Moranda describes Hueneme during this period of time as having "four or five stores . . . a bank, hotel and a restaurant, a post office, drug store, library, tennis court, the Berylwood office, a Women's Improvement Club and two street lights." The hope was that building a harbor would bring some life back into the town.

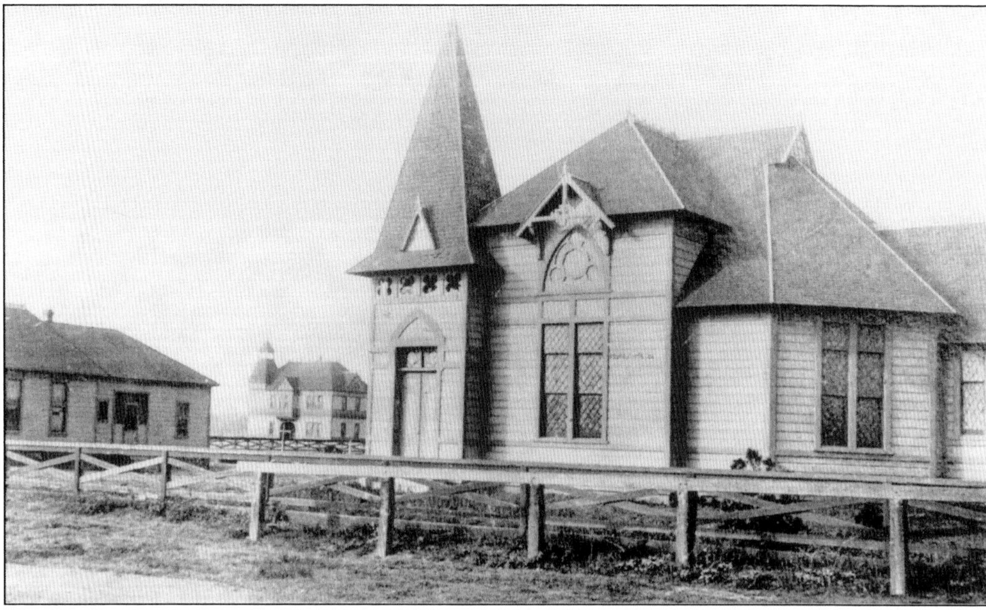

The Methodist Episcopal Church, built in 1884, was located at the corner of Scott and Third Streets. Thomas Bard donated the lot for the church and paid for one-third of the building costs. Bard was a member of the Presbyterian church.

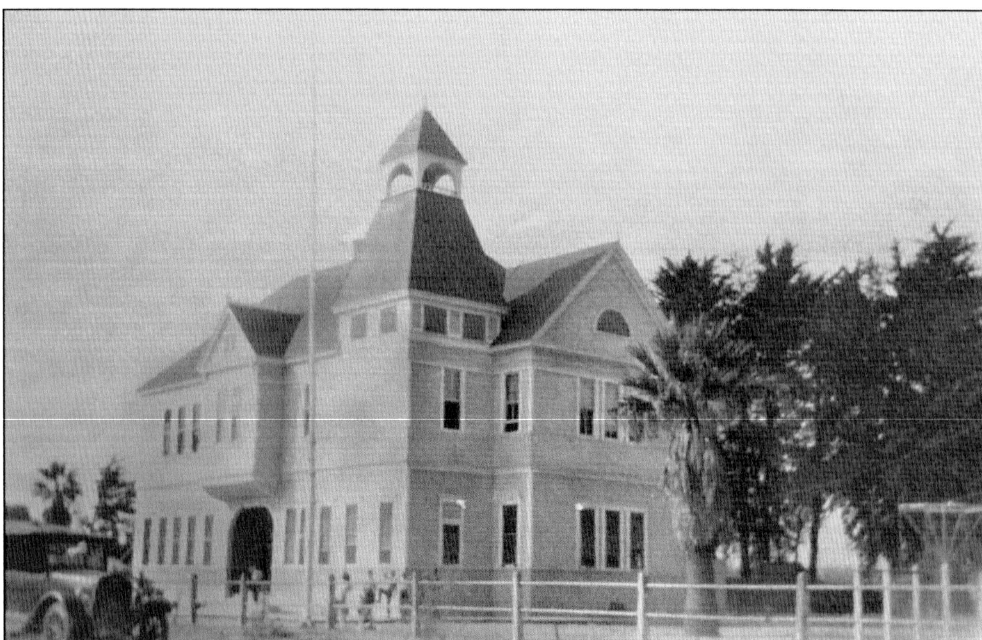

The Hueneme Grammar School was built in 1889 by Jens Rasmussen. Among the early teachers at the school were Charles Blackstock and Richard Haydock, and among the students during the 1880s were Fergus Fairbanks, Ben Korts, all five of the Peter Donlon's children, Albert F. Maulhardt, Ralph Hill, Charles Perkins, Mathew Lehman, Winnie Fairbanks, and Ella and Harry Bacon.

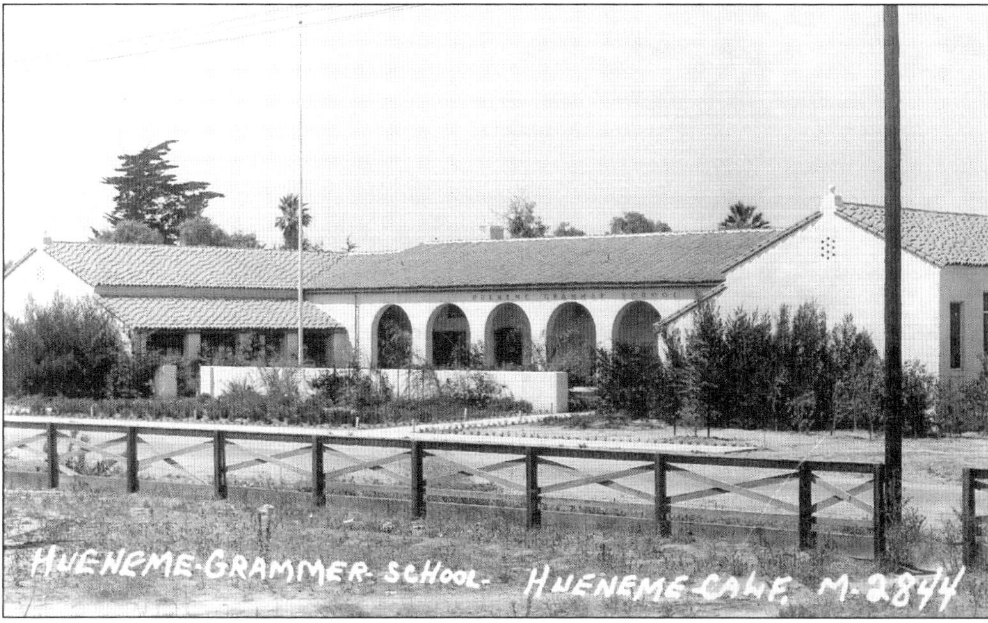

A "new" Hueneme Grammar School was built at 344 North Third Street and Ventura Road in 1928. In 1987, the school earned the designation of being named Ventura County Landmark No. 115.

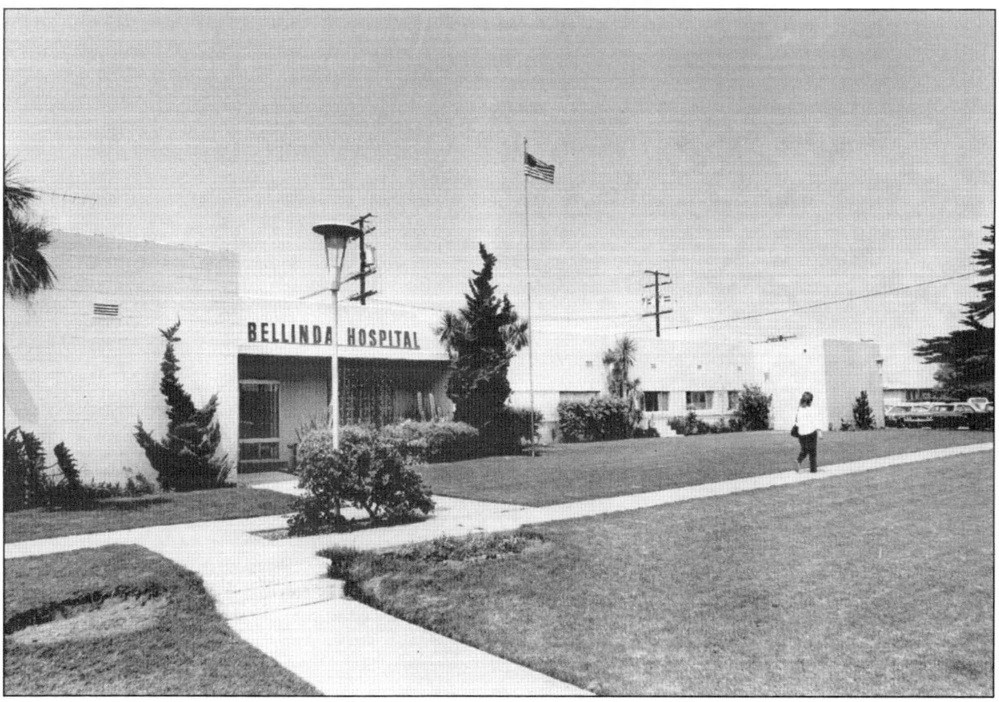

Hueneme's first hospital, the Belinda Hospital, at the corner of Clara and Fourth Streets, was dedicated in July 1955. The five-and-a-half-acre site offered 30-bed facilities, 3 surgery rooms, an x-ray department, a laboratory, and an administrative office.

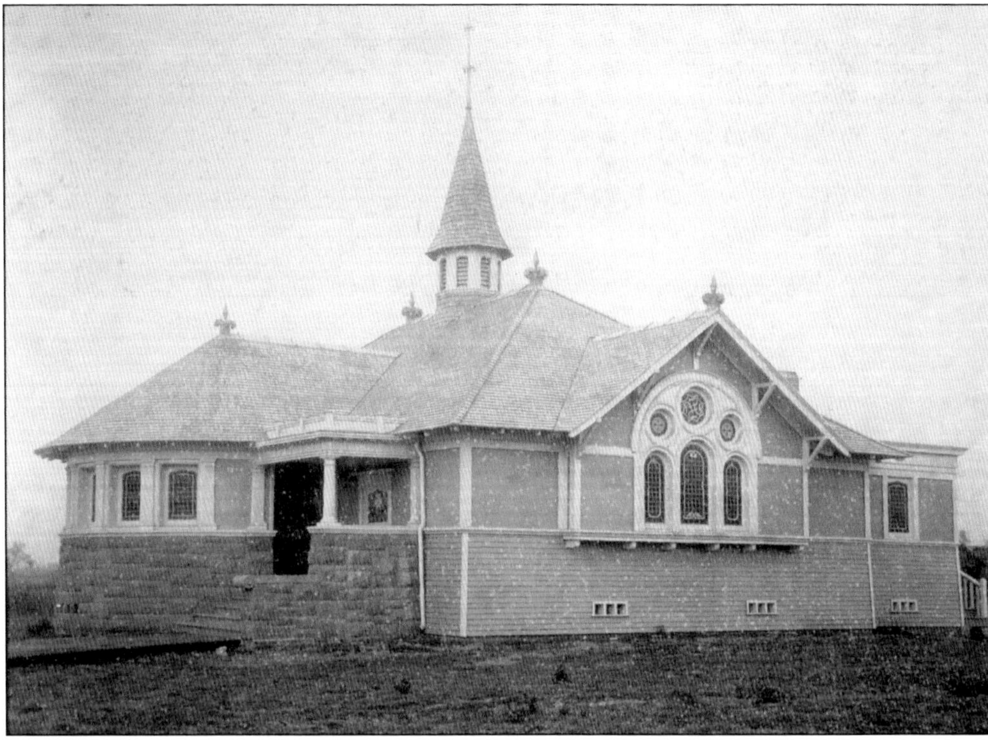

The Hueneme Presbyterian Church was built in 1891, but by the turn of the century, less than 50 members remained. A few years later, in 1905, only 15 members remained.

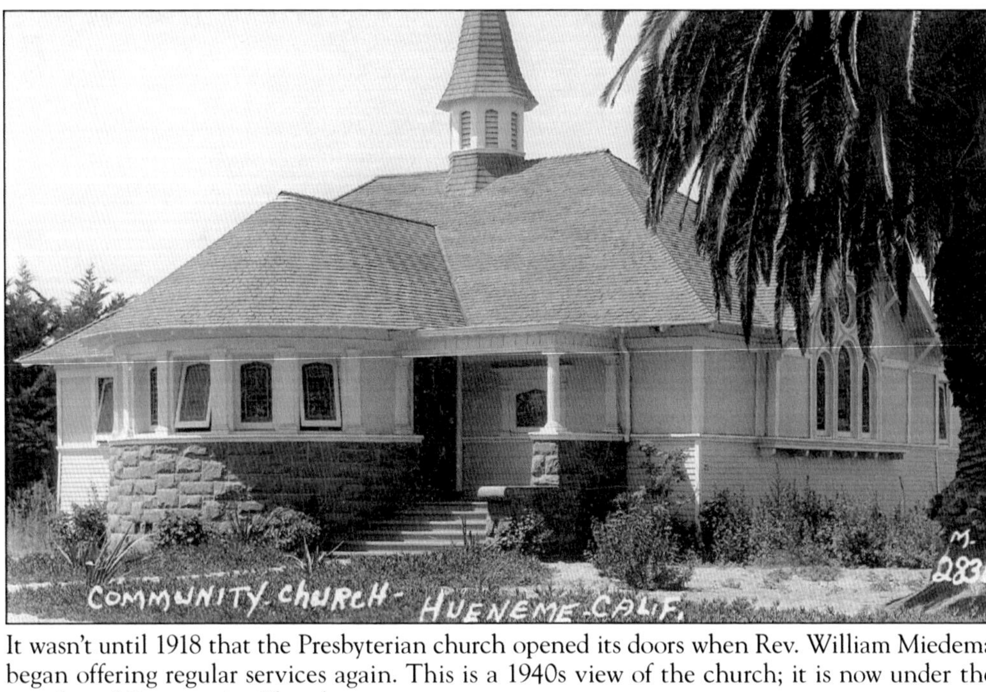

It wasn't until 1918 that the Presbyterian church opened its doors when Rev. William Miedema began offering regular services again. This is a 1940s view of the church; it is now under the moniker of Community Church.

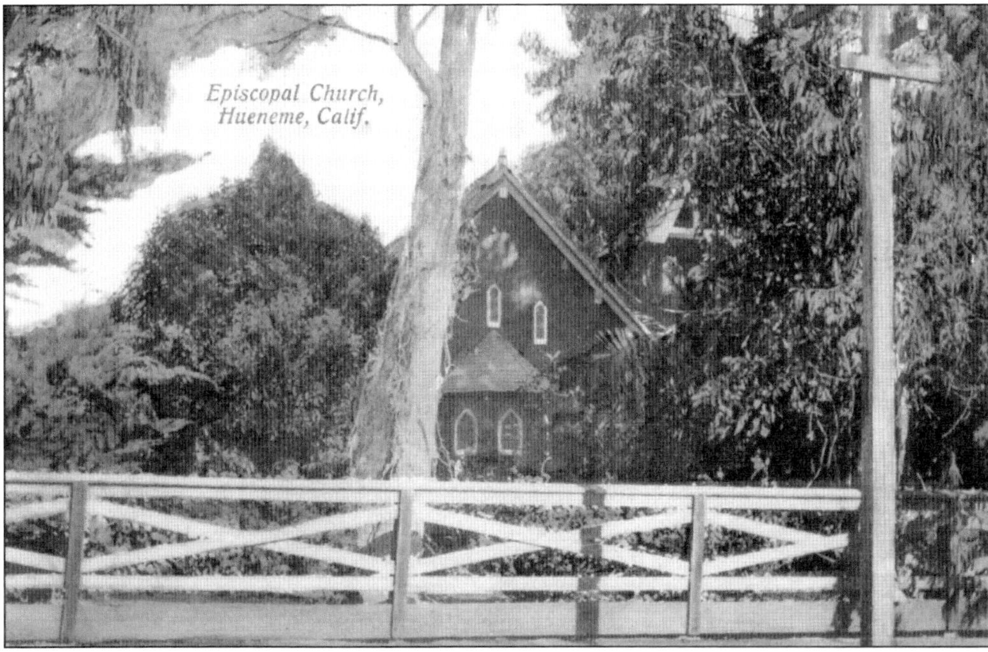

The Trinity Episcopal Church was built by Thomas Bard in 1901 and was located on the corner between Pleasant Valley Road and Clara Streets, on the east side of Ventura Road. The beautiful redwood chapel was moved to the town of Fillmore in 1933.

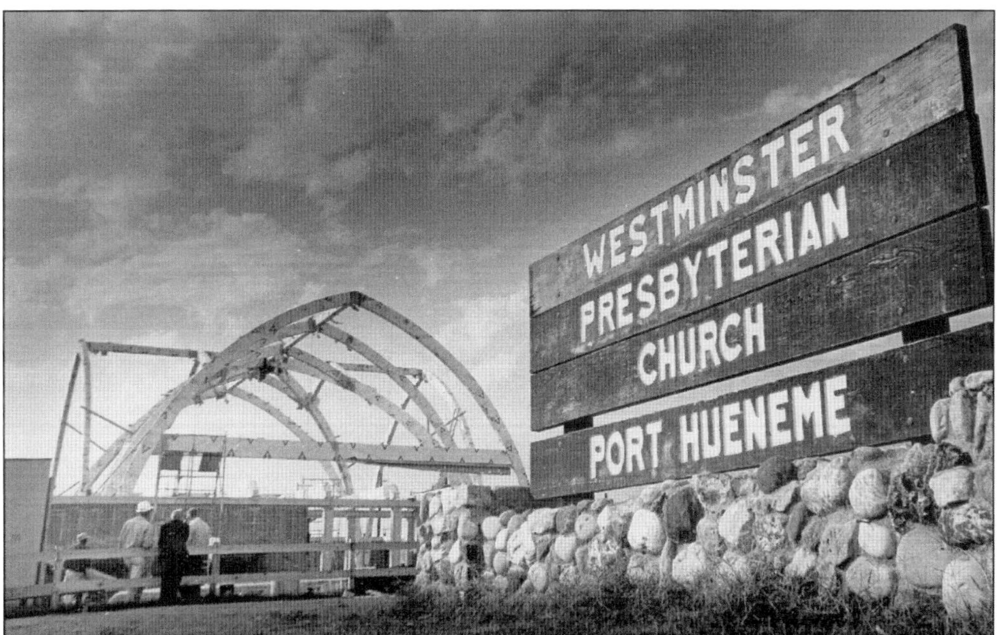

Construction of the Westminster Church, on the corner of Park Avenue and Bard Road, began in the fall of 1968 at a cost of $300,000. The new church was to replace the old, 74-year-old building at the corner of Second and Scott Streets.

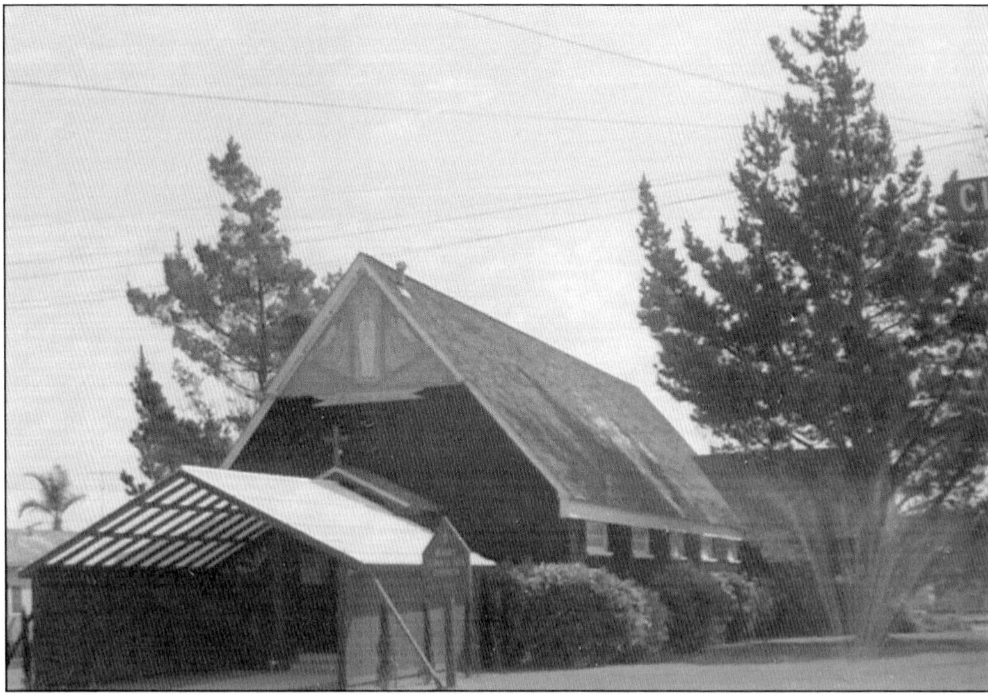

The first Mary Star of the Sea Church was built in 1942 off Pleasant Valley Road near Pacific Street in Hueneme. In 1962, the church, along with 180 families and 11 businesses, came under the influence of the 33-acre Urban Renewal project. The building found new life at a cemetery, relocating to the Conj Mountain Memorial Cemetery.

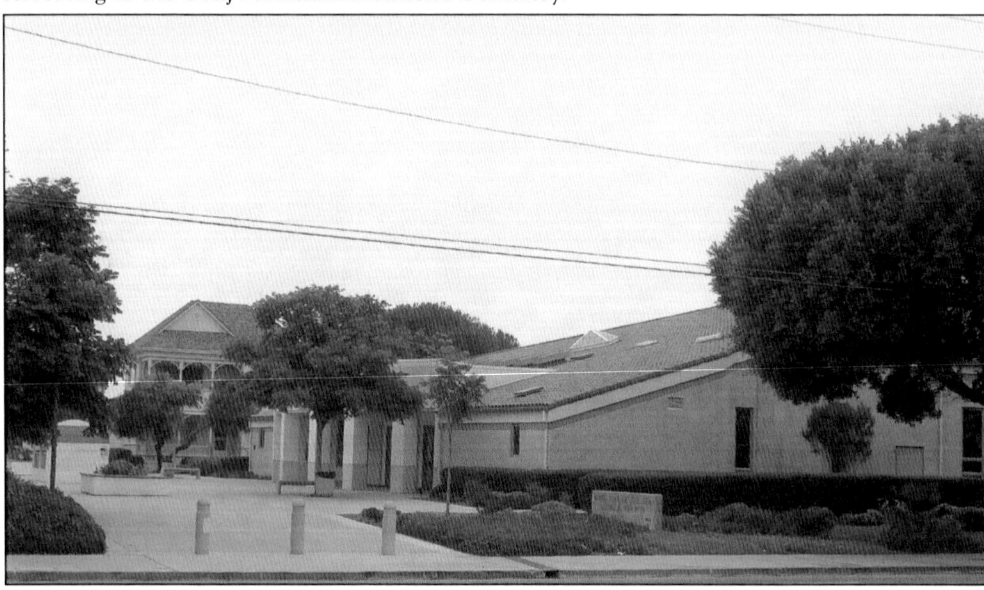

The second Mary Star of the Sea Church was located across the street from the Perkins house and on the former Zellar/Friedrich/Brucker ranch. The white masonry building served as the Catholic gathering place from the mid-1960s until the end of the century. A third church was build on the same property and just to the east of the second building. Behind the church is the Friedrich/Brucker house.

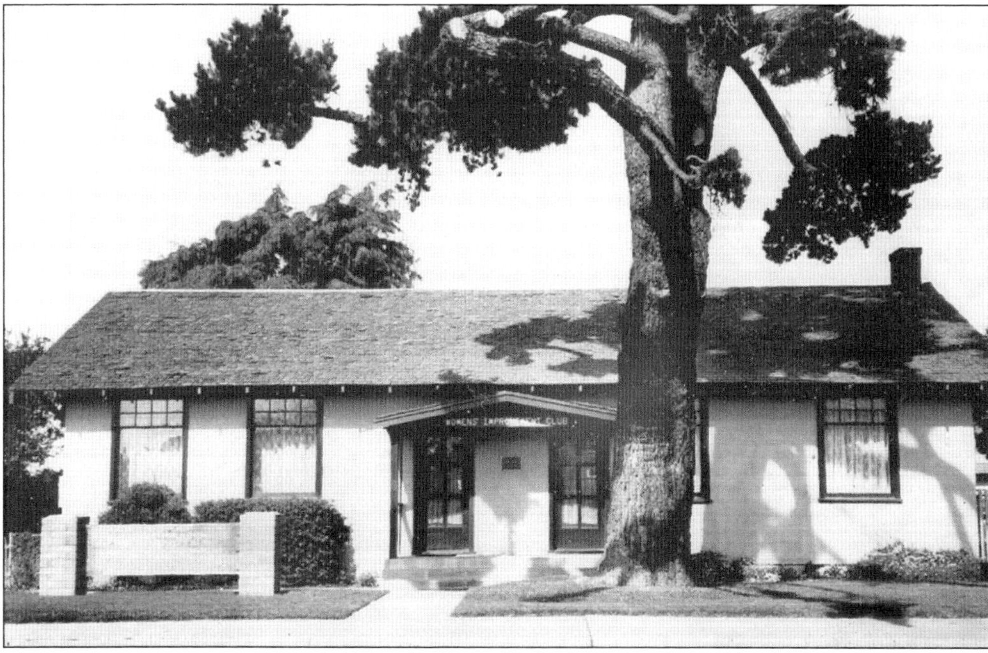

The Women's Improvement Club was built on the site of the demolished Methodist Episcopal Church. Mary Bard donated the land in 1909 and paid for the construction of the building. One of the projects the women took on was planting and watering trees along Ventura Road and throughout the community.

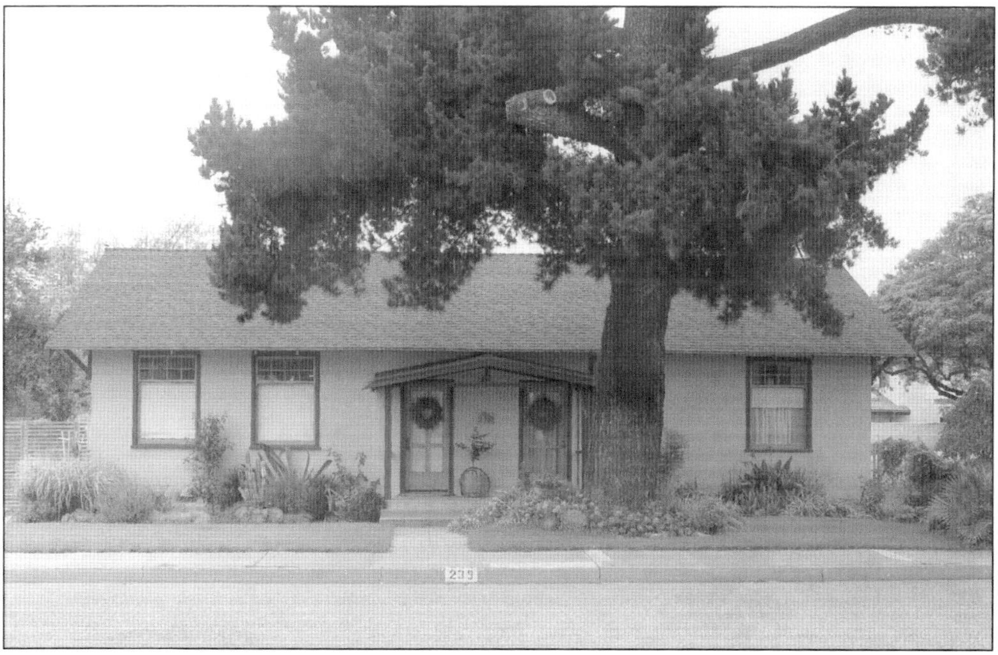

The Women's Club was located at 239 Scott Street. The site became so important to the community that the building was declared Ventura County Historical Landmark No. 19 in 1971. The current owner, architect David Kesterson, restored the building and converted it into a comfortable residence for his family.

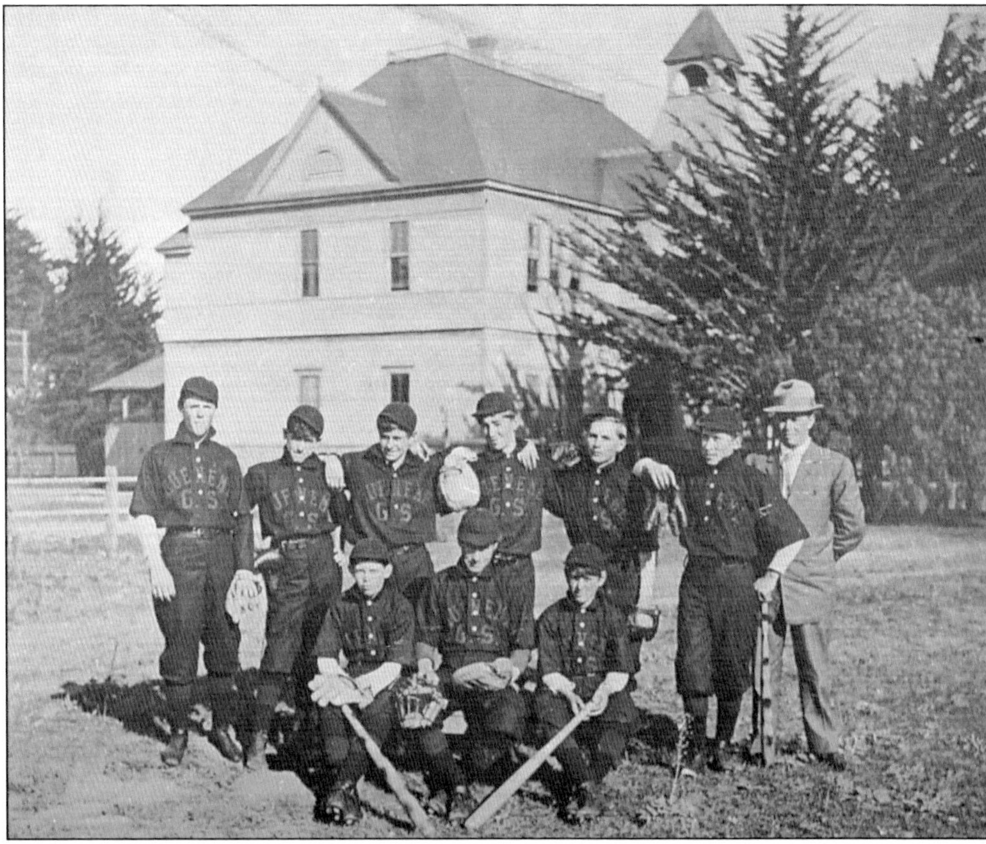

The baseball team at Hueneme Grammar School, *c.* 1912, barely had enough members for a full squad.

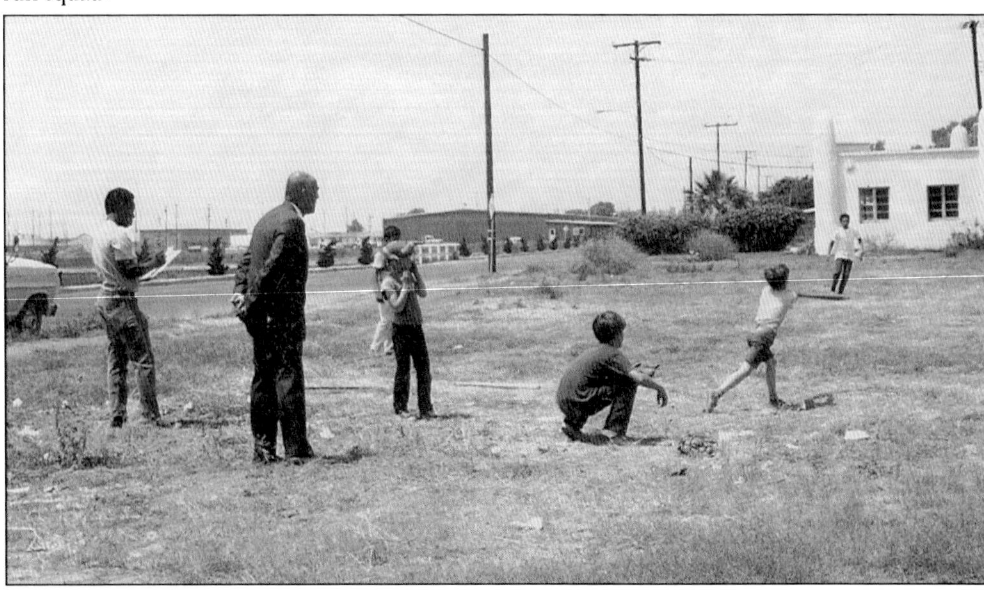

Police chief Al Jalaty oversees a pick-up game of baseball in a vacant in Hueneme. Jalaty would be instrumental in renovating the Hueneme Boys Club for the 125 boys who were members.

Pennie Prescott relaxes between serves while playing on the tennis court behind the Women's Improvement Club in the 1940s. Tennis became an important activity for the citizens of Hueneme. Ted Moranda claimed that the Prescotts, who lived next door to the court, were "without a doubt our town's leading tennis family."

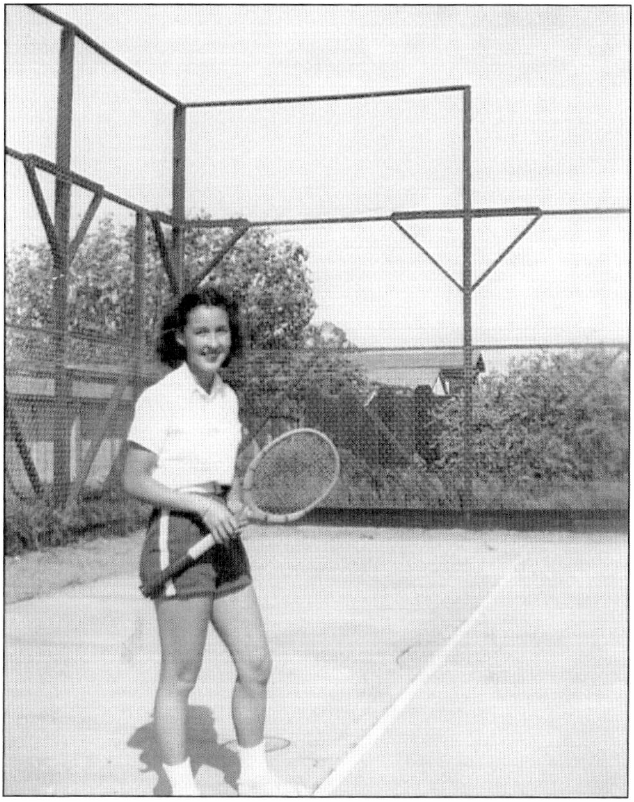

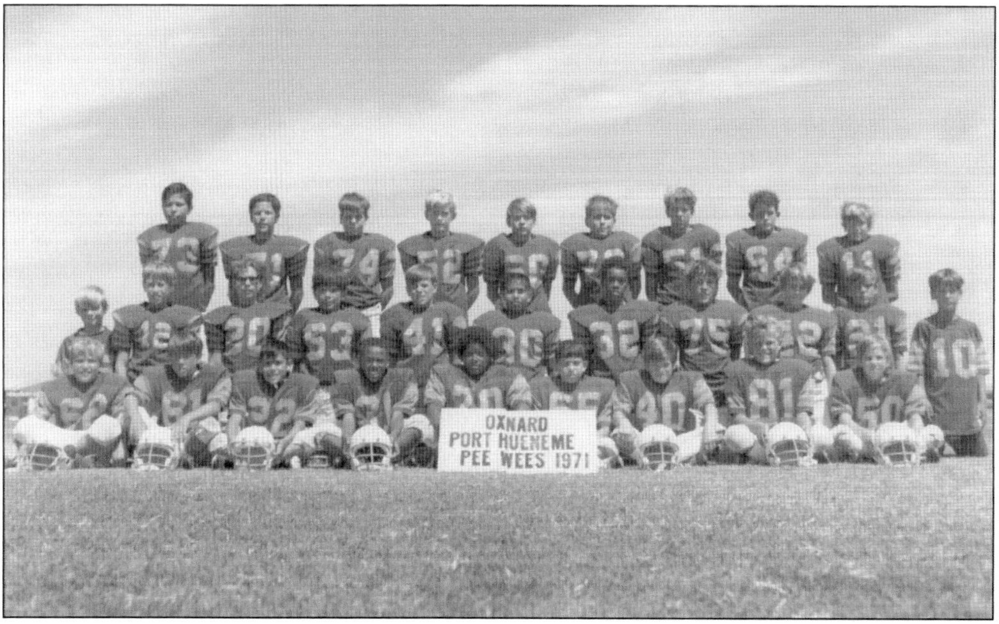

The communities of Port Hueneme and Oxnard have been intertwined in many ways over the years, including in sports. Among the successful coaches who helped shape the character of the boys in both Hueneme and Oxnard were J. T. Rogers Sr., Ray Burleson, and Mike Callazo Sr.

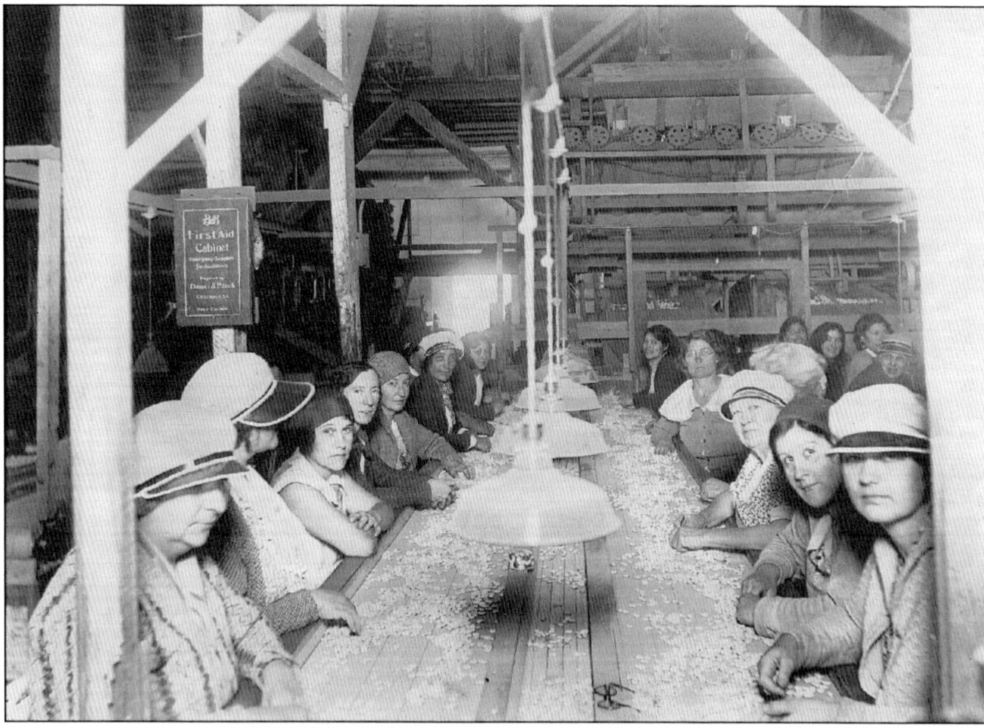

These girls at the Lima Bean Packing Plant, which was located on the wharf, are pictured in the 1930s. On the left side of the table, from front to back, are Camellia Miranda, unidentified, Amy Kier, Effie Cawelti, Lucy Cawelti, and two unidentified women. On the right side, from front to back, are Elsie Lykins, Amelia Sanders, and Mrs. ? Dempsey; the remainder are unidentified.

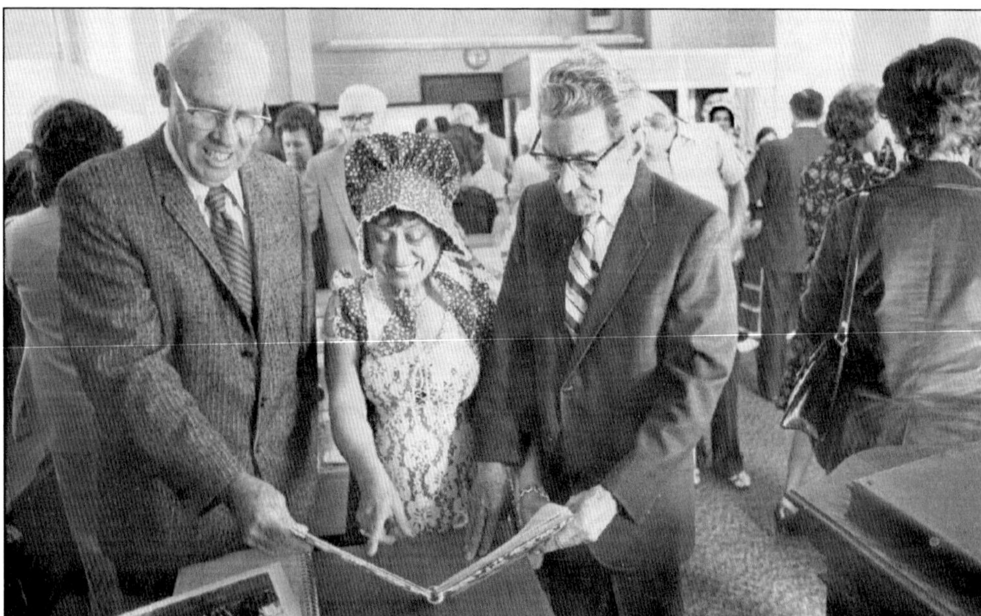

Dorothy Ramirez, dressed as an early Hueneme resident for a Harbor Days event at the old Hueneme bank, shares a few memories with Bob Nunn (left) and C. Dean Prescott (right).

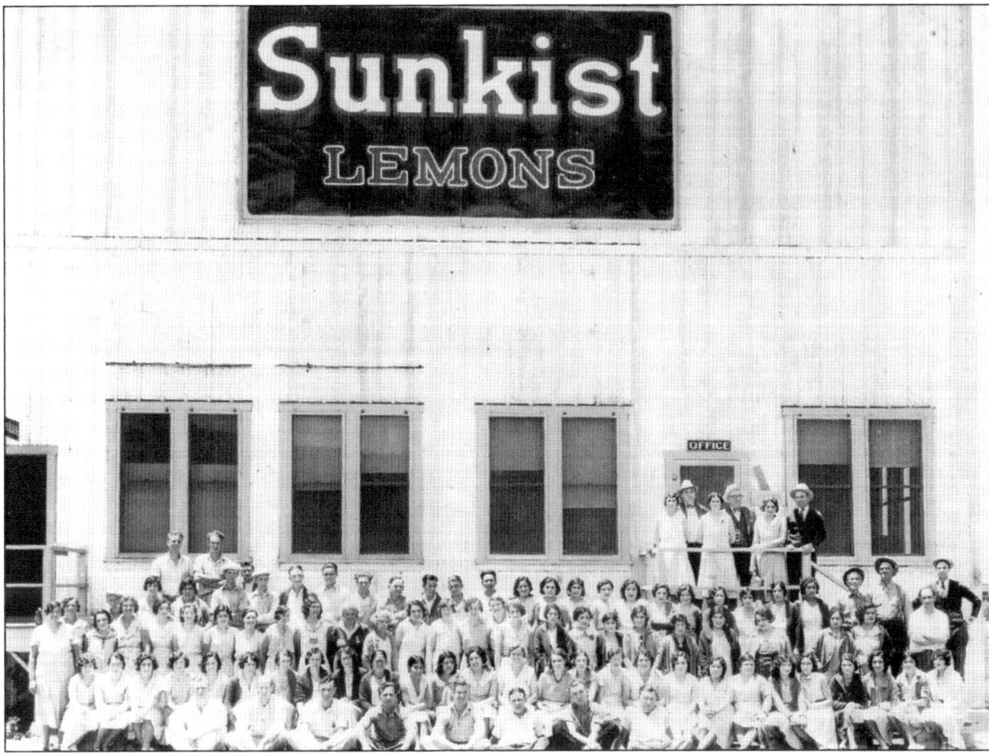

The Sunkist Lemon Packinghouse, built in 1922, brought new life into the community. The packinghouse became the largest employer during the 1920s through the 1930s.

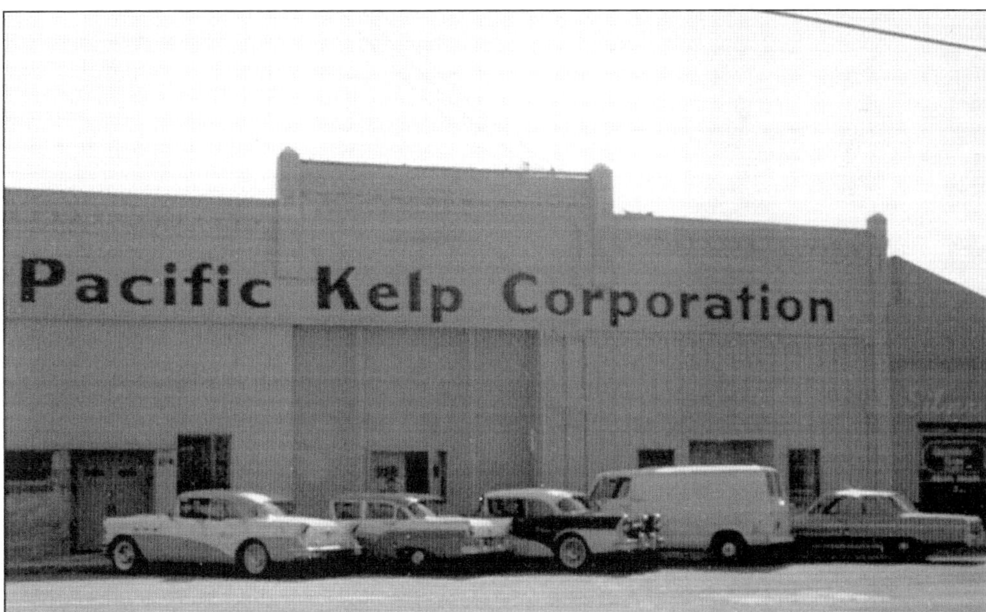

The Kelco Company was a kelp processing plant and was the first business to lease land from the Harbor District. The plant processed 300,000 tons of kelp annually. Up to 138 residents worked at the plant.

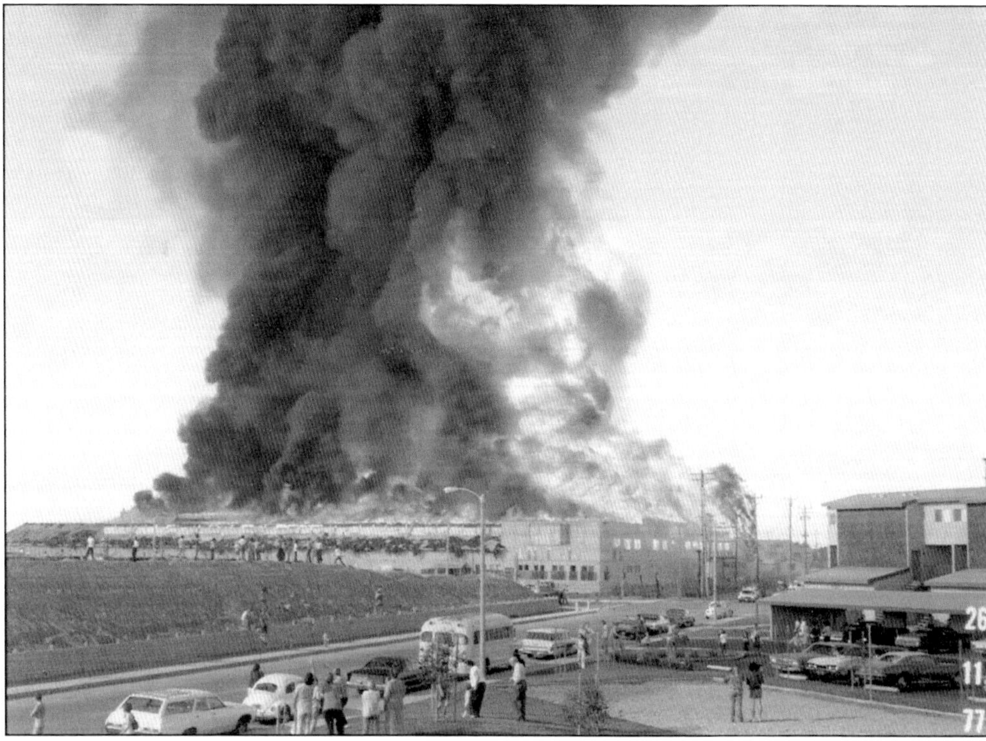

In 1978, Becky Haase was traveling down the Conejo Grade to visit the Moranda family when she noticed a great cloud of smoke off in the distance towards Hueneme. When she arrived, Becky took this picture of the 56-year-old lemon packinghouse going up in smoke.

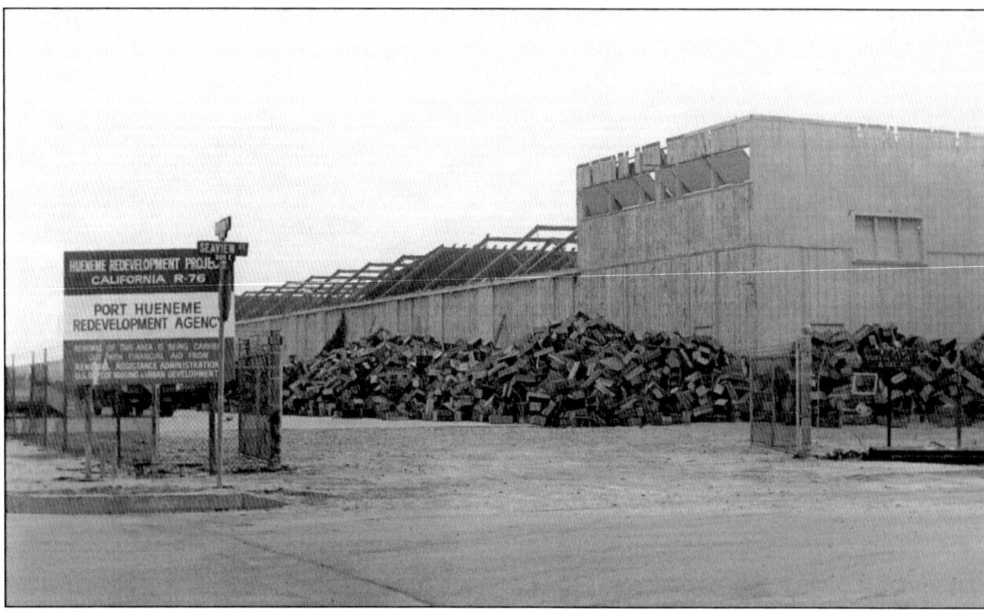

Damaged beyond repair, the packinghouse No. 1 was demolished in 1978.

Seven

STREET SCENES

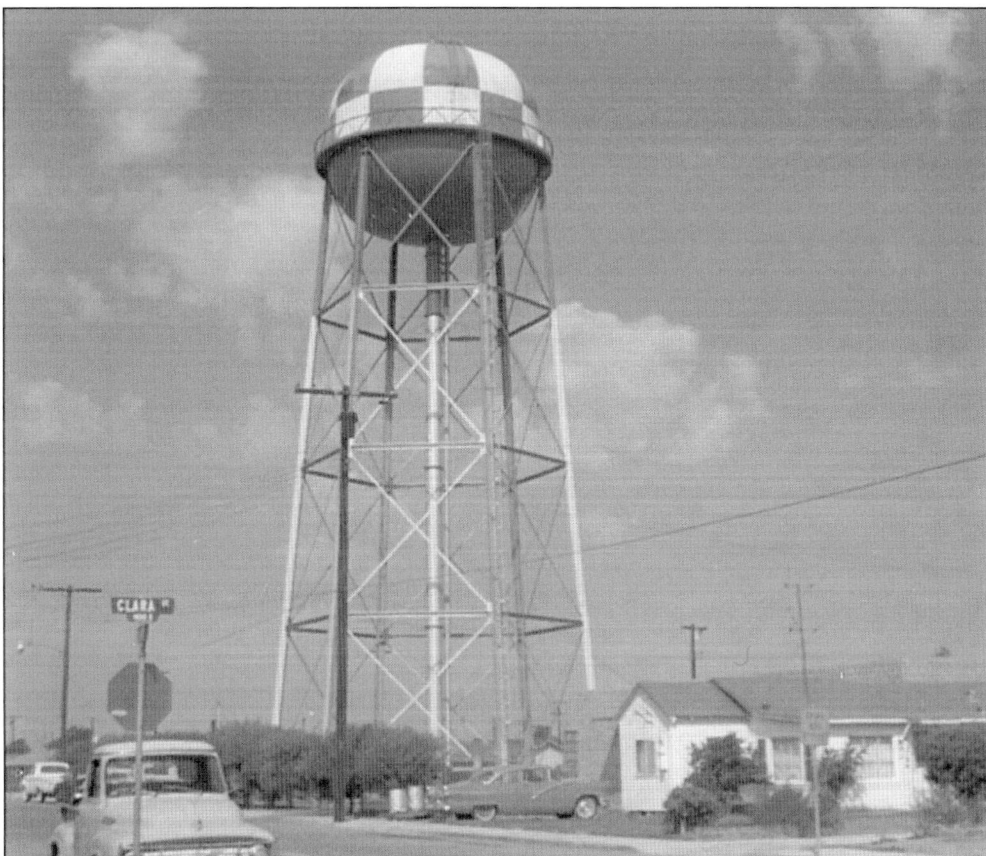

The water tower, located at Fifth Street near Clara Street, was a project spearheaded by Walter Bill Moranda. For years, the residents of Port Hueneme and South Oxnard could look up towards the western sky and see the tower decorated in Christmas lights. The tower was torn down in 2000.

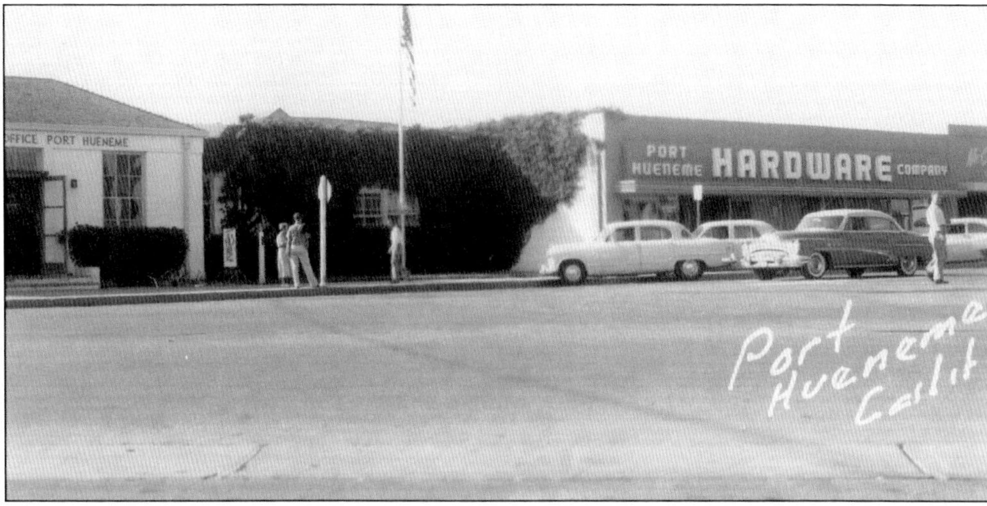

The Port Hueneme Post Office, constructed in 1941, was located at 231 Market Street next to the Berylwood Investment Company. The Cape Cod–style building was designed by Austin Pierpont. The post office was replaced in 1968 by a new location at 560 East Pleasant Valley Road.

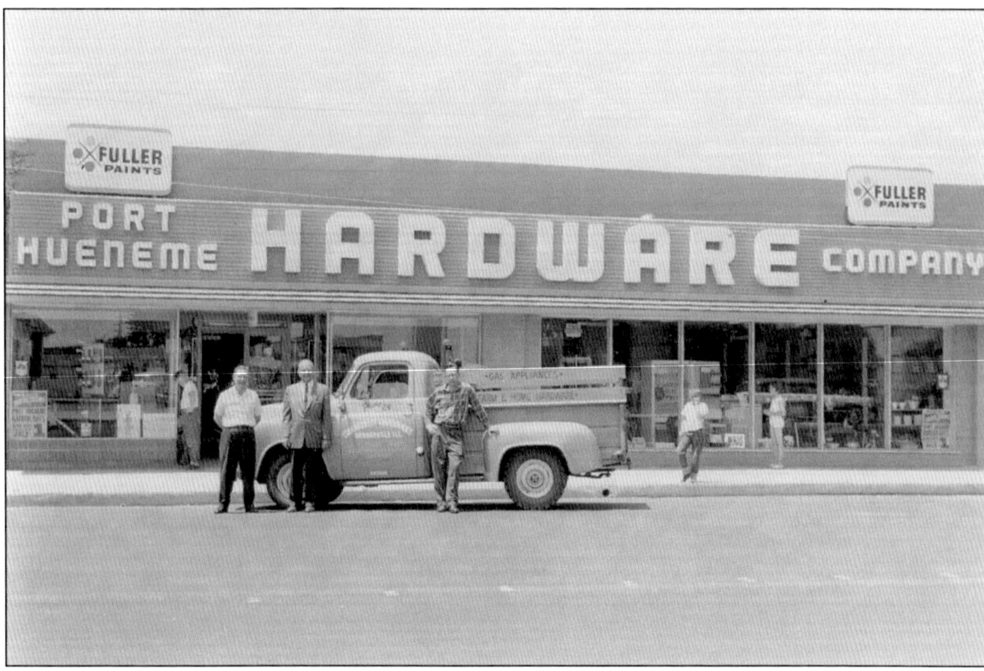

The Port Hueneme Hardware Company was located on Market Street. Several buildings on the block were torn down in the late 1960s during the renovation of downtown.

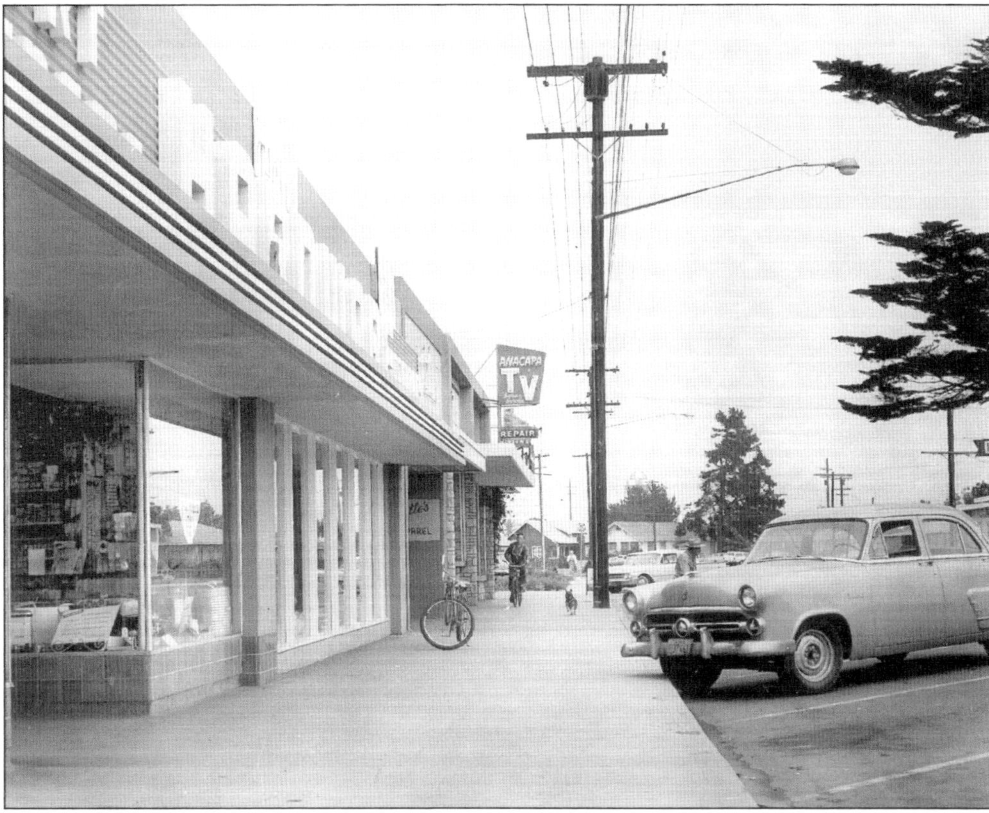

This second view of Market Street, looking toward Scott Street, includes a sign for Anacapa TV.

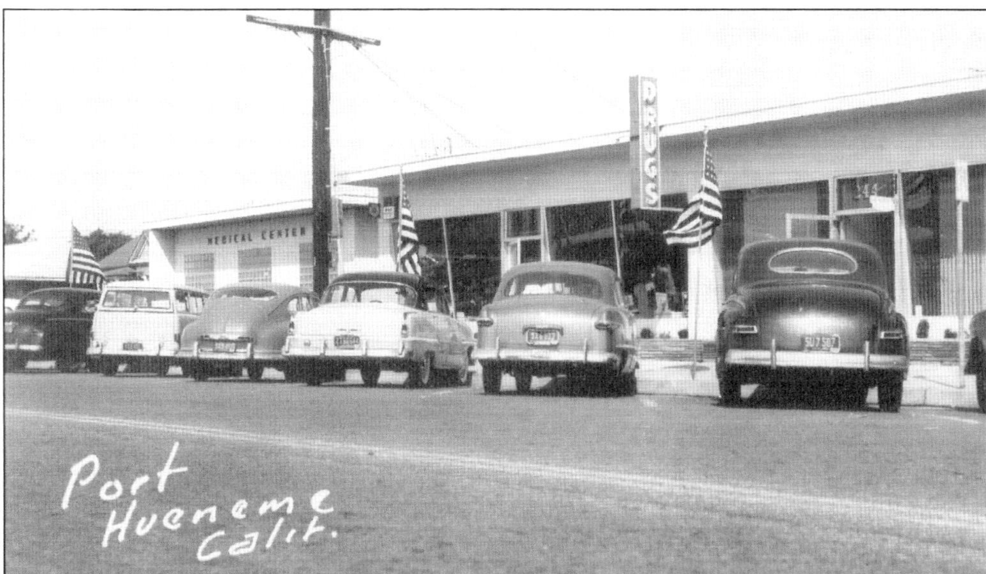

This 1950s scene at the corner of Market and Main Streets shows the Oxnard Harbor District building, located in the original Bank of Hueneme and next to the Sunkist Lemon Packinghouse No. 1.

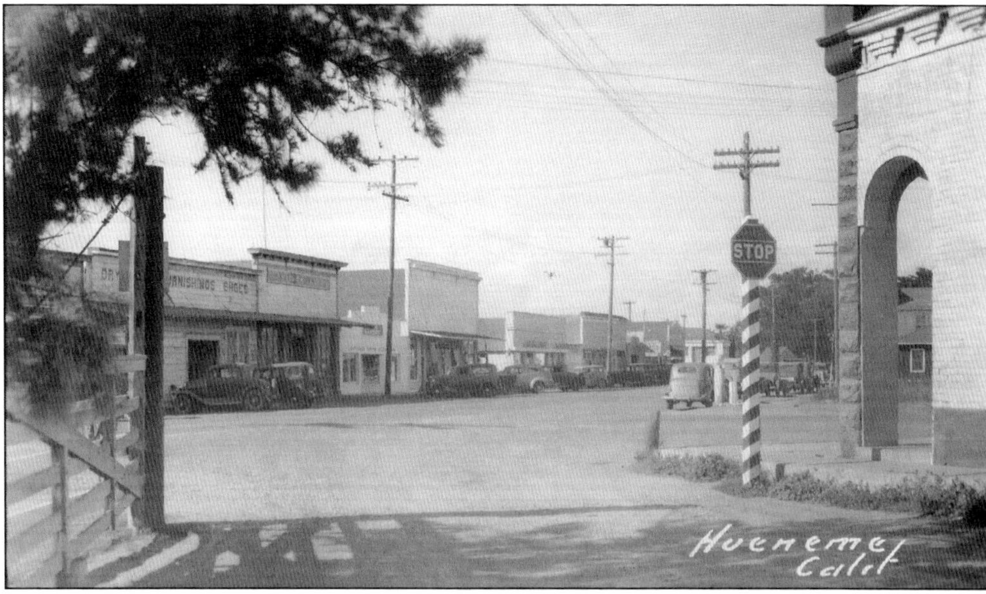

This view, looking on to Market Street, was taken from between the Sunkist Lemon Packinghouse No. 1 and the Harbor District building. The arch of the Oxnard Harbor District building is on the right. The original commissioners for the district were Eugene H. Agee, Elmer O. Green, and Fred M. Aggen.

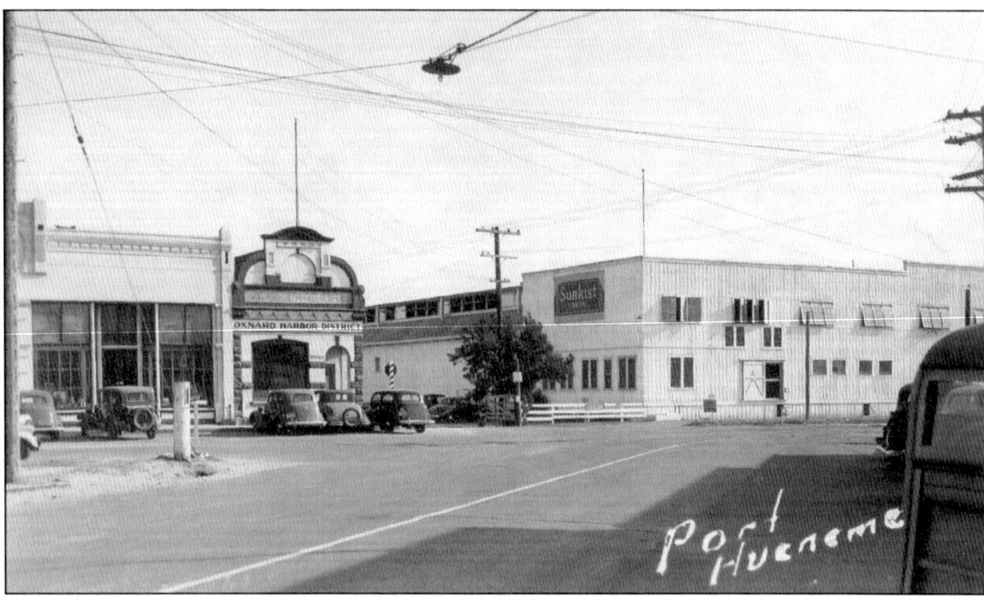

In this view of the Sunkist Lemon Packinghouse No. 1 at Main Street, the Oxnard Harbor District, formed in 1937, is visible across the street. The building was originally constructed for the Hueneme Bank.

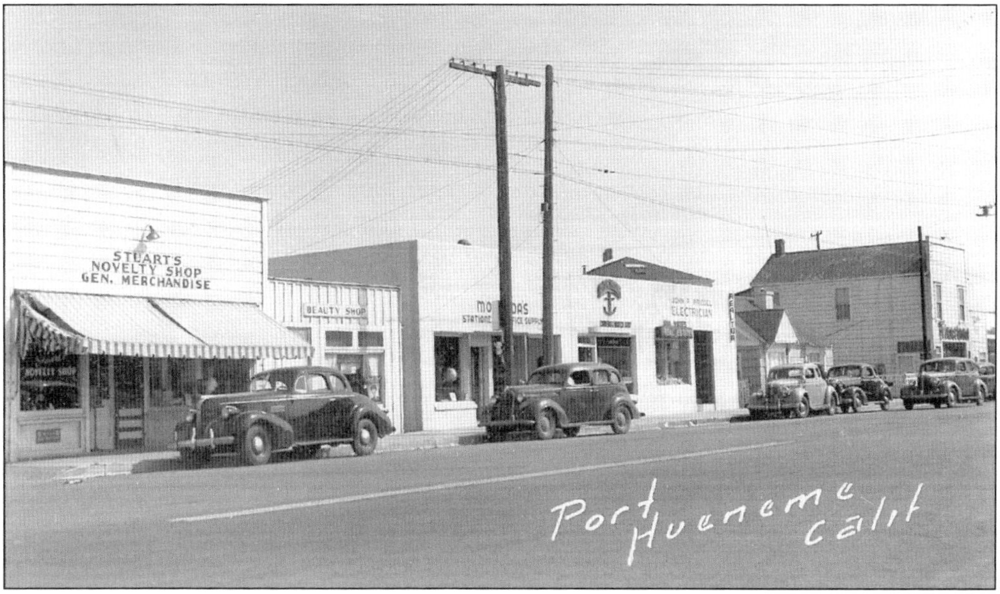

Among the businesses along Market Street are the following: Stuart's General Merchandise Store, Mapes Beauty Salon, Moranda's Stationery and Office Supplies, and John Priegle's electric shop.

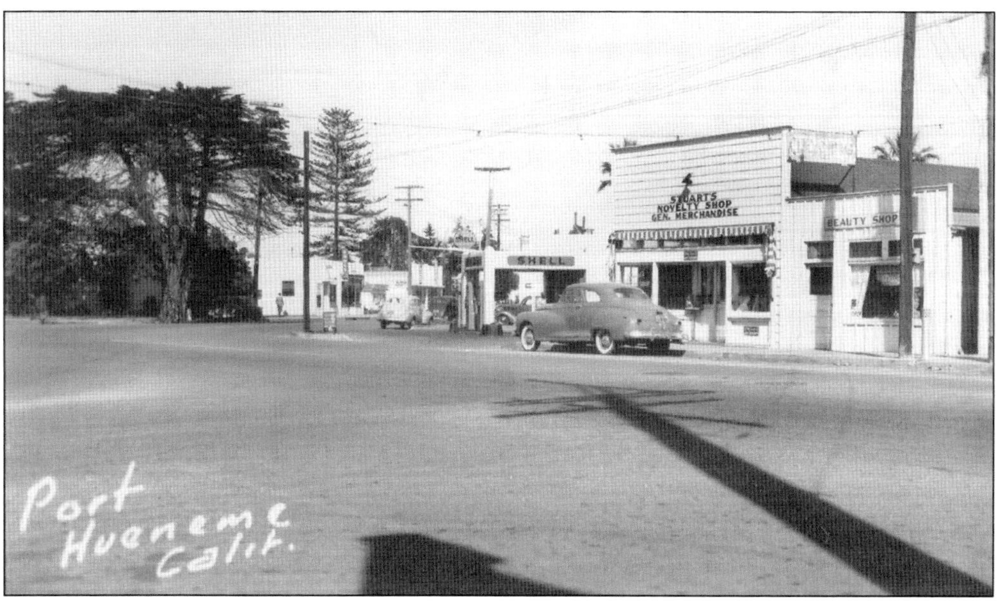

Farther down the street is Bert Dahl's Shell station.

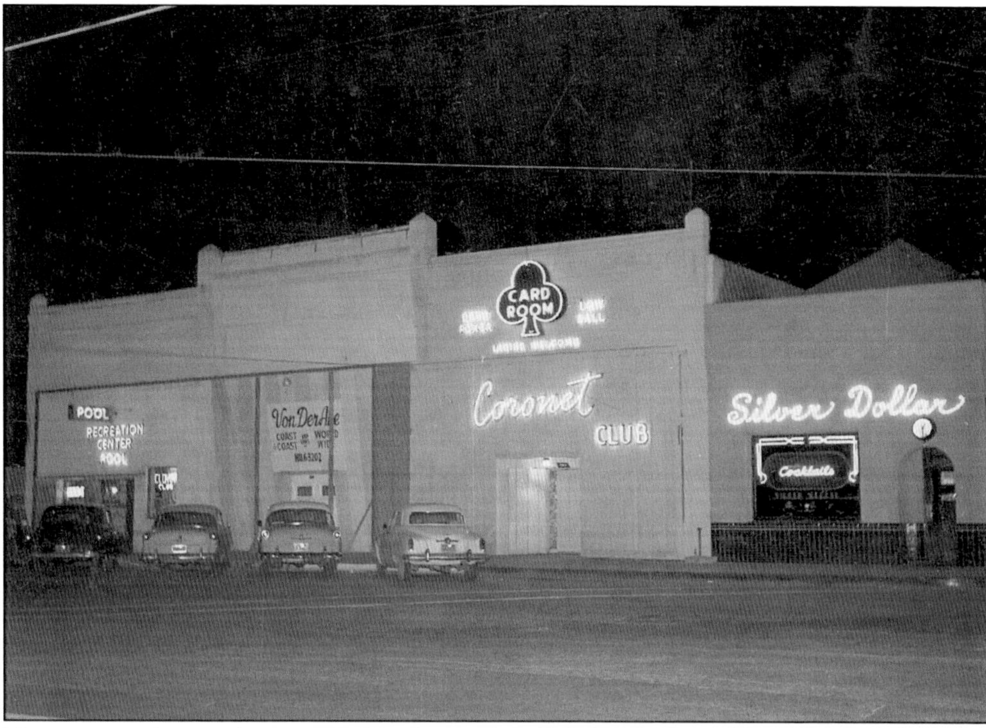

Hueneme was known for its card clubs during the 1950s. With the influx of military personnel, the need for a nightlife and adult entertainment also increased. The Silver Dollar was next door to the Coronet Club, which was next to a pool hall.

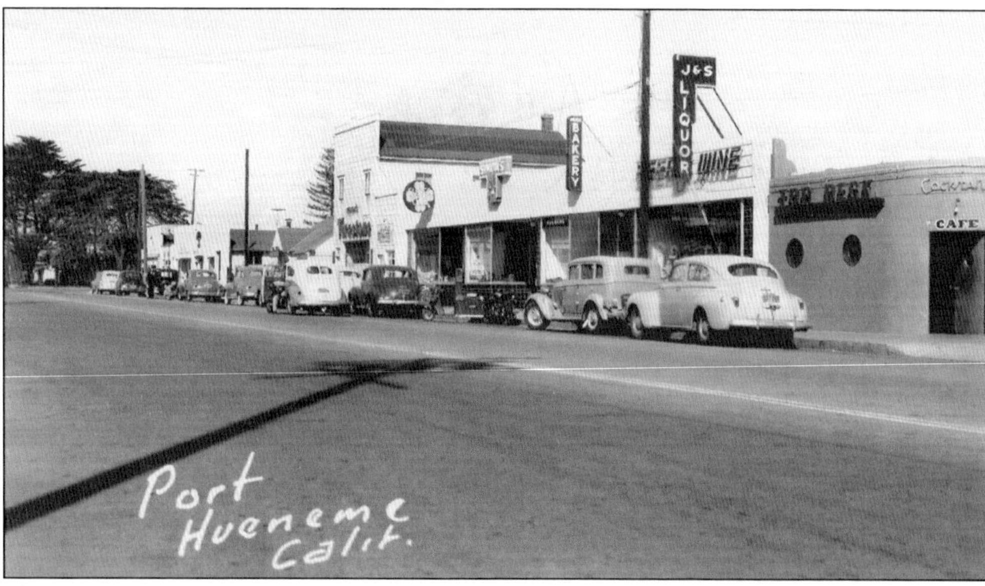

The Top Deck was another local watering hole. The bar opened in 1942 and claimed to have the longest bar in the county, at 60 feet. By October 3, 1961, the citizens of Hueneme voted in favor of eliminating card rooms from the city by a two-to-one vote. Police chief Al Jalaty was determined to support the community's spirit and also initiated the "Block Parent Program" to get more parents involved in making the area a more desirable place to live.

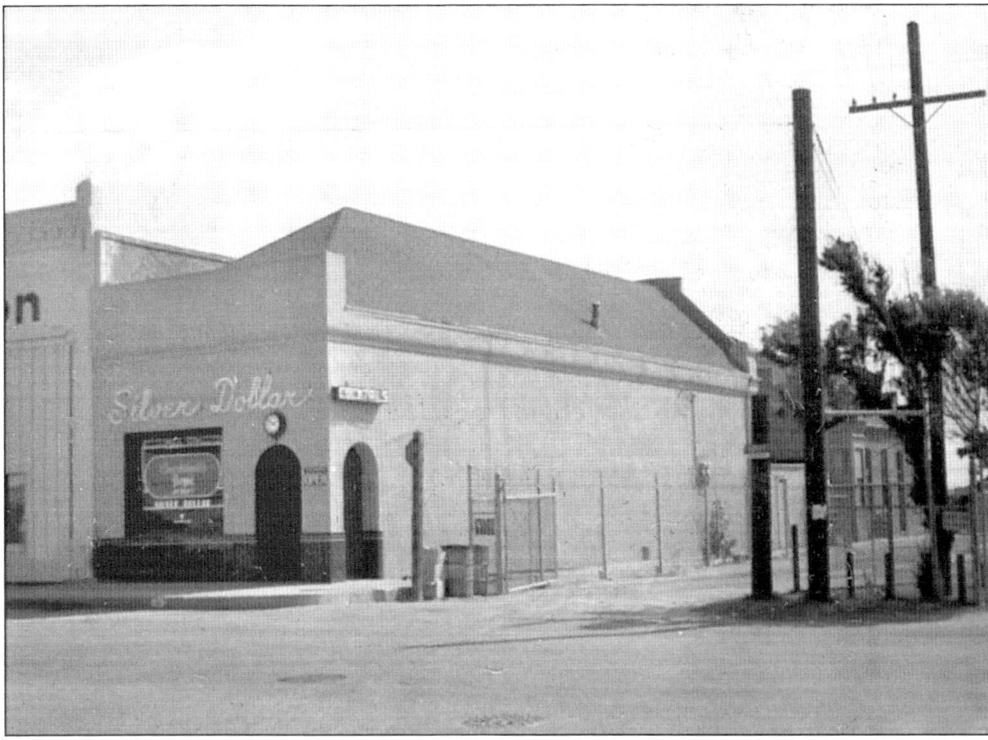

The Silver Dollar was the last incarnation of the original Bank of Hueneme. Behind the bar was the original weigh station that was across the street from the Lima Bean House.

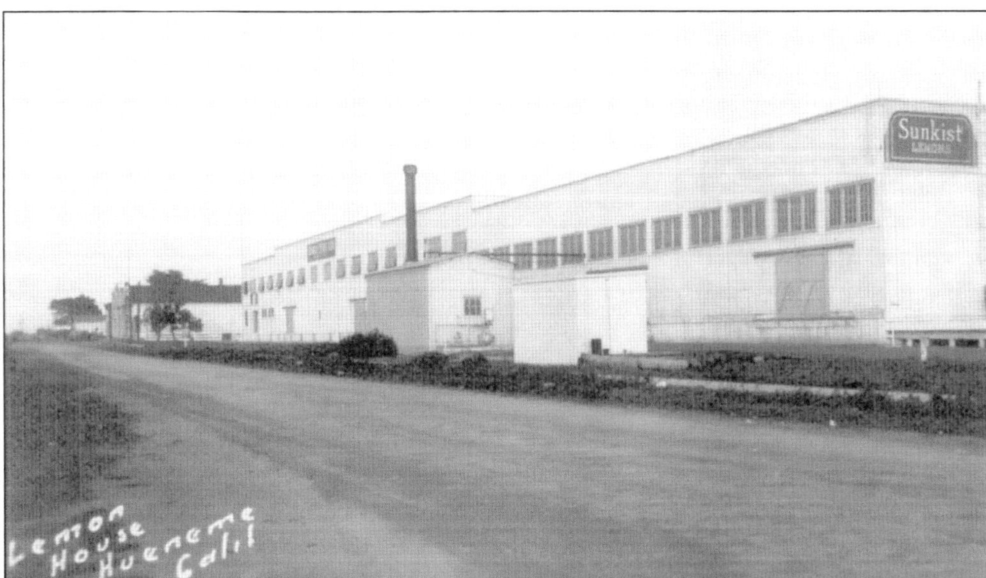

This image, looking south along Main Street, provides another view of Sunkist Lemon Packinghouse No. 2, part of the Oxnard Citrus Association. Neither the packinghouse nor Main Street remains.

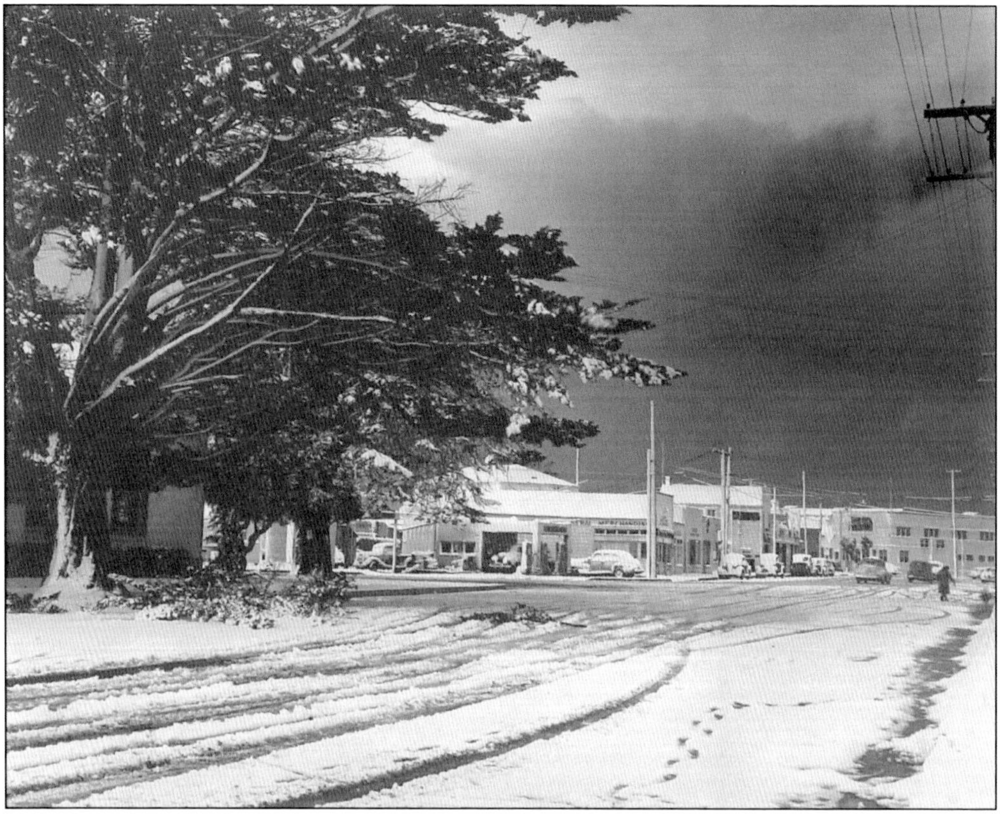

Snow fell on Southern California on January 11, 1949. This view of Market Street looks toward the lemon packinghouse No. 2.

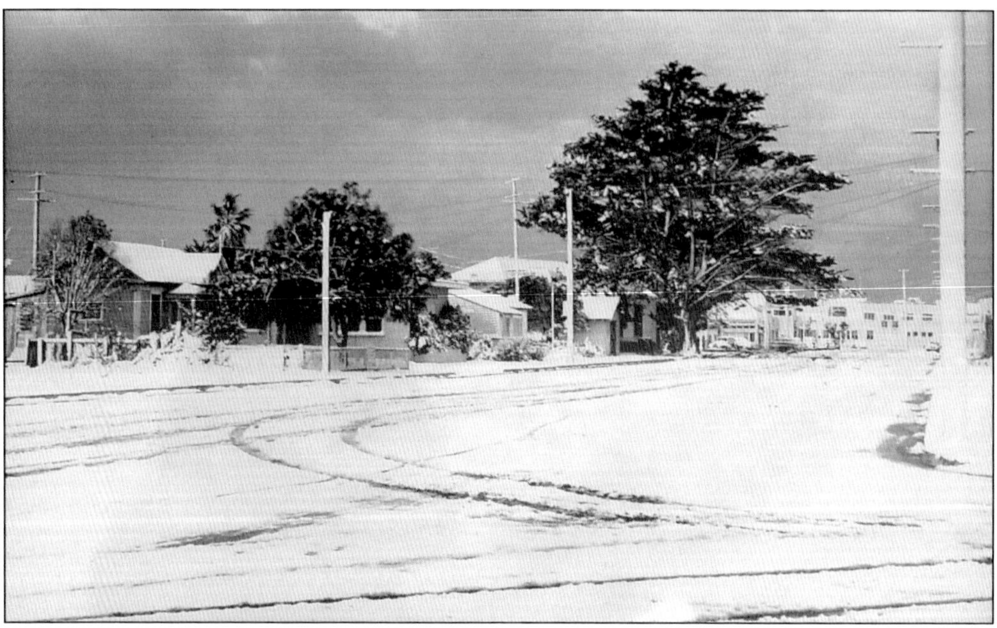

Here is a similar view as above, but taken from farther back.

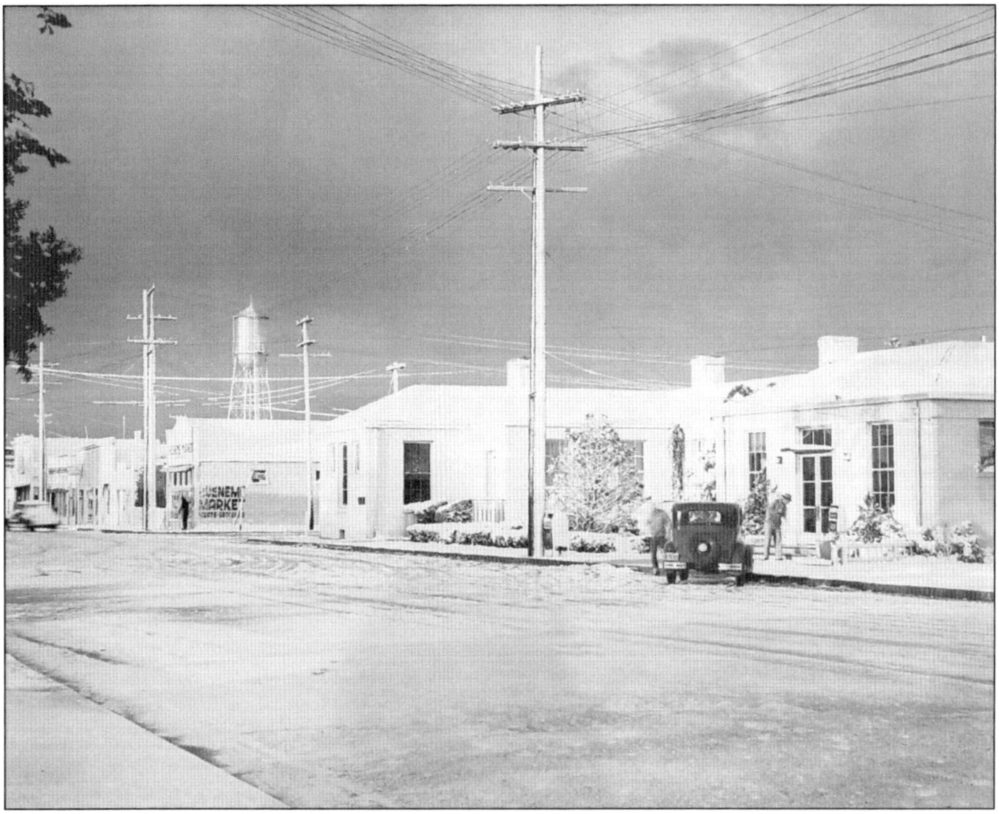

This view also shows Market Street, this time taken from the U.S. Post Office, looking past the Berylwood Investment Company and towards Arosteguey's Market.

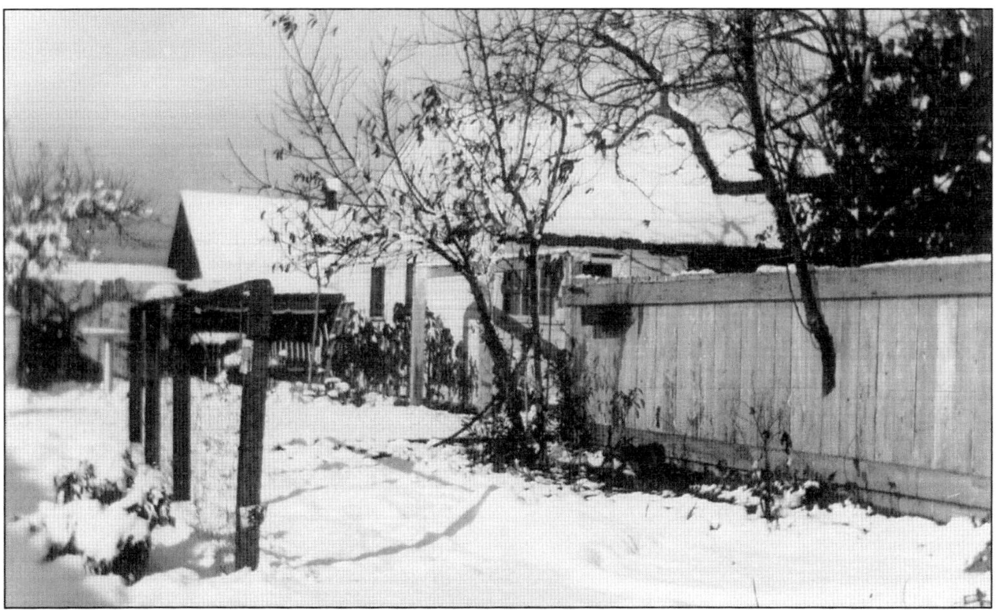

This undocumented view may be of San Pedro Street.

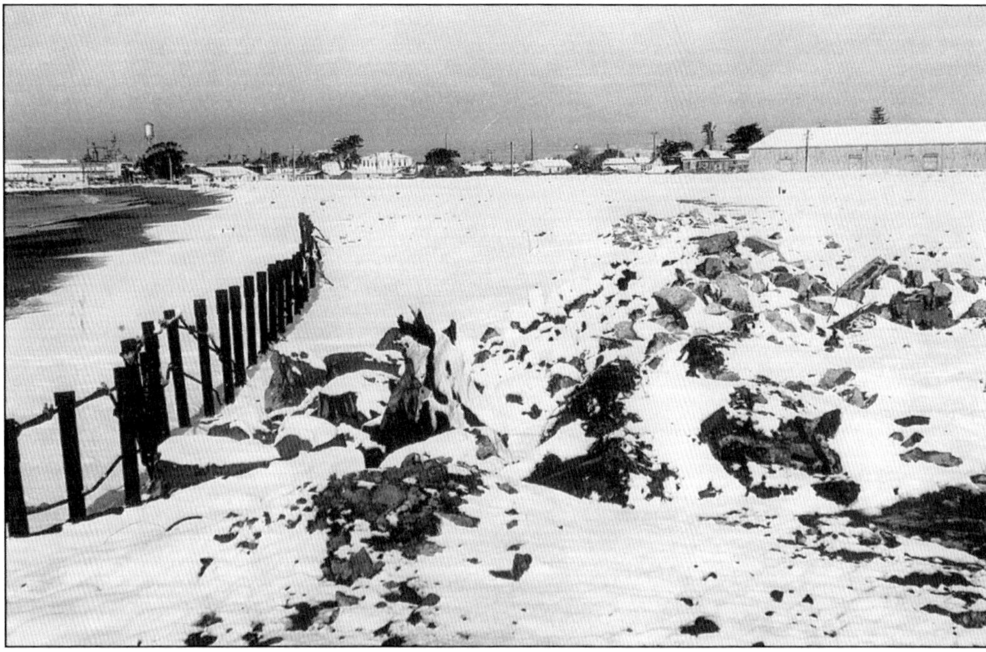

Even the snow at the beach stuck around long enough to be photographed. The tower at Main Street is visible in the distance.

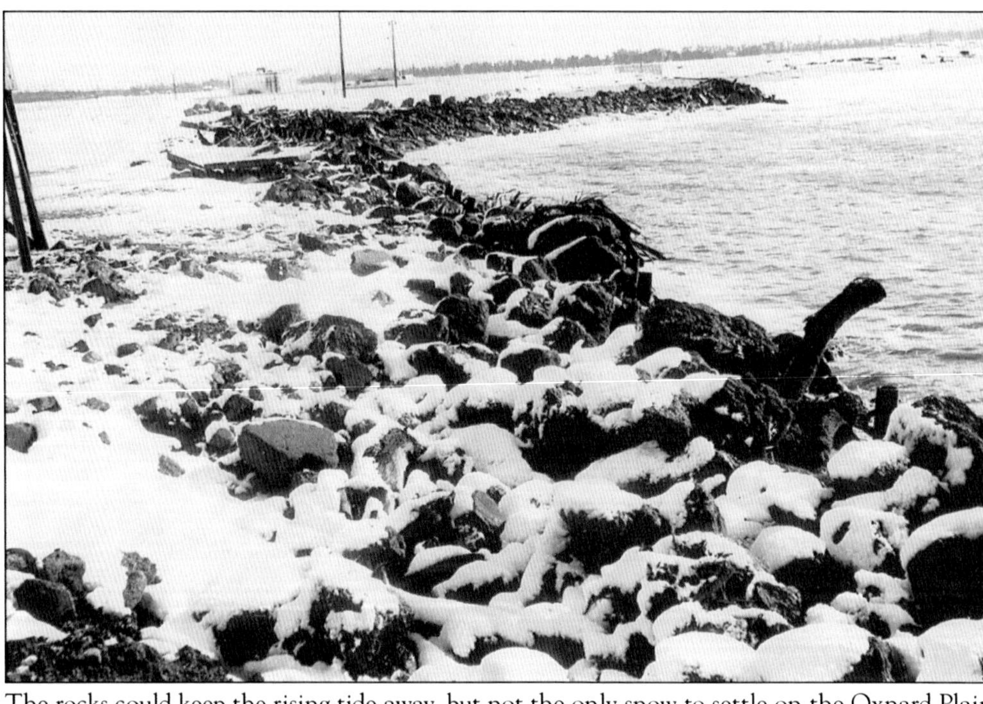

The rocks could keep the rising tide away, but not the only snow to settle on the Oxnard Plain during the 20th century.

Eight

The Seabees

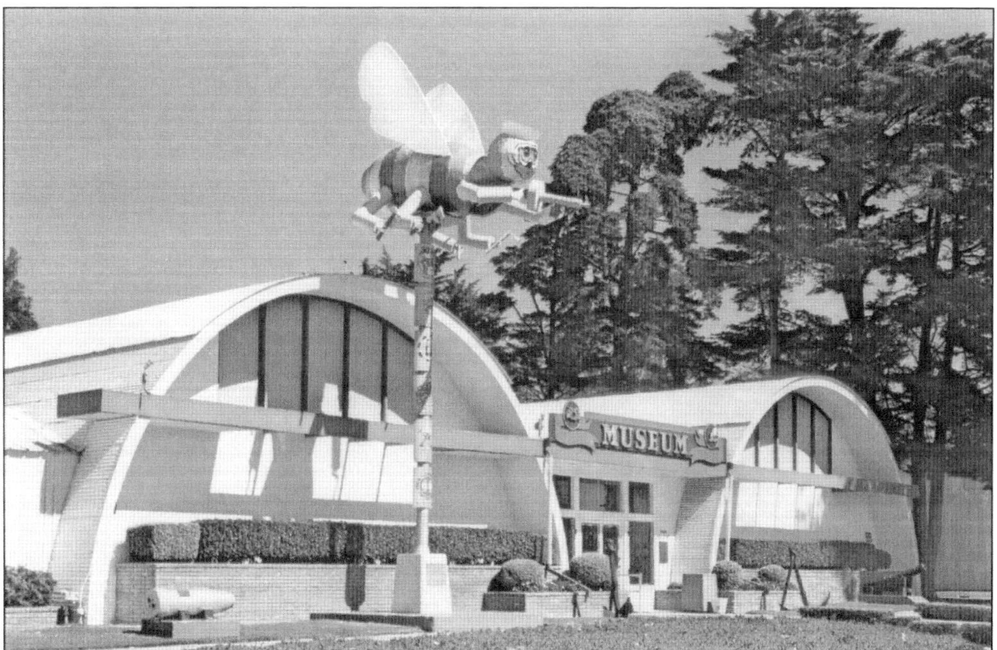

The second Seabee Museum, located in building 99 on Twenty-third Street, was constructed on the 25th anniversary of the Seabees in 1967. Construction of a newer and larger museum began in 2005. The museum exhibits the accomplishments of the Seabees, as well as those of the Civil Engineer Corps.

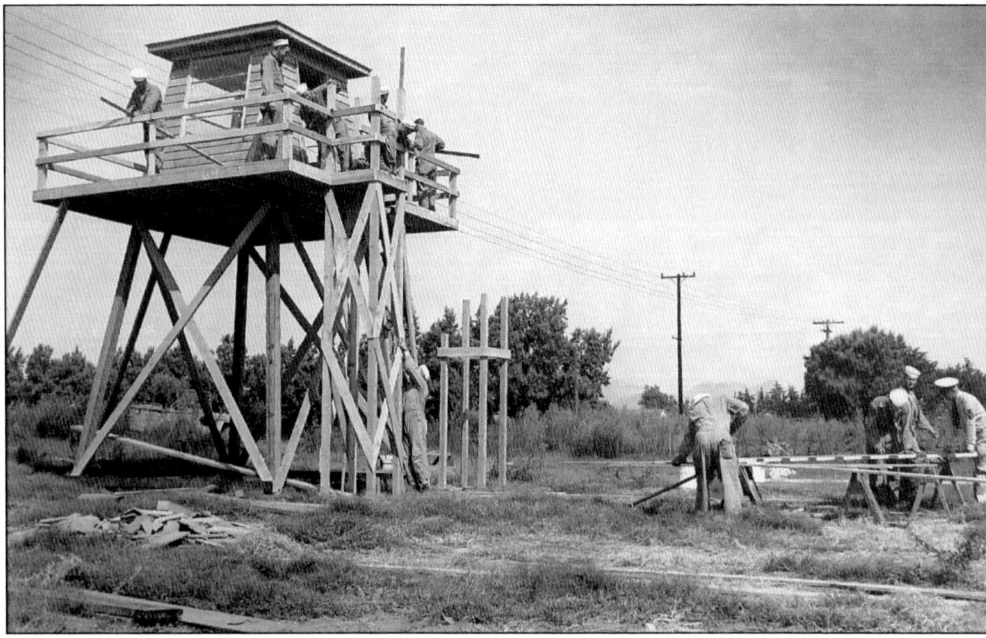

The Seabees at the Naval Battalion Construction Center would build structures like the tower in this picture, test its reliability, and then take the structure apart for the next group of Seabees to practice.

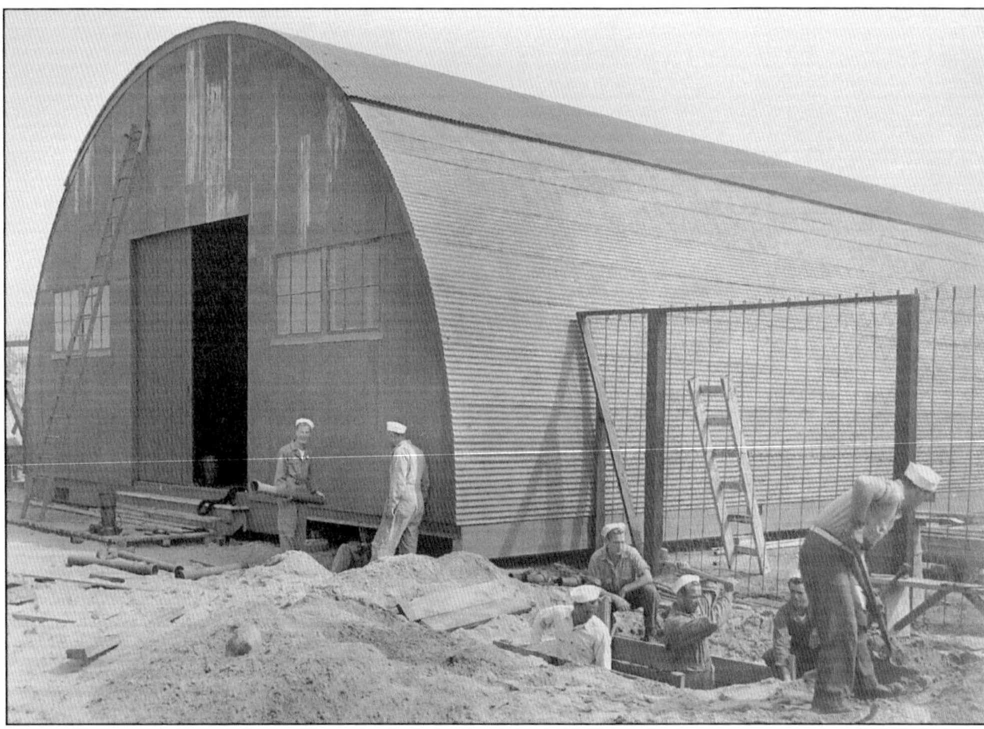

The Seabees constructed thousands of Quonset huts during the war years. Remnants of their buildings could be seen throughout the county during and after the war, as building materials were in short supply.

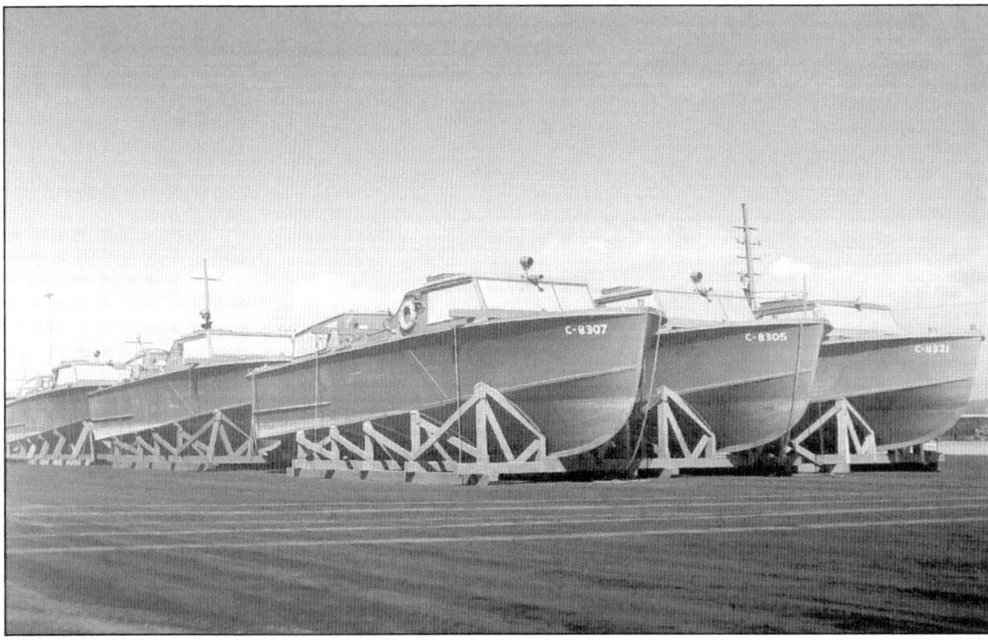

This fleet appears to be made up of Patrol Torpedo, or PT, boats. These were small, wooden craft that carried enough firepower to sink a battleship. They were the fastest on the water and were also used for rescue missions.

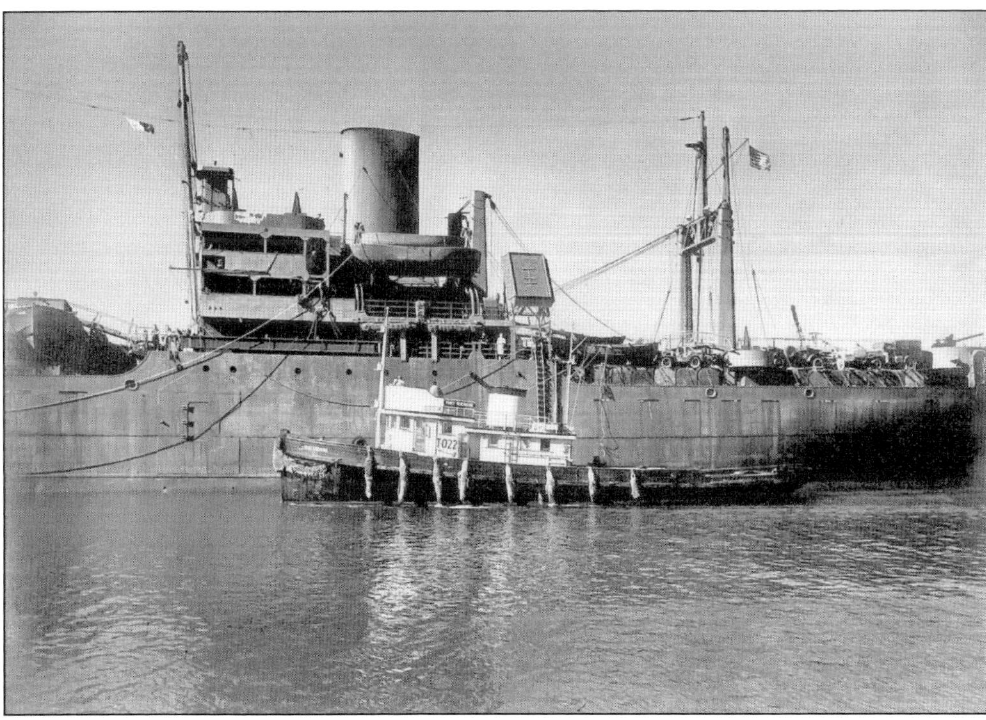

The Hueneme tugboat was in service 24 hours a day.

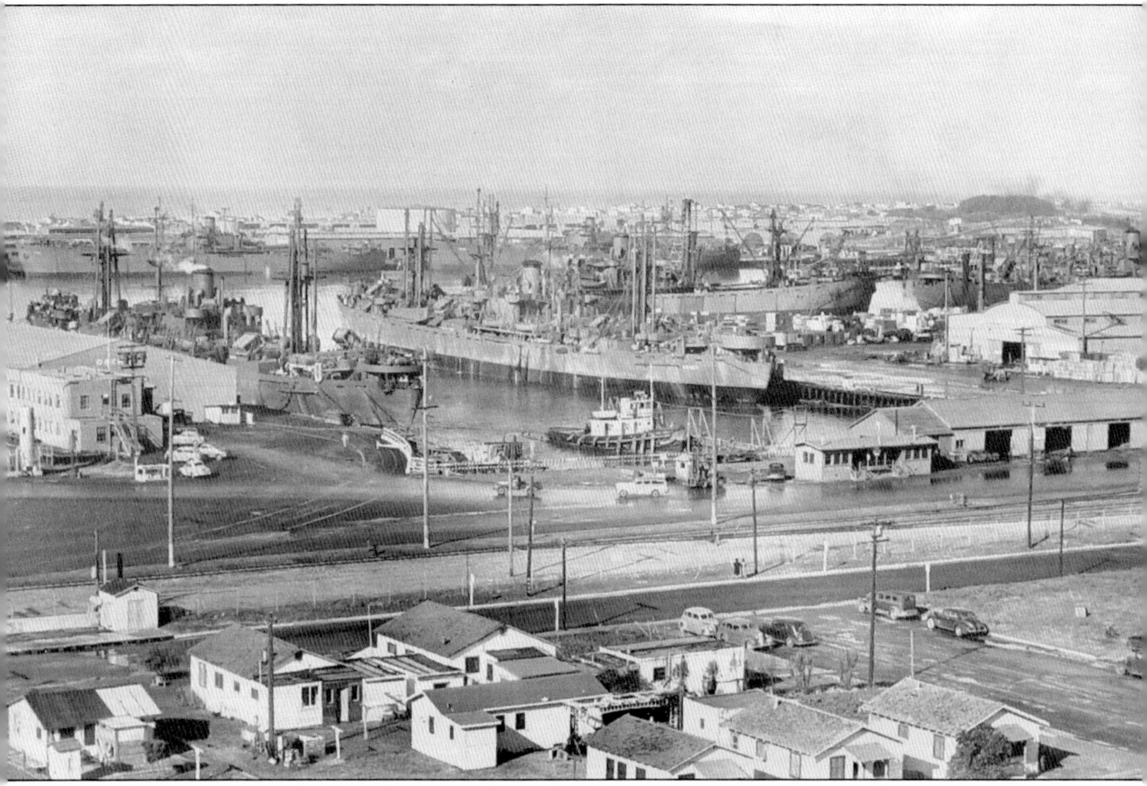

This 1940s view of the harbor was taken after the government took over the site.

Nine

FUN, FOLLIES, AND PEACE

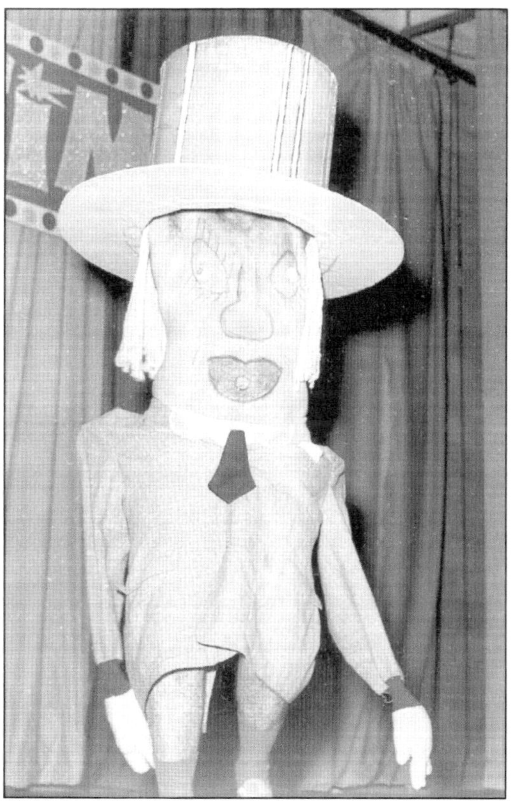

An unidentified belly performs at the Follies during the annual Harbor Days festivities. Harbor Days began in July 1955 in celebration of the 15th anniversary of the construction of the harbor. By 1961, over 200,000 people were attending the several-day event that included a parade down Main Street in Hueneme.

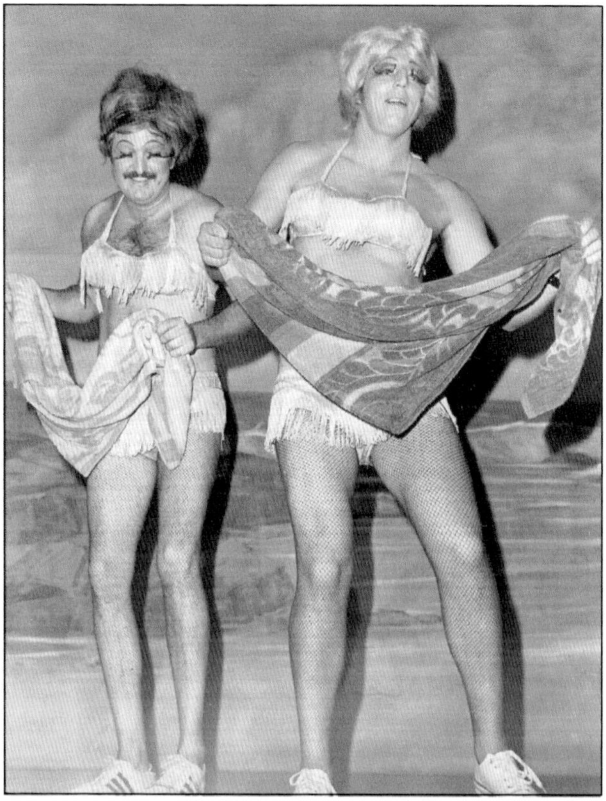

Hueneme High teachers and coaches Jim Laine (left) and Sam Antcliffe take the stage in a 1972 performance during the Follies to raise money for community organizations and projects. Fortunately for Laine and Antcliffe, their students never found out about the appearance.

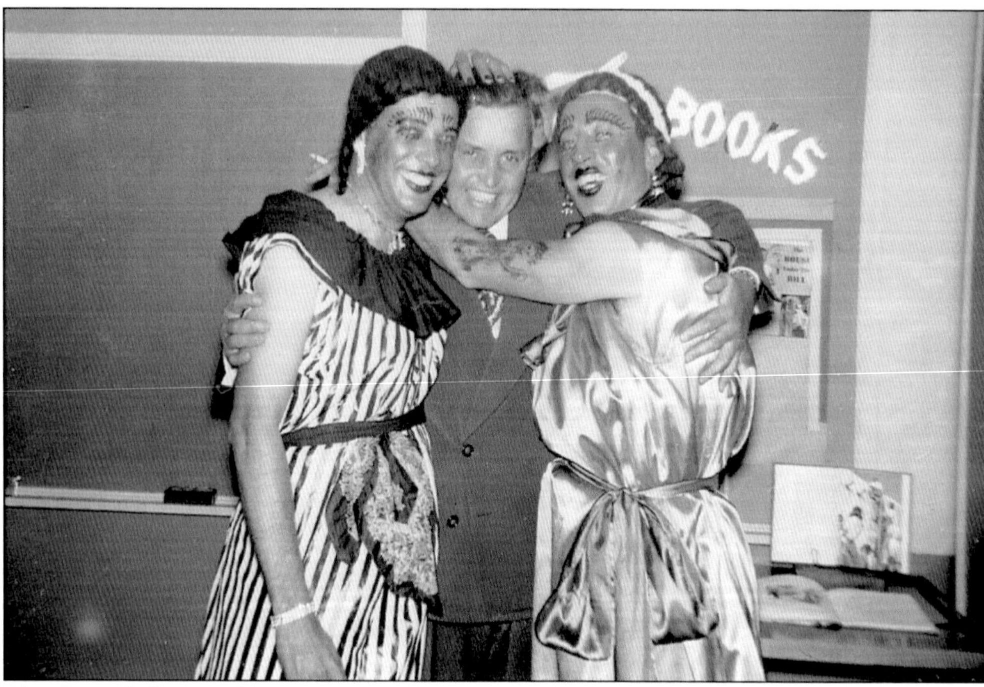

The three "ladies" in this picture getting ready to perform at the Follies are, from left to right, Ray Prueter, Ralph McKeehan, and Bob Brant.

There did not seem to be a shortage of female impersonators in Hueneme.

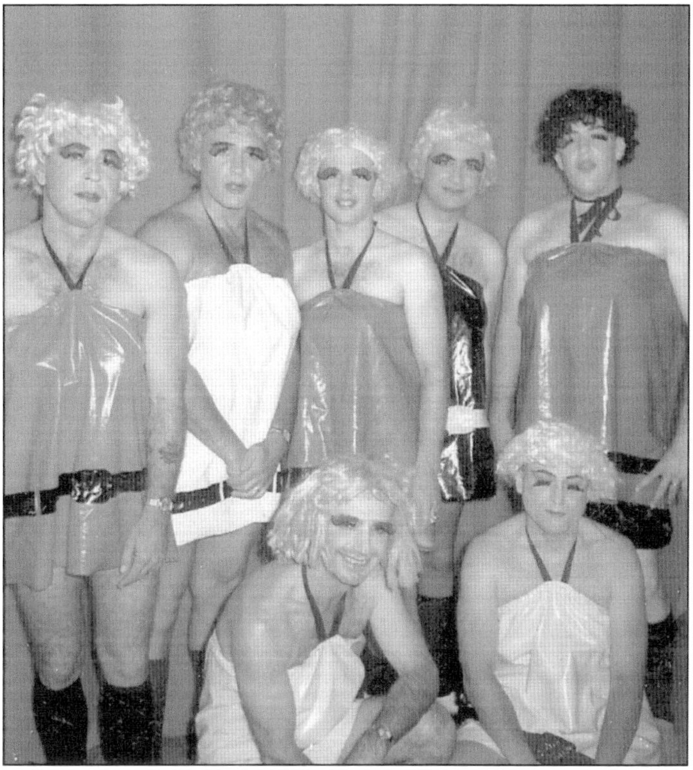

Many of the community's top professionals took part in the annual ritual. On the far left is longtime Hueneme optometrist Dr. Ralph Moses.

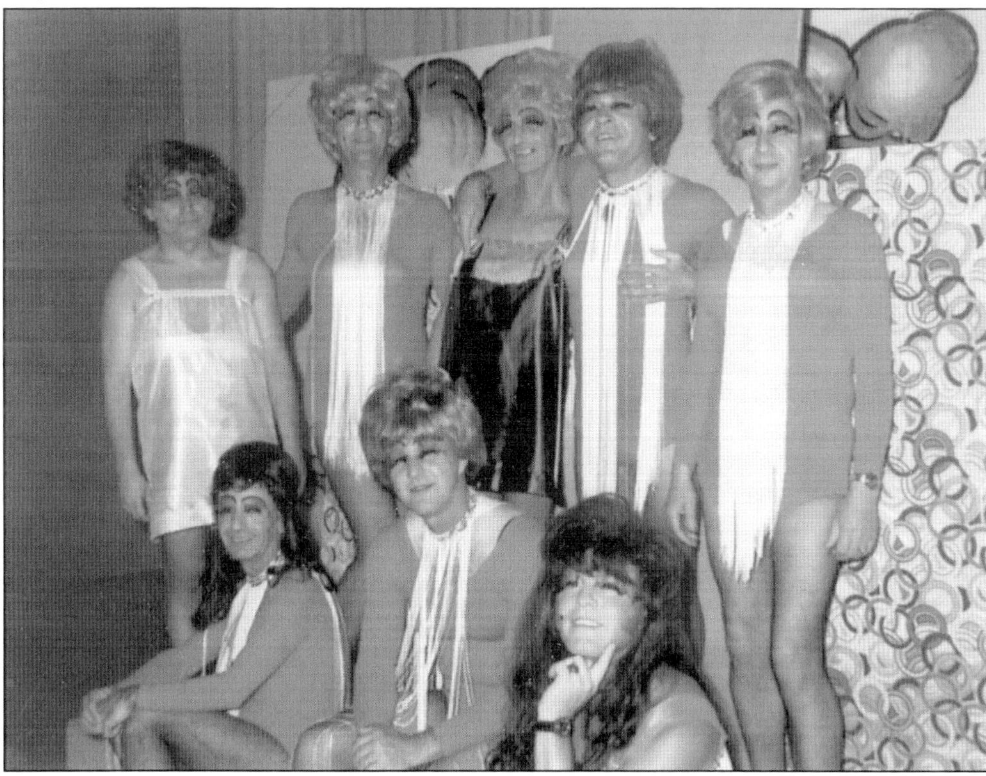

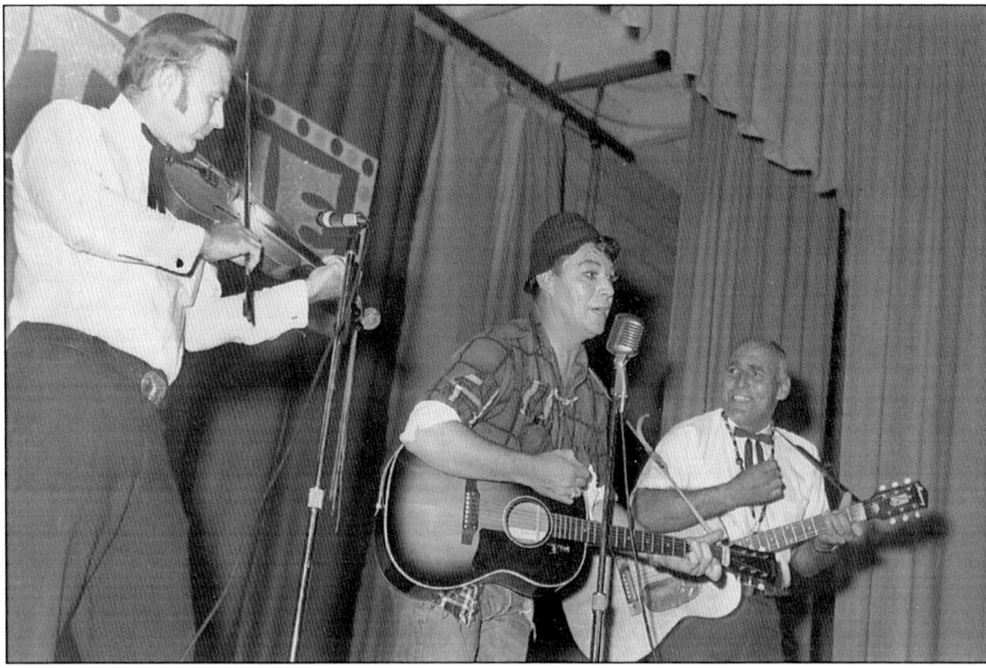

Another popular feature of the Harbor Days was the musical portion, and this performance showcased the talents of Ralph McKeehan (center) and police chief Al Jalaty. Jalaty was a lieutenant with the sheriff's department for 12 years before taking on the role of police chief in 1961. He was instrumental in cleaning up gambling and prostitution, which had increased in Hueneme throughout the preceding years.

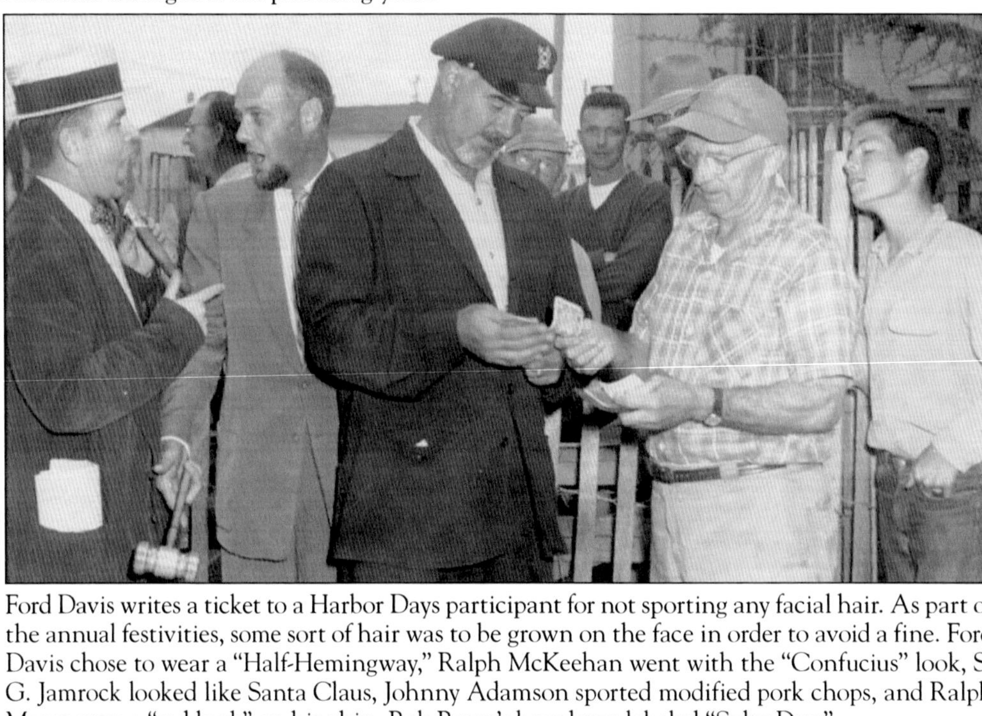

Ford Davis writes a ticket to a Harbor Days participant for not sporting any facial hair. As part of the annual festivities, some sort of hair was to be grown on the face in order to avoid a fine. Ford Davis chose to wear a "Half-Hemingway," Ralph McKeehan went with the "Confucius" look, S. G. Jamrock looked like Santa Claus, Johnny Adamson sported modified pork chops, and Ralph Moses grew a "red bush" on his chin. Bob Brant's beard was labeled "Salty Dog."

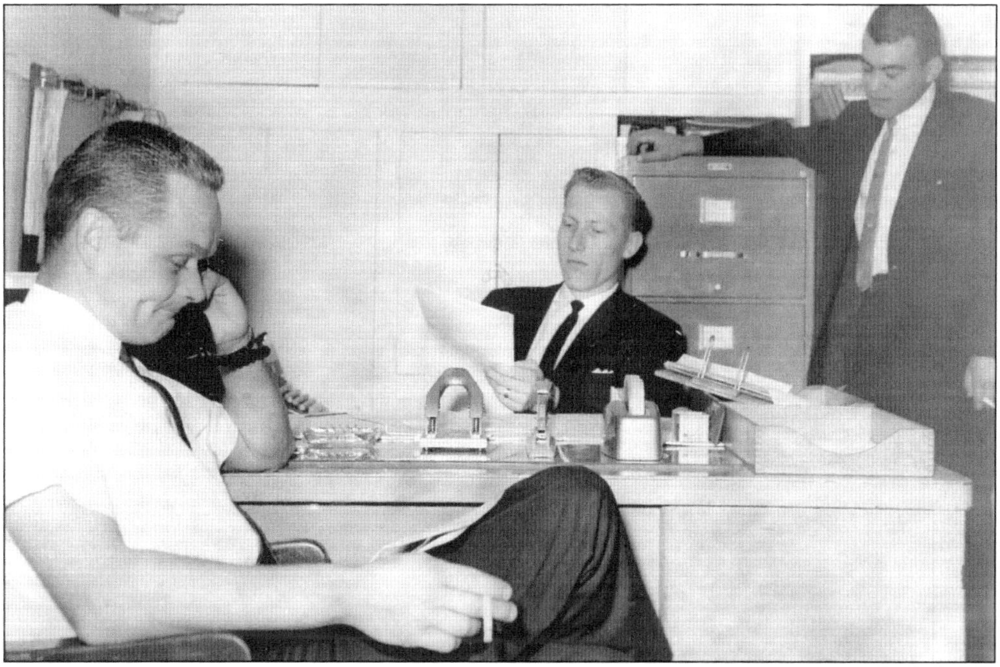
Det. M. G. Moeschler contemplates the latest facts of the case while his colleagues look over another case.

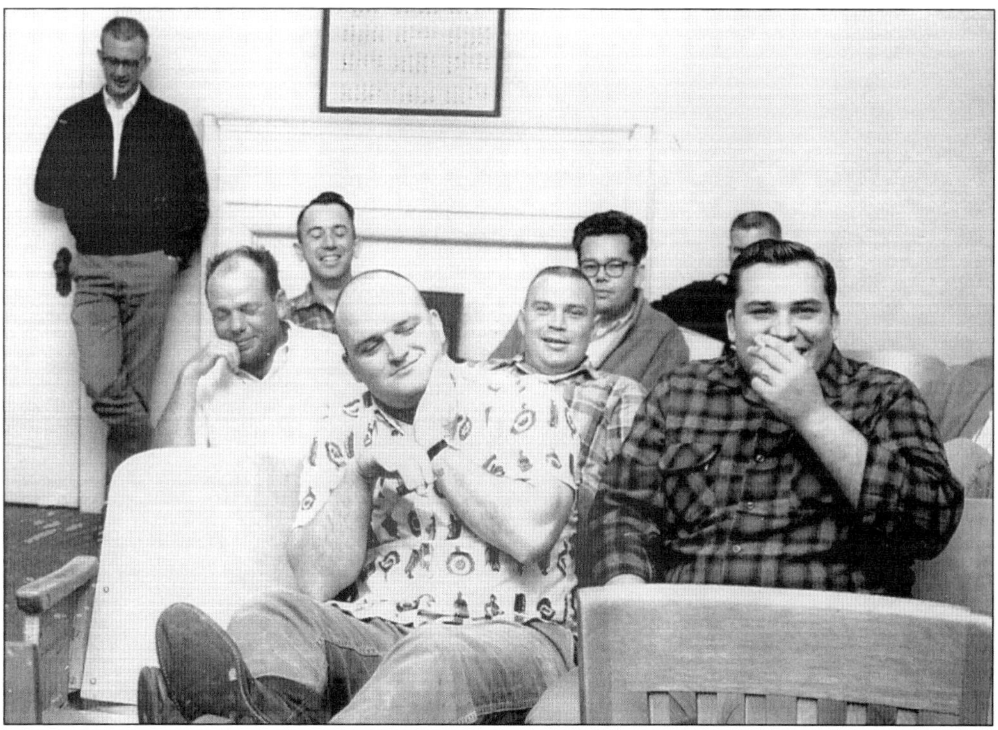
Hueneme police officer reserves share a light moment before a meeting at the station in the 1960s. From left to right are (first row) Chuck Melaney and Leo St. Hillar; (second row) Stan Wyatt Sr. and Mark Mellenchamp; (third row) Bill Nugent and Troy Baker.

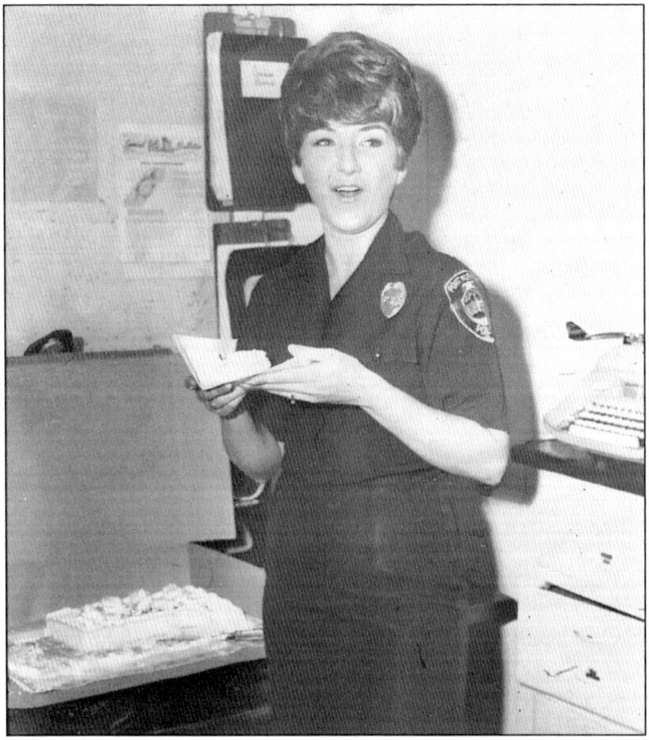

Eileen St. Hillar joined her husband on the force, c. 1960s.

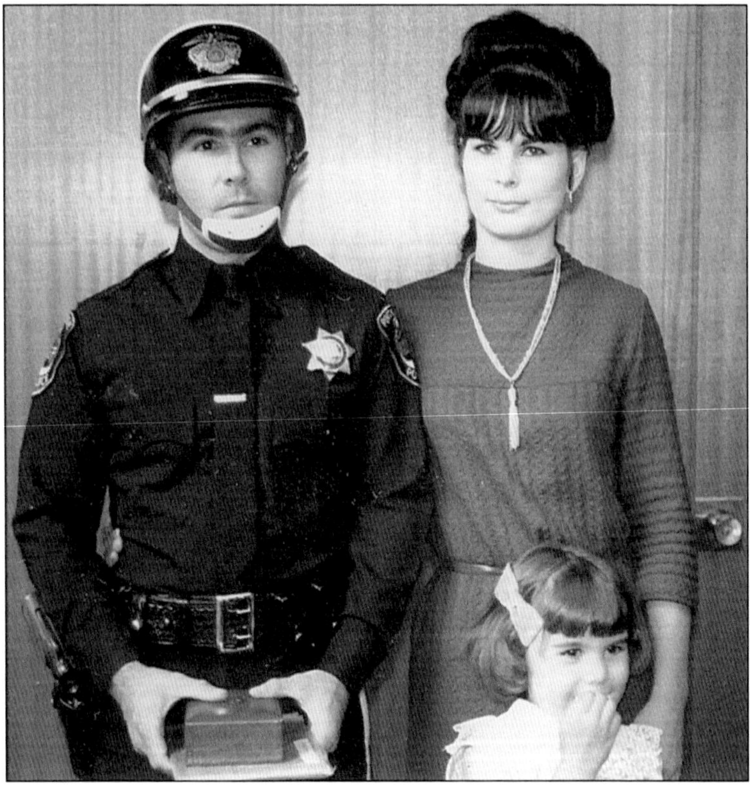

Sergeant Fitzgerald and his family take a moment to pose for the camera.

Jeanette Brown served as secretary for police chief Al Jalaty in the 1960s and 1970s.

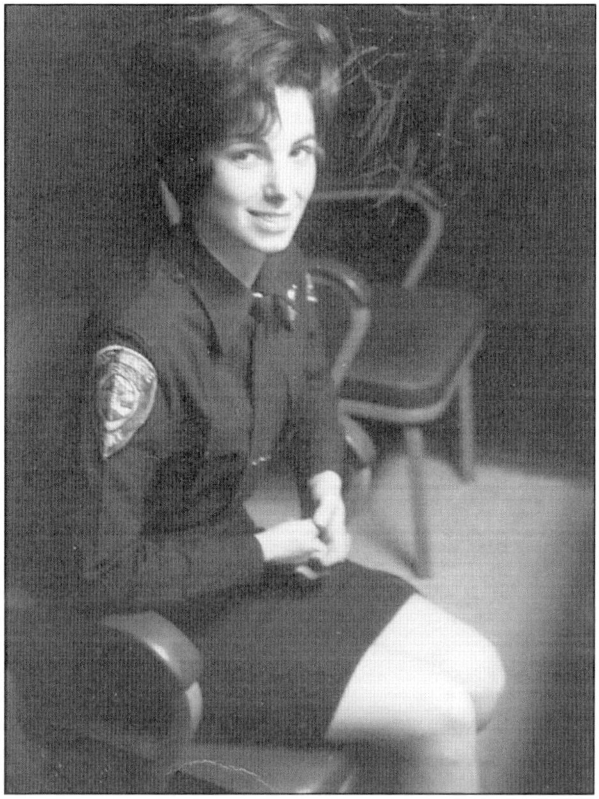

Carolyn Rosso worked as a police dispatcher for the Hueneme Police Department and is pictured here c. 1965.

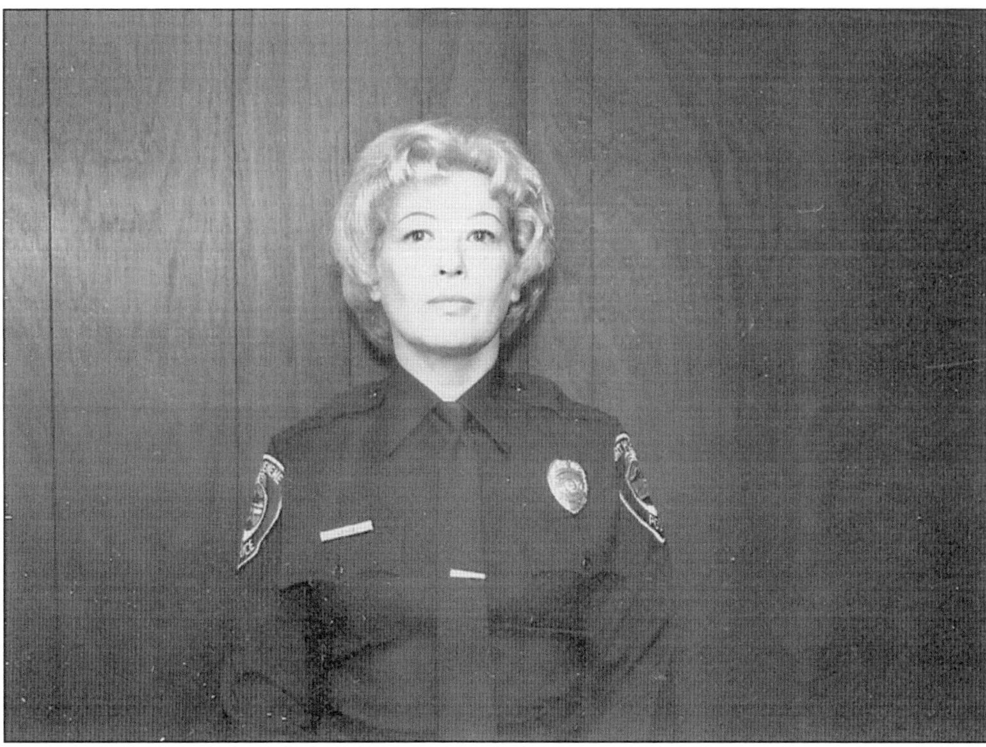

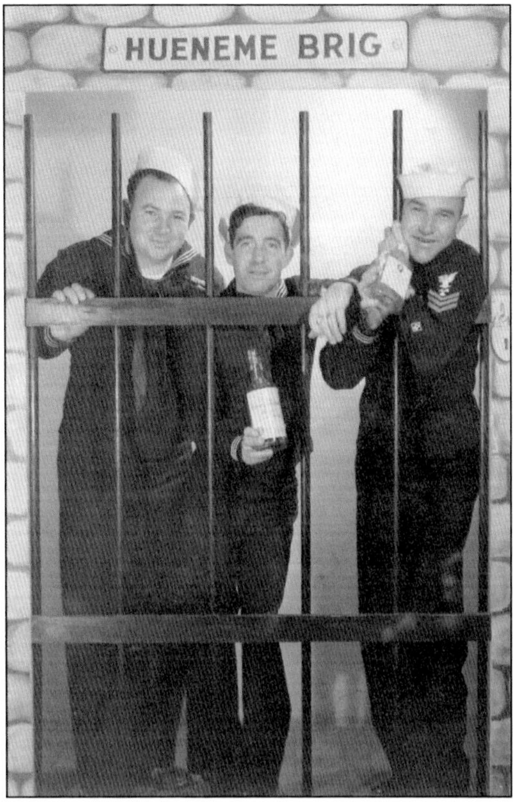

One of the many activities during Harbor Days was having one's picture taken in "the jail." This group shot was captured around 1955.

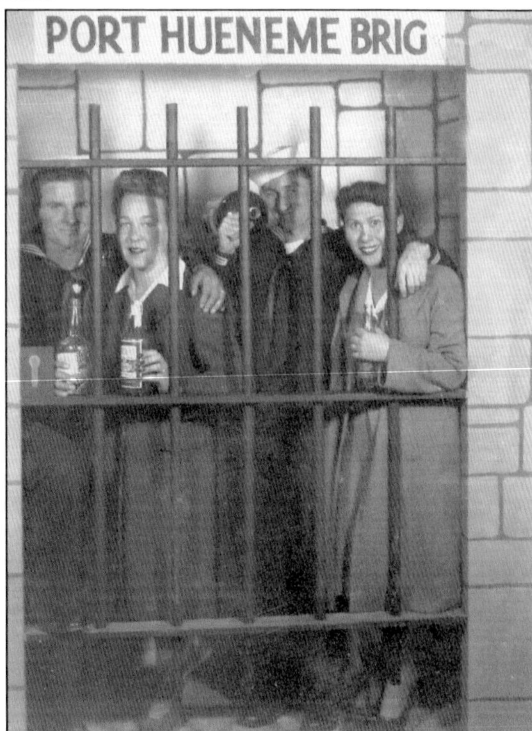

A parade that started near the 23-acre Bubbling Springs Park traveled down Market Street and towards a carnival area at the end of street. Too much fun and you could end up in the "brig."

Postmaster Arthur Haycox, who took the position in 1935, accepts the keys to a new mail truck from Congressman Charles Teague, c. 1950s. After a lifetime devoted to community service, Haycox was honored by having an elementary school named after him.

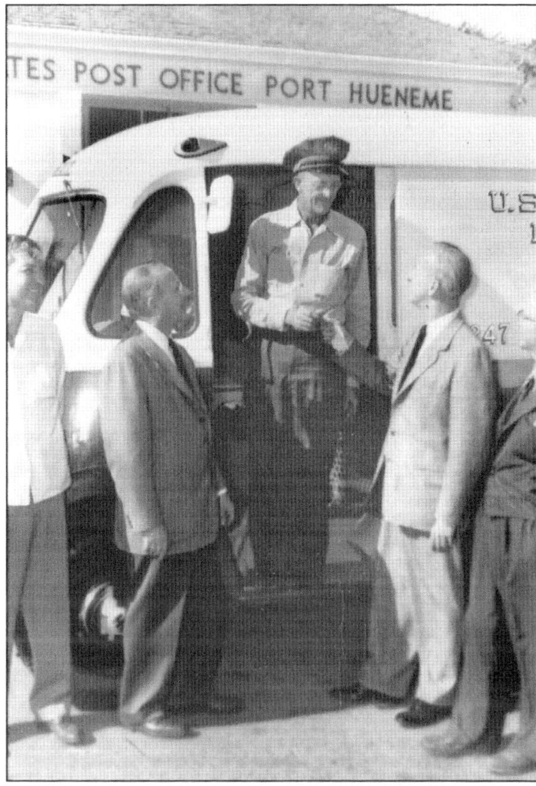

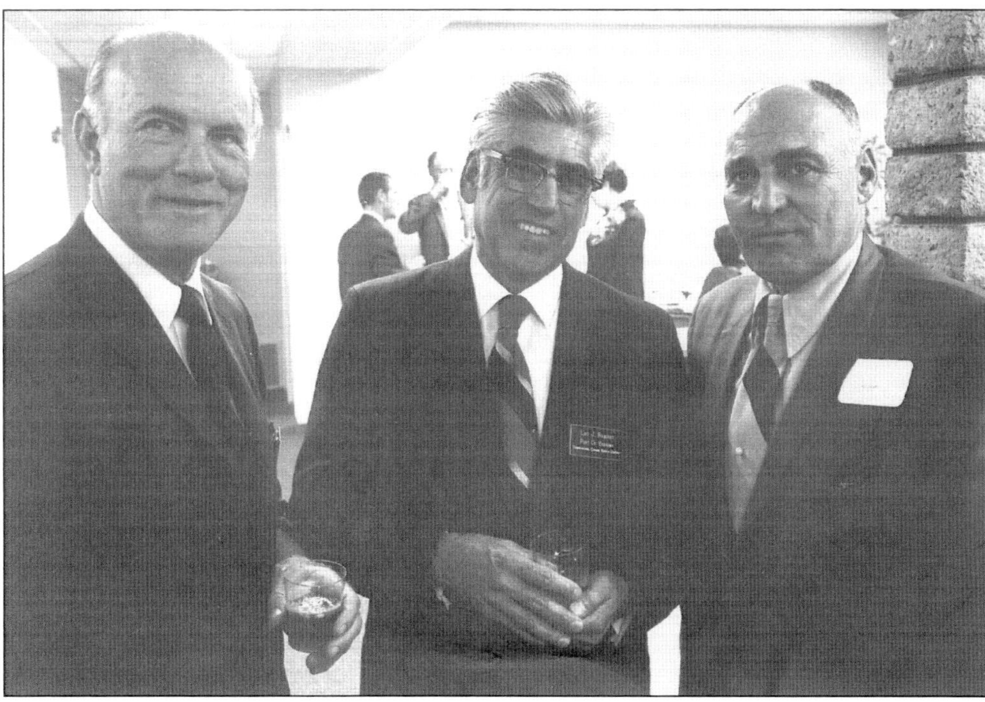

From left to right are Captain Bennett, who served on the Port Hueneme City Council; Leo Ramirez, a longtime board member for the Harbor District; and Al Jalaty, the police chief.

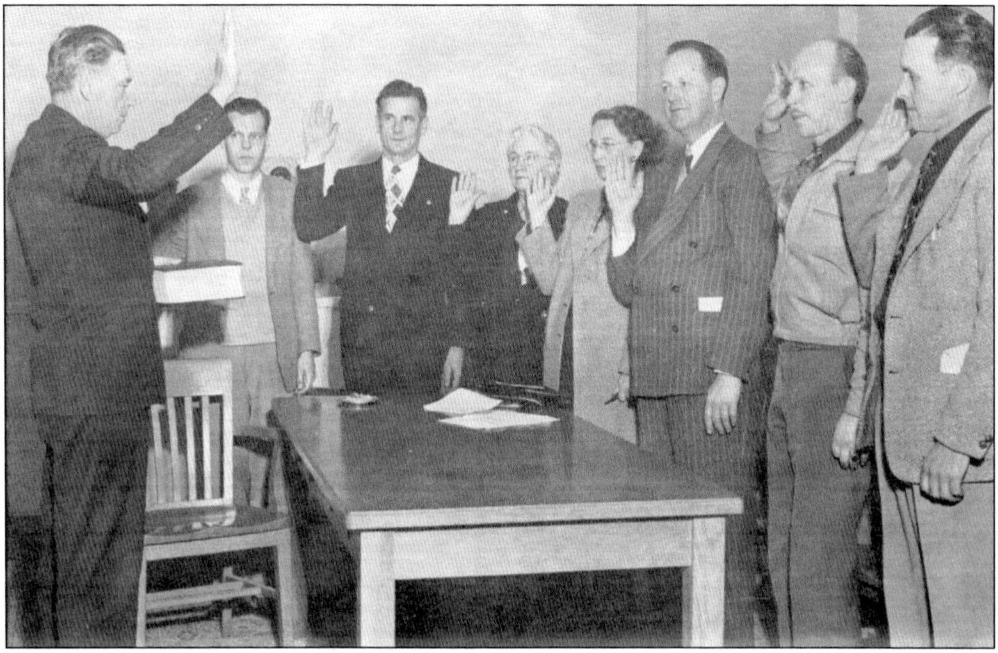

On March 16, 1948, the majority of the 2,875 residents of Port Hueneme voted in favor of incorporation. Judge Louis A. Peterson performed the duty of swearing in the first city council.

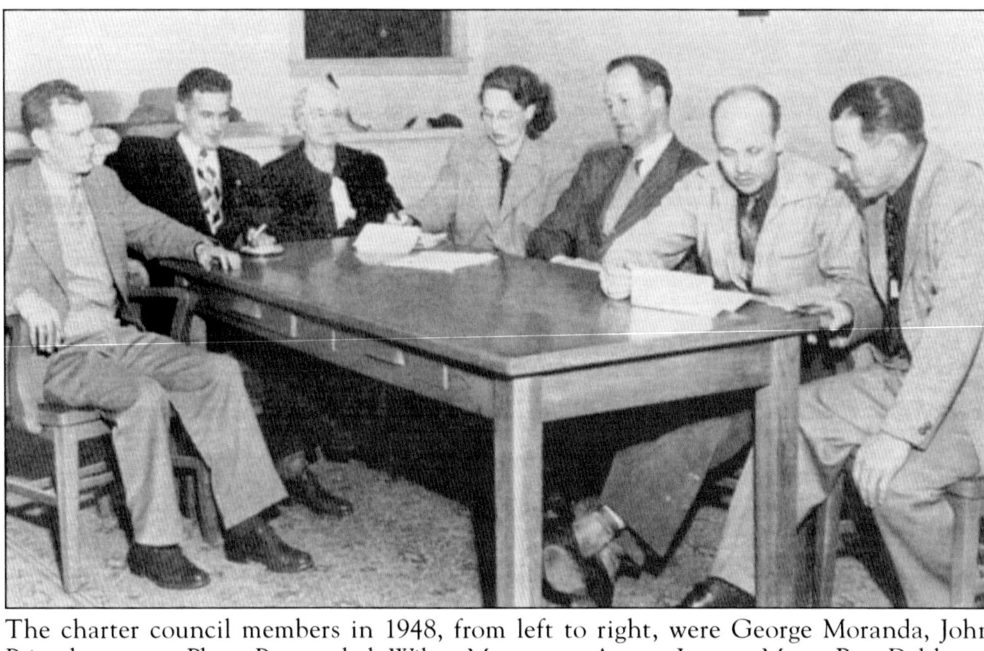

The charter council members in 1948, from left to right, were George Moranda, John Priegal, treasurer Phosa Porter, clerk Wilma Merryman, Ansgar Larsen, Mayor Bert Dahl, and Ralph McKeehan.

Ten

Going Forward

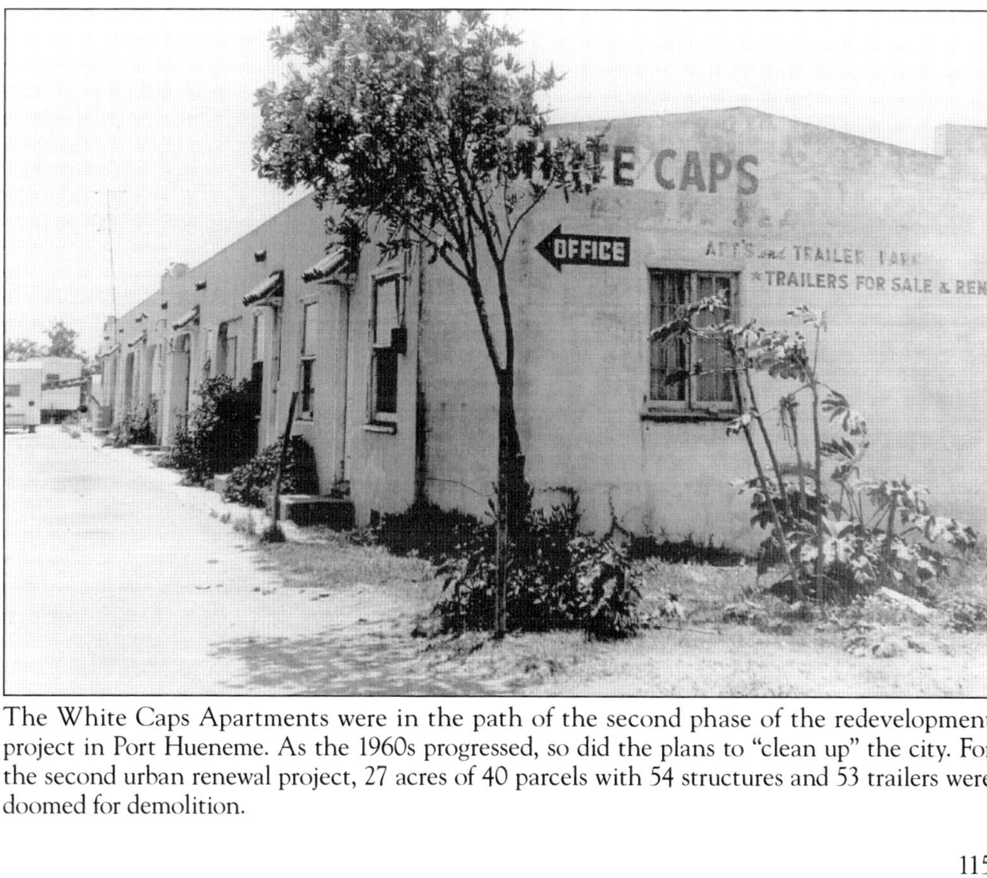

The White Caps Apartments were in the path of the second phase of the redevelopment project in Port Hueneme. As the 1960s progressed, so did the plans to "clean up" the city. For the second urban renewal project, 27 acres of 40 parcels with 54 structures and 53 trailers were doomed for demolition.

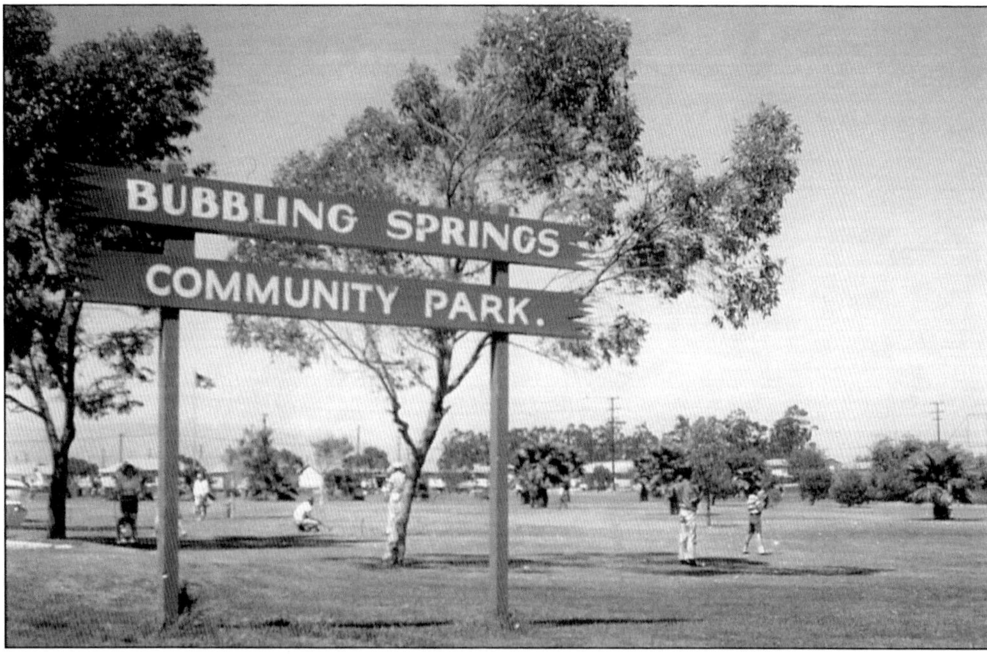

Bubbling Springs Community Park was dedicated on Memorial Day in 1957. Present at the ceremony were Ansgar Larson, superintendent of the Hueneme Elementary School District, and Richard Bard, keynote speaker at the event. Bubbling Springs became the home for picnics, guppies and crawdads, over-the-line baseball games (in which a line is used to designate the beginning of the infield, and teams of two or more hit between the lines of half a field), cakewalks, and the Hueneme Little League.

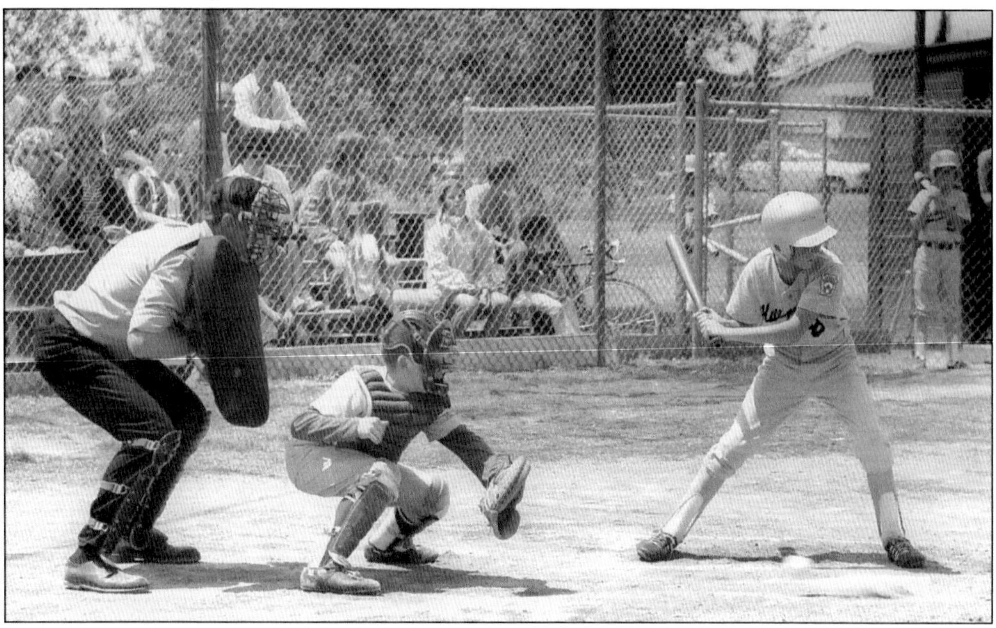
Hueneme Little League not only produced many successful players, including future Major Leaguer Jerry Willard (catching), but also lifelong friendships, like the one between Craig Maulhardt (batting) and Willard. The umpire is Russel Buhay.

In 1962, the developers of the 120-acre Hueneme Bay community off Channel Islands Boulevard and Ventura Road came up with an advertising campaign to entice people throughout the Southland to buy one of the more than 1,000 garden-patio dwellings. The idea was to have a walk-a-thon from Los Angles to Hueneme to emphasize that "Hueneme Bay was within walking distance of L.A."

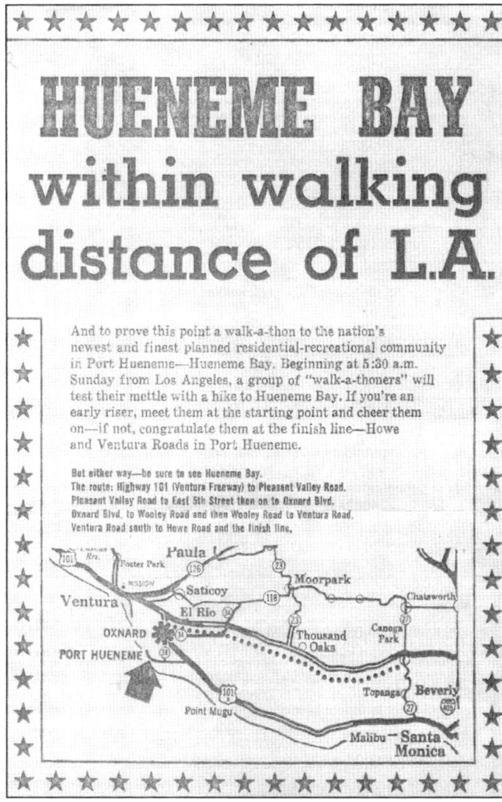

HUENEME BAY
within walking distance of L.A.

And to prove this point a walk-a-thon to the nation's newest and finest planned residential-recreational community in Port Hueneme—Hueneme Bay. Beginning at 5:30 a.m. Sunday from Los Angeles, a group of "walk-a-thoners" will test their mettle with a hike to Hueneme Bay. If you're an early riser, meet them at the starting point and cheer them on—if not, congratulate them at the finish line—Howe and Ventura Roads in Port Hueneme.

But either way—be sure to see Hueneme Bay.
The route: Highway 101 (Ventura Freeway) to Pleasant Valley Road.
Pleasant Valley Road to East 5th Street then on to Oxnard Blvd.
Oxnard Blvd. to Wooley Road and then Wooley Road to Ventura Road.
Ventura Road south to Howe Road and the finish line.

There to greet and meet the walkers were, from left to right, Walter Bilynsky, the physical director; Bill Moranda, Port Hueneme city administrator; unidentified; Ernest George, president of William E. Doud Company; and Art Vienna, president of the California Springs Company.

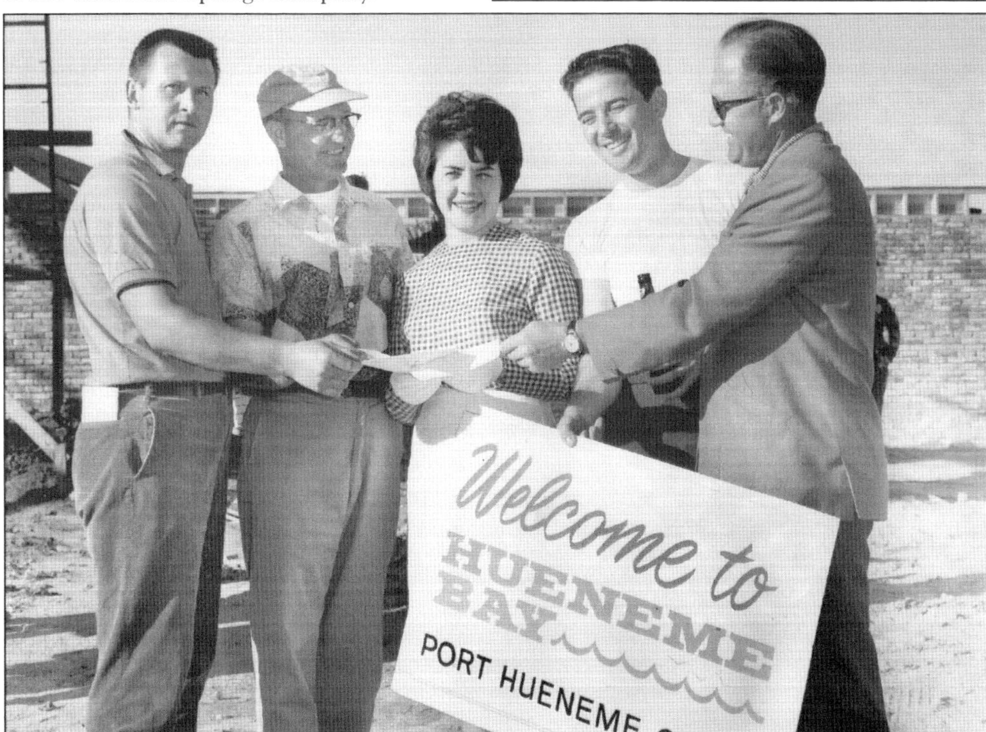

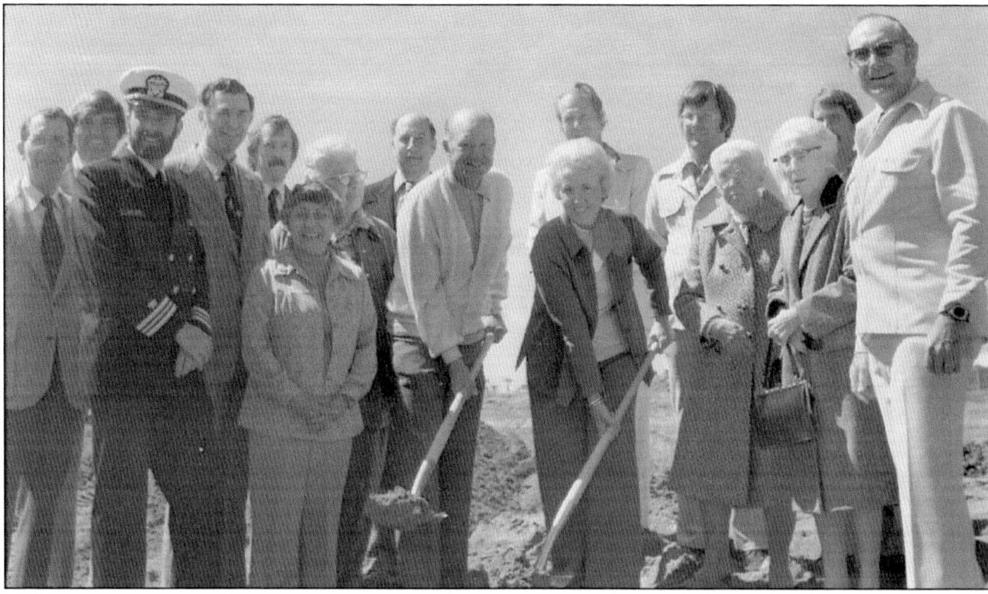

The groundbreaking for Moranda Park took place shortly after Walter Bill Moranda announced his retirement in 1975, after serving 20 years as the chief administrative officer for the city of Port Hueneme. Moranda also took on duties as supervisor of the sanitary district and served several terms as a city councilman. With the two shovels are Walter Bill Moranda and his wife, Jeannette. To the right of Jeannette are their mothers, and to the left of Bill is Dorothy Ramirez.

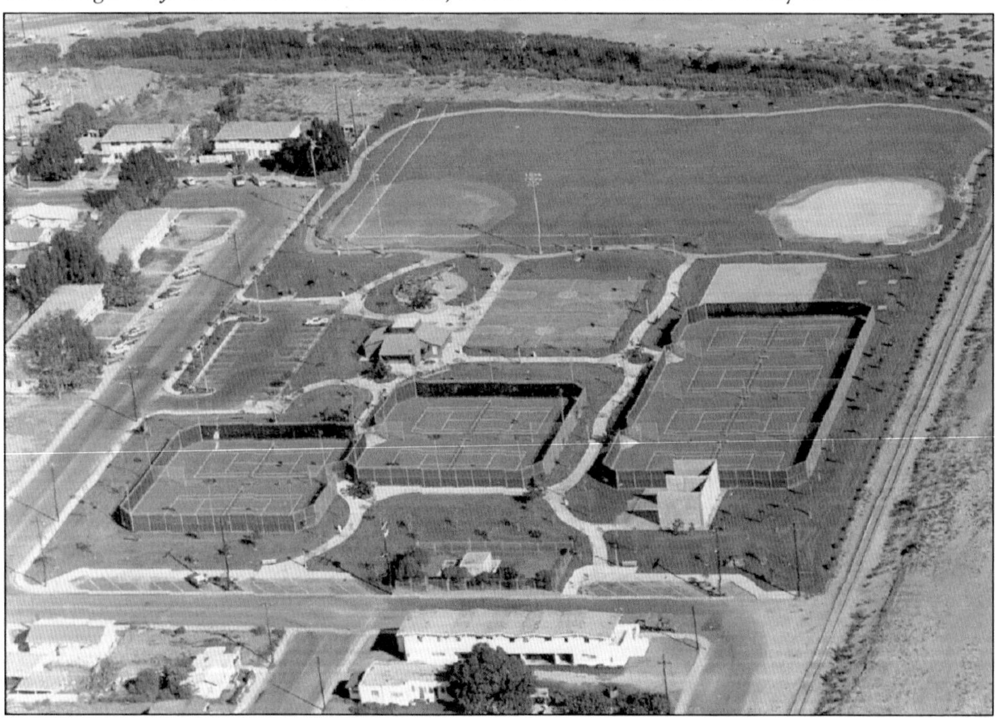

The park is located near the corner of Anacapa Street and Hueneme Road and is only a half a block from the beach. The all-inclusive park includes eight tennis courts, two full basketball courts, and a softball field.

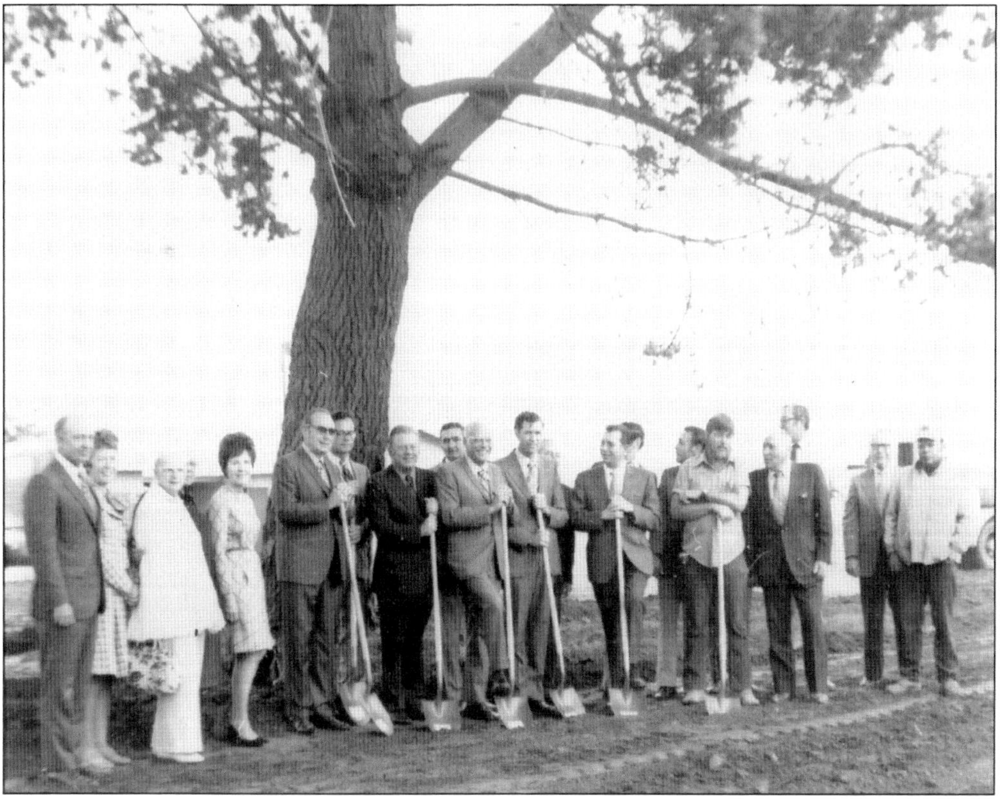

Groundbreaking for the city hall took place in 1972. Holding shovels, from left to right, are Orvene Carpenter, Herbert Templemen, Ray Prueter, two council members, Ike Baldwin, and, with one hand in his pocket, Al Jalaty.

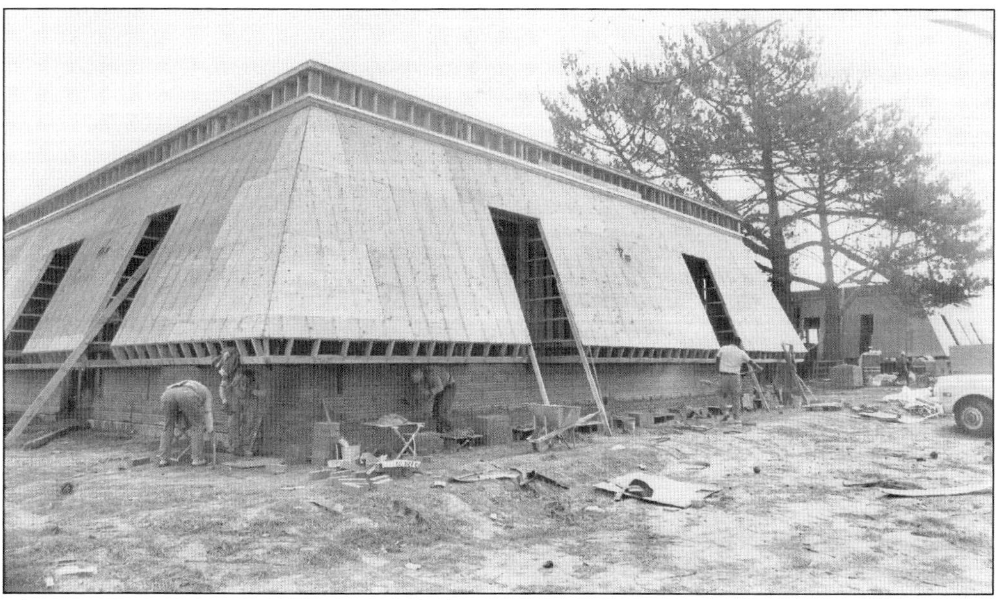

The Port Hueneme civic center was ready for occupation by 1973 and became the new home for city hall, as well as for the Hueneme Police Department.

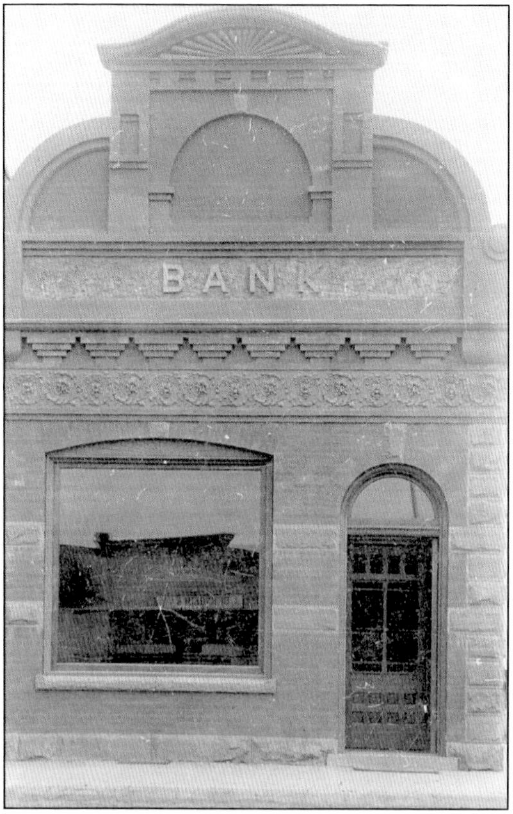

The original Bank of Hueneme was incorporated in 1889. Its building became the first brick structure in Hueneme when it was erected in 1894 by Jens Rasmussen. The bank was also the first business to feature a cement sidewalk. The bank was later used by the Oxnard Harbor District and, finally, by the Silver Dollar Saloon.

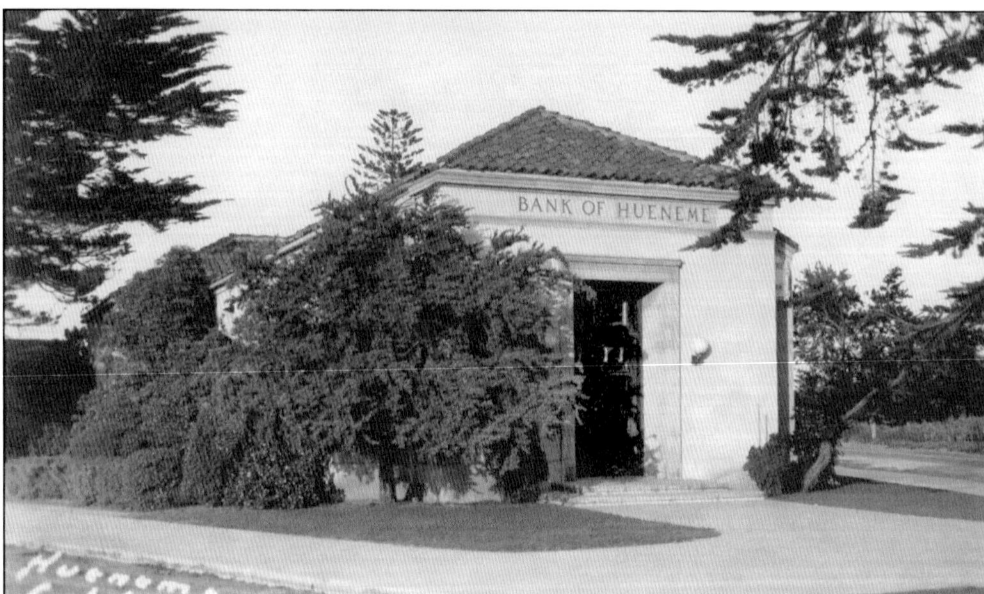

In 1925, Myron Hunt designed the Hueneme Bank at 220 North Market Street; Hunt had also been the architect of the Bard Mansion and the Huntington Library. The bank building was purchased in 1952 by the Security First National Bank of Los Angeles. In 1959, the city of Port Hueneme bought the building and, by 1961, had converted it to a new city hall.

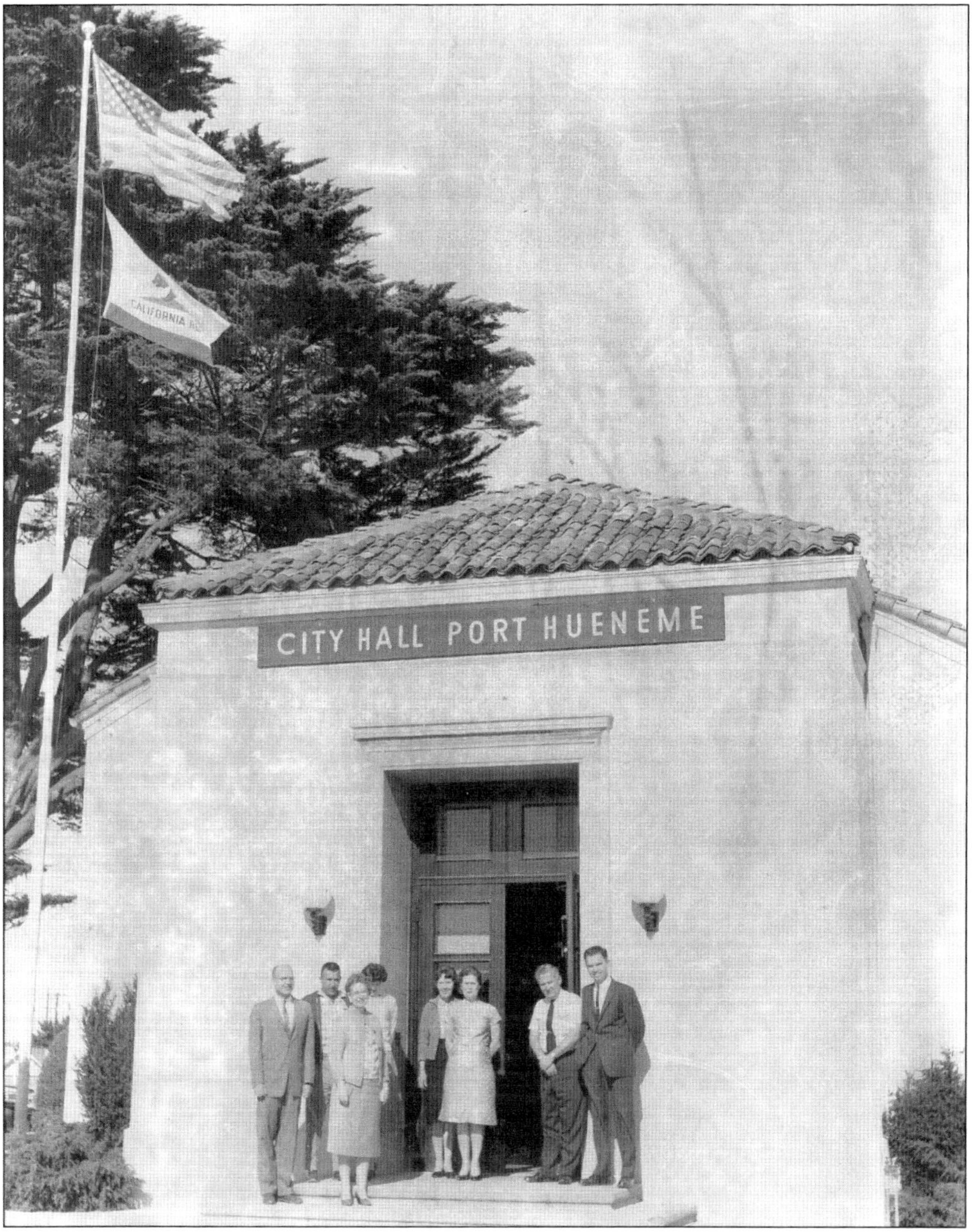

In 1976, the building earned the designation of Ventura County Landmark No. 32, and today it is used by the Hueneme Historical Society and the chamber of commerce. Appearing in this 1960s picture are some of the members of the council and its staff. From left to right are Bill Moranda, Andy Nicholds, Wilma Merryman, unidentified (with her head down), Celia Eccles, Louis Graham, John Nickerson, and unidentified.

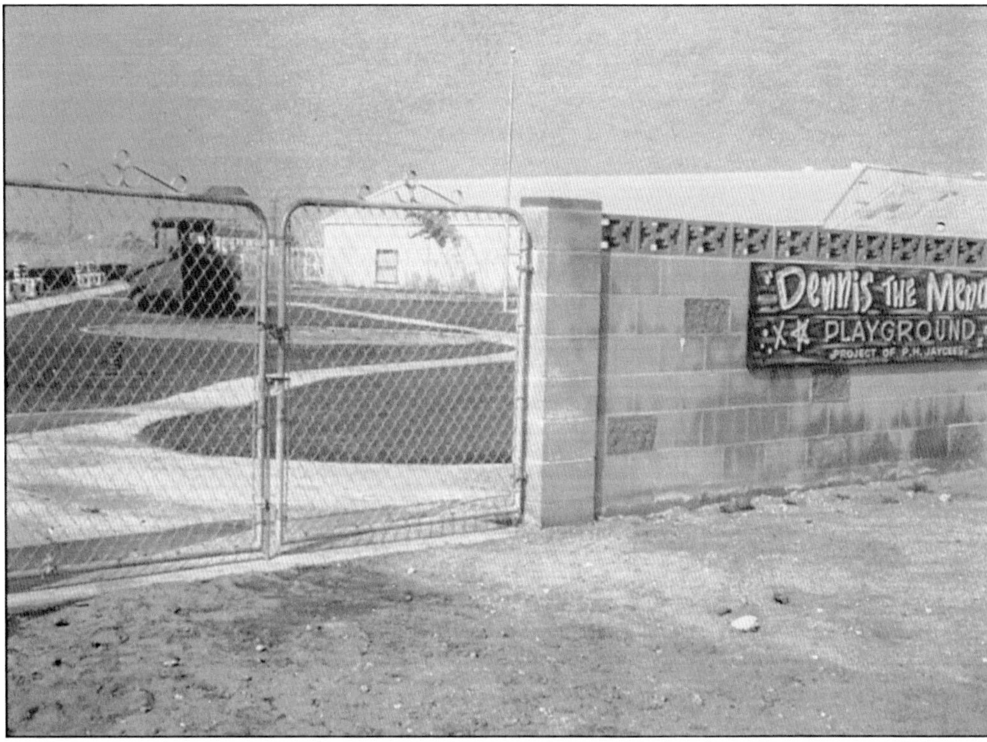

By the spring of 1963, Dennis the Menace Playground was ready for play. The playground, located at the end of Ventura Road and the beach, was guarded by a block wall and chain-link fence. The park was a joint project of the Port Hueneme Junior Chamber of Commerce, the Jaycees, and the Navy Seabees.

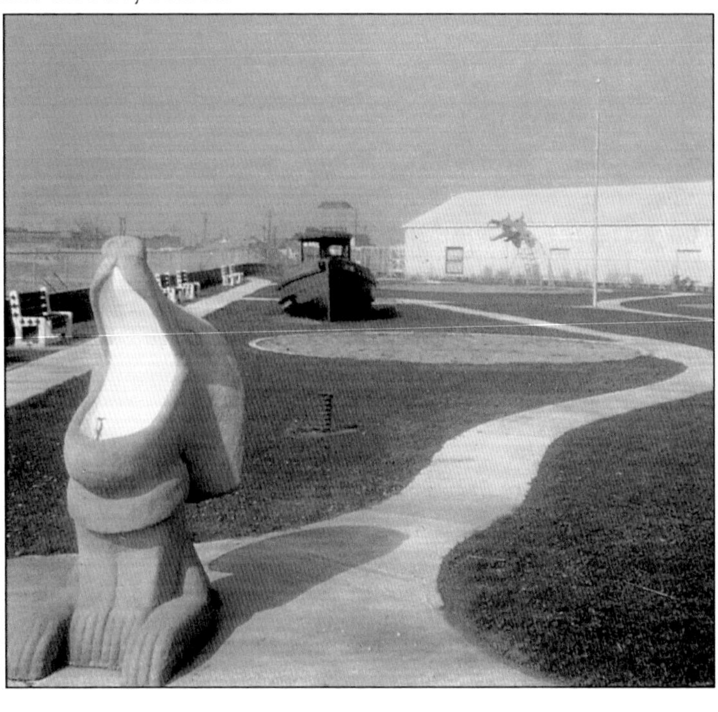

The Dennis the Menace Playground offered a merry-go-round, a balancing bridge, a boat, a lion-shaped drinking fountain, an umbrella tree, a plastic horse and donkey on a thick springs, a wading pool, and a climbing dragon.

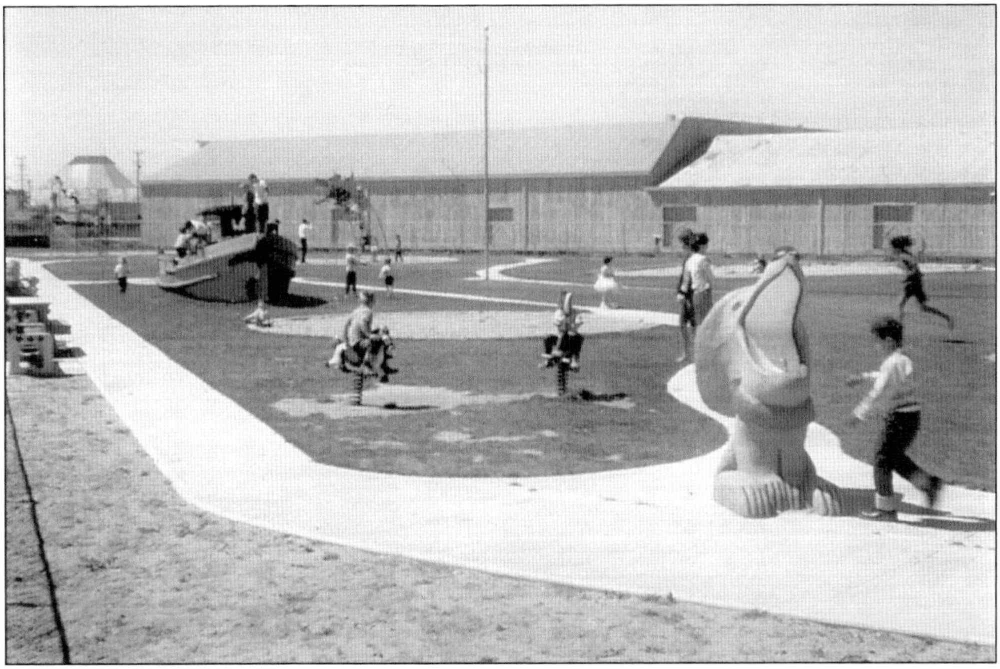

Photographs of this short-lived but much-remembered playground were hard to come by. Many residents remember a piece of equipment that looked like a skeletal plane, but these rare images don't support that memory. Maybe the plane was added later.

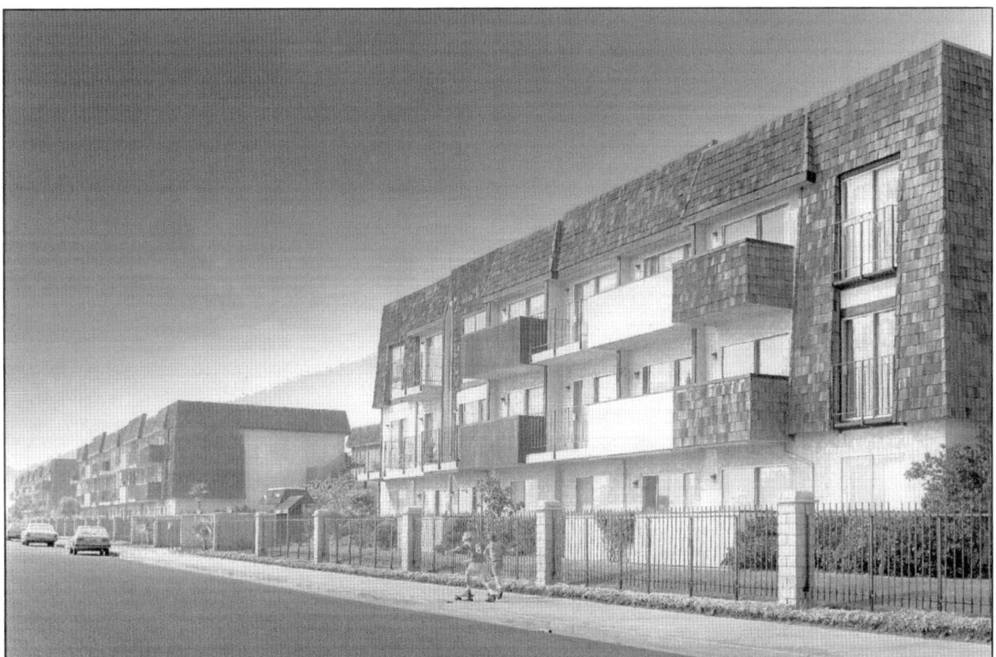

In the 1970s, the site of the Dennis the Menace Playground was converted to hold condominiums. Many housing projects followed, including Surfside Village, Surfside IV, Beachport Villas, Port Harbor Town Homes, Weston Pacific Collection, and La Entrada Villas.

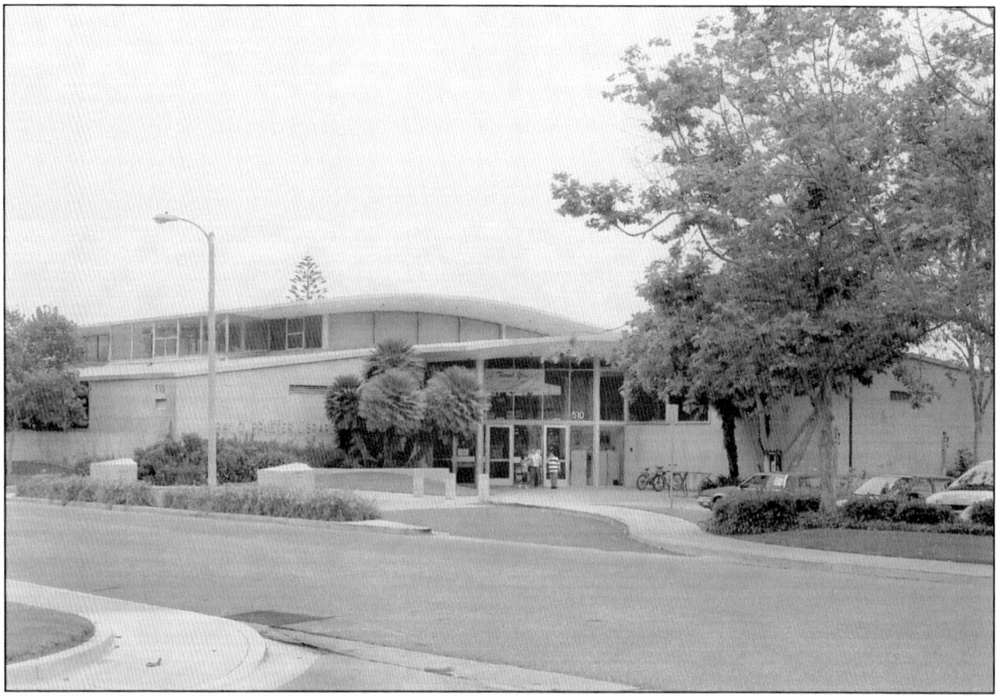

The Ray D. Prueter Library replaced the old library at Bubbling Springs Park and was named after the longtime community leader and former mayor.

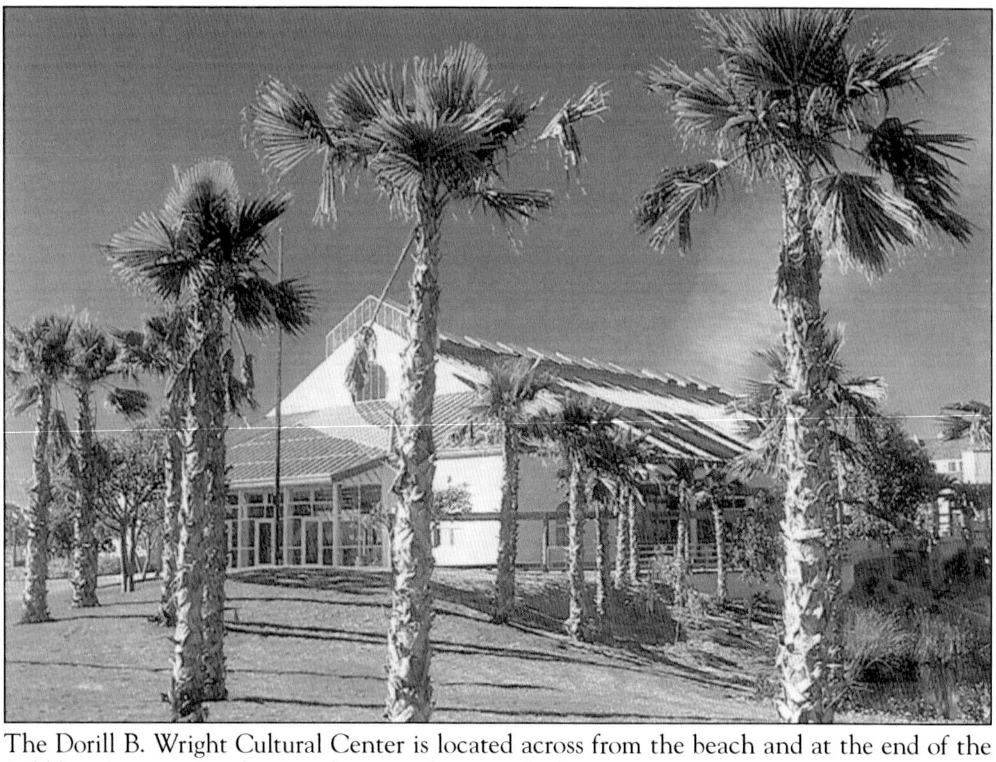

The Dorill B. Wright Cultural Center is located across from the beach and at the end of the Bubbling Springs corridor. Wright was a distinguished engineer and mayor of Port Hueneme.

Eleven

SPORTS

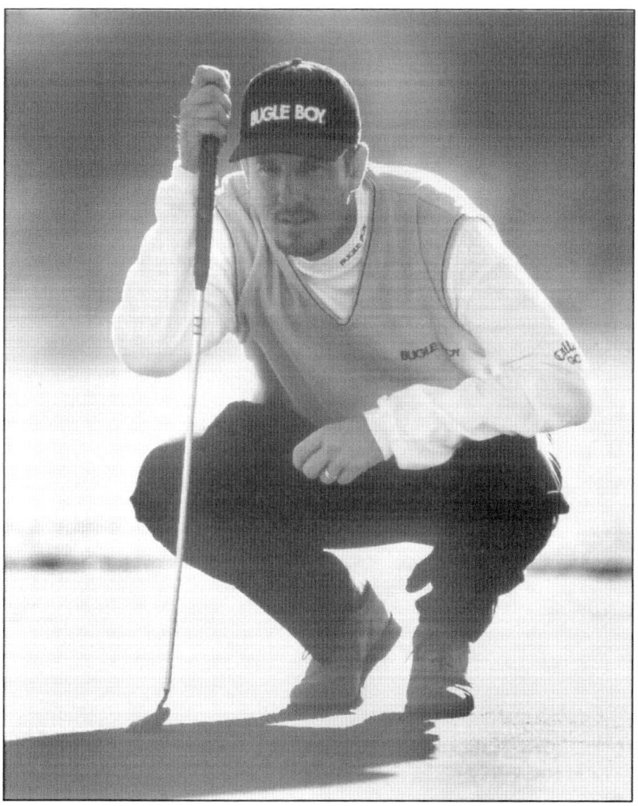

Hueneme grad Paul Stankowski continued his education at the University of Texas, El Paso, where he was a three-time All-American. He won the Western Athletic Conference championship in 1990 and turned pro in 1991. Stankowski finished first on the PGA Tour twice, in 1996 and 1997.

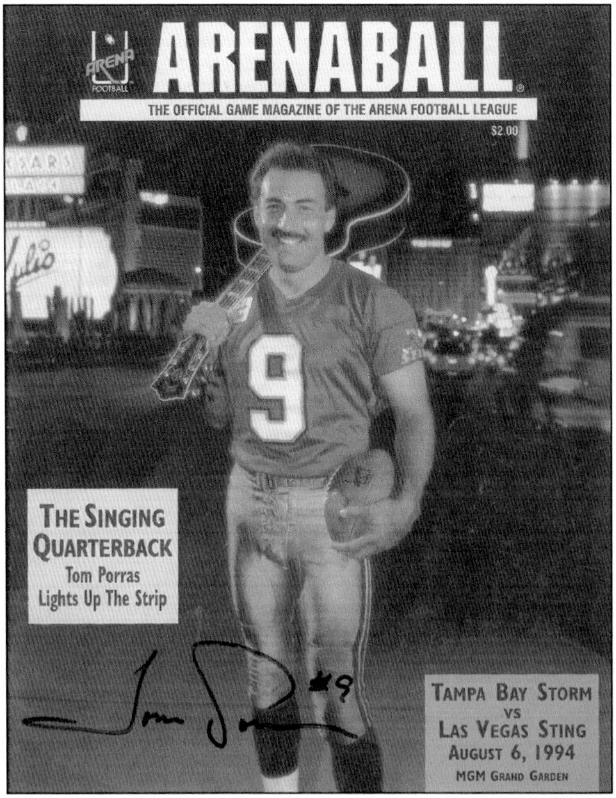

Tom Porras, known during his playing days as "The Singing Quarterback," began slinging footballs for Hueneme High School in the mid-1970s, graduating in 1976. He went on to star at Ventura College in 1977–1978, and lead the University of Washington Huskies squad to the 1979 Sun Bowl. Porras proceeded to accumulate 17 years of professional experience in the USFL, CFL, and AFL. Porras has stayed in the game as a scout for various professional teams.

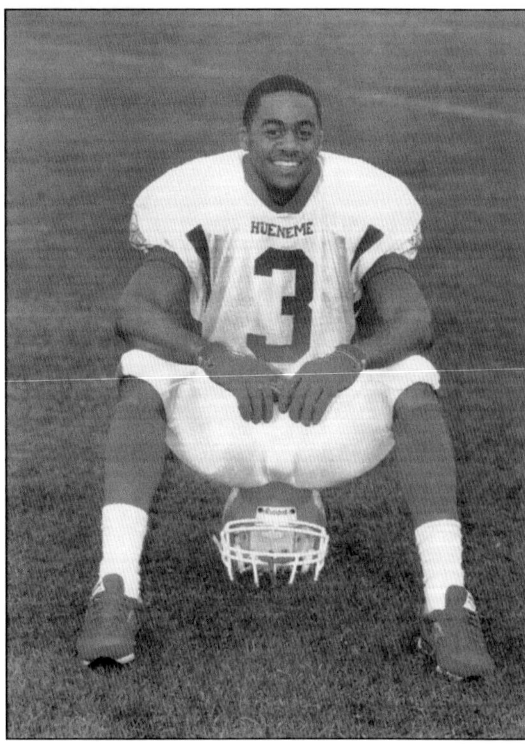

Keary Colbert graduated from Hueneme in 1999 and earned Super Prep All-American and All-CIF Division IV first team awards, among many others. At Hueneme, Colbert caught 25 passes for 600 yards that averaged 24 yards per catch, with 10 touchdowns. Colbert went on the break the University of Southern California reception record with 207 career catches and 2,964 receiving yards, putting him in the top three of all time. Colbert's great abilities, work ethic, and reliable personality helped him land a second-round selection by the Carolina Panthers. In his rookie season, Colbert played in 15 games, caught 47 passes for 754 yards averaging 16 yards per catch, and scored 5 touchdowns.

Josh Towers graduated from Hueneme High School and starred at Oxnard College, where he played for Hueneme graduates Jon Larson, Jerry Willard, and his uncle, Roger Frash. Towers made his professional debut with the Baltimore Orioles during the 2001 season. In 2003, Towers posted an eight-win, one-loss record with the Toronto Blue Jays and earned another nine victories in 2004. Towers has been one of many former Hueneme stars who have come back to the community to donate their time and participate in fund-raising efforts.

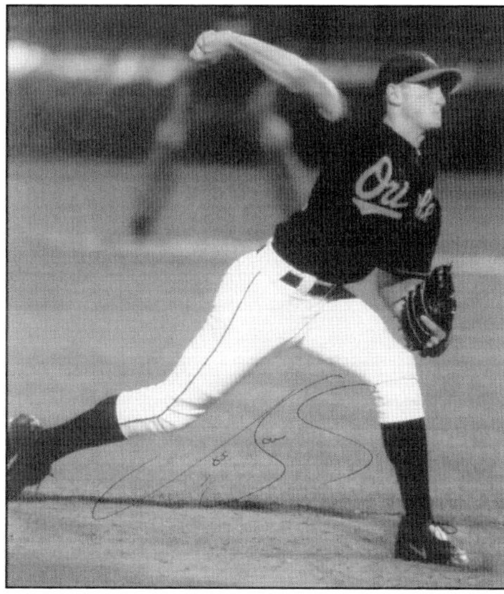

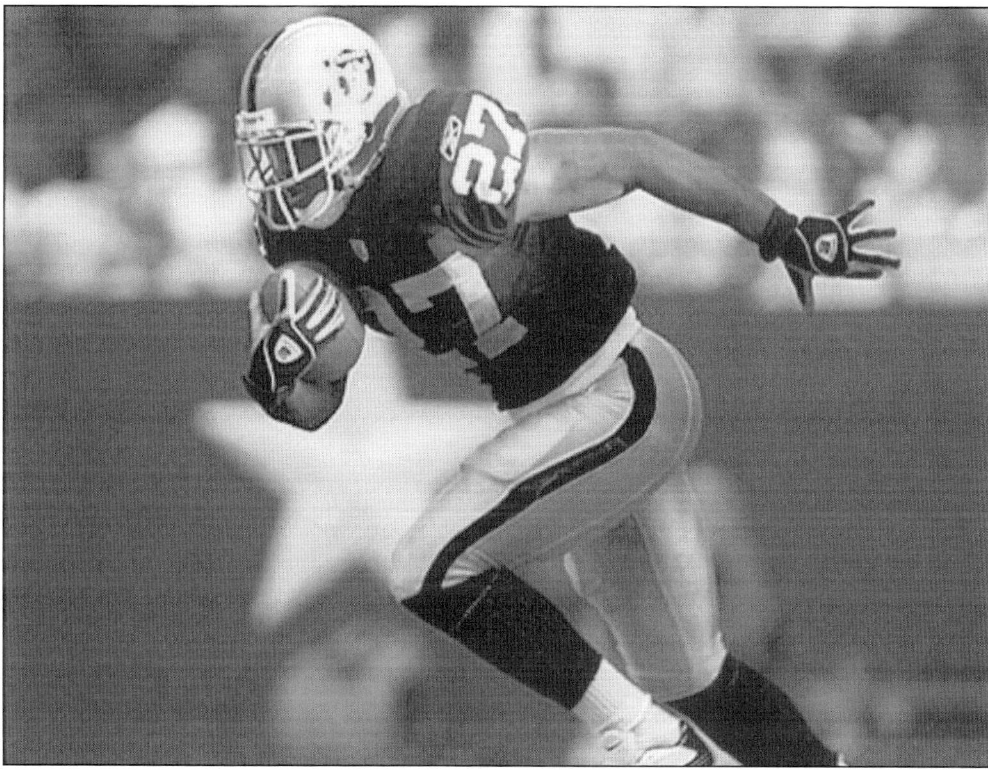

Ronney Jenkins graduated from Hueneme High in 1996. Coached by former Viking running back Larry Miller, Jenkins ran 619 yards to earn the national high-school record for single-game rushing. That's 619 yards in one game, which took place on November 9, 1995, versus Rio Mesa High School. At Brigham Young University, Jenkins was chosen second team All-WAC in 1998 after rushing for 1,307 yards and making 12 touchdowns. From 2000 to 2002, Ronney Jenkins led the San Diego Chargers in kickoff returns. He ran for 925 yards in 2002 and earned alternate Pro Bowl honors in 2001, when he led the NFL with a 26.6-yard average on kickoff returns. In 2003, Jenkins played for the Raiders, and in 2004, he was on the roster for the New Orleans Saints.

BIBLIOGRAPHY

I used several sources in putting together this publication, but, as always, my choice of material was limited to the information and photographs archived at area libraries and museums. I have tried to supplement this collection by contacting as many people as time permitted, but there is never enough time. I am extremely indebted to Powell Greenland for his comprehensive publication on the history of Hueneme. I hope this publication serves as an inspiration to others to continue documenting our local history.

Bolton, Barbara A., project director. *Bank of A. Levy: A History*. Virginia Beach, VA: Donning Company, 1991.

Greenland, Powell. *Port Hueneme: A History*. Ventura County Maritime Museum, 1994.

Hutchinson, W. H. *Oil, Land and Politics*. University of Oklahoma Press, 1965.

Maulhardt, Jeffrey Wayne. *Beans, Beets & Babies*. MOBOOKS, 2001.

———. *The Day the New York Giants Came to Oxnard*. MOBOOKS, 1997.

———. *The First Farmers of the Oxnard Plain*. MOBOOKS, 1999.

Moranda, Ted. *Me 'n Paul and Old Hueneme*. Self-published, 1999.

Moranda, Walter B. *The City of Port Hueneme History*. Eight-page article.

Ventura County Historical Society Quarterly. Volumes II, No. 3; III, No. 1; IV, No. 2; IX, No. 1; X, No. 1; XI, No. 2; XII, No. 3; XVII, No. 4; XVIII, No. 1; XIX, No. 1; XXII, No. 1; XXIII, No. 4; XXV, No. 3; XLVI, Nos. 1–4.

The Way-Nay-Me Harbor News, supplement to the *Port Hueneme Pilot* newspaper, July 4, 1957.

For more information on my local history writings,
please visit http://www.jeffmaulhardt.com or e-mail me at jeffmohart@aol.com.